American Society for Training & Development

IN ACTION

Developing High-Performance Work Teams

VOLUME 2

THIRTEEN

CASE STUDIES

FROM THE

REAL WORLD

OF TRAINING

JACK J. PHILLIPS
SERIES EDITOR

STEVEN D. JONES

MICHAEL M. BEYERLEIN
EDITORS

ASTD

Ordering information: Books published by the American Society for Training & Development can be ordered by calling 800.628.2783 or 703.683.8100.

Library of Congress Catalog Card Number: 97-78237
ISBN: 1-56286-113-1

Table of Contents

Introduction to the
In Action Series

The people involved in human resource development (HRD) are, like most professionals, eager to see practical applications of the models, techniques, theories, strategies, and issues relevant to their craft. In recent years, practitioners have developed an intense desire to learn about the first-hand experiences of organizations implementing HRD programs. To fill this critical void, the Publishing Review Committee of the American Society for Training & Development established the *In Action* casebook series. Issue editors are experienced professionals, and topics are carefully selected to ensure that they represent important and timely issues. Covering a variety of HRD topics, the series significantly broadens the scope of currently available literature.

The objectives of the *In Action* series are

- *To provide real-world examples of HRD program application and implementation.* Each case describes significant issues, events, actions, and activities. When possible, actual names of organizations and individuals are used. Where names are disguised, the events are factual.
- *To focus on challenging and difficult issues confronting the HRD field.* These cases explore areas where it is difficult to find information, or where processes or techniques are not standardized or fully developed. Emerging issues critical to success are also explored.
- *To recognize the work of professionals in the HRD field by presenting best practices.* Each casebook represents the most effective examples available. Cases are written by highly respected HRD practitioners, authors, researchers, and consultants. The authors focus on many high profile organizations—names you will quickly recognize.
- *To serve as a self-teaching tool for people learning about the HRD field.* As a stand-alone reference, each volume is a practical learning tool that fully explores numerous topics and issues.
- *To present a medium for teaching groups about the practical aspects of HRD.* Each book is a useful supplement to general and specialized HRD

textbooks and serves as a discussion guide to enhance learning in formal and informal settings.

As you read, the cases will no doubt challenge and motivate you. The new insights will serve as an impetus for positive change in your organization. If you have a case that might serve the same purpose for other HRD professionals, please contact me. New casebooks are always being developed. And if you have suggestions on ways to improve the *In Action* series, your input will be welcomed.

Jack J. Phillips
Series Editor
Performance Resources Organization
Box 380637
Birmingham, AL 35238-0637

Preface

This is our second book of case studies on developing high-performance work teams. The purpose of this casebook is to give readers an interior view of work teams as they have struggled to become high-performance teams. There is much to be learned from these efforts, and we thank the case authors for allowing us this view into their organizations.

Target Audience

This book is designed for any practitioner interested in teams. Thus, it may be of interest to human resource development (HRD) professionals, trainers, organization development (OD) practitioners, managers, supervisors, design teams, and team members. Consultants also may find the book valuable because it covers a wide range of team issues and discusses specific interventions.

Lessons Learned

Generally, this book presents success stories. The case studies are from the real world, however, and so they describe some aspects of teaming that failed. By examining these struggles along with those aspects that were successful, we can gain insights for implementing teams in our own organizations. Perhaps these cases can help us to avoid some problems. One lesson is clear: We cannot exactly duplicate another organization's implementation. Although there are basic principles in developing high-performance work teams, the details of each intervention are unique to the culture of each organization, as each of these cases demonstrates.

Acknowledgments

We would like to thank Melanie Bullock of the Center for the Study of Work Teams and Patti Pulliam and Terry Cantrell of Performance Resources Organization for their assistance with this casebook.

We dedicate this book to our children: Caitlin, Lindsay, and Chris (for Steve) and Marisa (for Mike).

Steven D. Jones
Murfreesboro, TN

Michael M. Beyerlein
Denton, TX

April 1999

How to Use This Casebook

Think of this book as an armchair benchmarking adventure into a variety of settings, union and nonunion, domestic and international, manufacturing and service. The cases present a variety of approaches to implementing teams in the workplace. Collectively, the cases offer a wide range of settings, methods, techniques, strategies, and approaches, representing manufacturing, service, and government organizations. Target groups for the programs vary, ranging from all employees to managers to specialists. As a group, these cases represent a rich source of information on the strategies of some of the best practitioners, consultants, and researchers in the field.

Each case does not necessarily represent the optimum or ideal approach for the specific situation. In every case, it is possible to identify areas that could benefit from refinement and improvement. That is part of the learning process—to build on the work of other people. Although the evaluation approach is contextual, other organizations can use these methods and techniques.

Table 1 presents basic descriptions of the cases in the order in which they appear in the book. This table can serve as a quick reference for readers who want to examine the evaluation approach for a particular type of program, audience, or industry.

Using the Cases

This book will be helpful to anyone who wants to see real-life examples of team implementation. Readers may wish to choose among these four approaches to using the book:

- Human resource development (HRD) professionals can use it as a basic reference for practical applications. They can analyze and dissect each of the cases to develop an understanding of the issues, approaches, and, most of all, refinements and improvements that could be made.
- In group discussions, interested individuals can react to the material, offer different perspectives, and draw conclusions about ap-

Table 1. Overview of the case studies.

Case	Industry	Key Features	Target Audience
Mobil Oil Corporation	Petroleum/United States	Culture change, work redesign, cross-functional teams, executive team building, training	HRD staff, design team, managers, supervisors, and consultants
Pall Gelman Sciences	Manufacturing/United States	Culture change from traditional management style, redesign, continuous improvement, training, lean manufacturing, performance measurement	HRD staff, design team, managers, supervisors, and consultants
ETHICON Endo-Surgery, Inc., a Johnson & Johnson company	Health-care manufacturing/United States	Learning organization, aligning training with organization's objectives	Training staff, management, design team, organization development (OD) consultants
Advanced Micro Devices	Semiconductor/United States	Learning organization, transformational management training, examining differences between stated mission and actions	Trainers, HRD staff, OD consultants
Ohio State Manufacturers	Manufacturing/United States	Team continuum, training, steering committee, work redesign, performance management, implementation guidelines	HRD staff, design team, managers, supervisors, and consultants

Organization	Industry/Country	Topics	Participants
Sydney Water Corporation Pty Ltd.	Water/Australia	Union-management cooperation, culture change, reduction in force, sociotechnical systems design, performance measurement	Design team, steering committee, union leadership, and managers
Malden Mills Industries	Textile/United States	Union support, organizational change, management and supervisory support, team performance measures	Union leadership, HRD staff, design team, managers, supervisors, and facilitators
Chemainus Sawmill	Timber/Canada	Union support, pay for knowledge and skills	Union leadership, HRD staff, design team, managers, and facilitators
Fernco, Inc.	Manufacturing/United States and England	Sustaining teams over the long run, organization development, survey feedback, team leadership training, pilot teams, pay system	HRD staff, OD practitioners, trainers, and steering committee
Automobile Parts Manufacturer	Automobile parts manufacturing/Japan	Survey measurement of team work dynamics, relation to productivity	HRD staff and researchers
United Kingdom National Health Service	Health care/United Kingdom	Reasons for team failure, organizational support	HRD staff, OD practitioners, managers, and steering committee
Blue Cross Blue Shield of South Carolina	Insurance/United States	Work redesign, team support systems, training, ground rules, and role expectations	HRD staff, design team, managers, and facilitators
United States Navy	Defense/United States	Culture change, management teams, office redesign, reorganization, privatization	Managers, OD consultants, and HRD staff

proaches and techniques. The questions at the end of each case can serve as a beginning point for lively and entertaining discussions.

- As a supplement to other training and development or evaluation textbooks, this book provides the extra dimensions of real-life cases that show the outcomes of team building and implementation.
- Managers who do not have primary training responsibility will find this book extremely useful. These managers provide support and assistance to the HRD staff, and it is helpful for them to understand the results that HRD programs can yield.

It is important to remember that each organization and its program implementation are unique. What works well for one may not work for another, even if both are in similar settings. This book offers a variety of approaches and provides an arsenal of tools from which to choose.

Follow-Up

Space limitations have required that some cases be shorter than the author and editors would prefer. It has been necessary to omit some information about background, assumptions, strategies, and results. If readers need additional information on a case, they may contact the lead author directly. They'll find information on how to contact lead authors in the biographical section at the end of each case.

Five Principles of Team Implementation

Steven D. Jones and Michael M. Beyerlein

Trainers often say there is no magic formula for team success and that each organization has to implement teams in accordance with its own culture. Although this is true to some extent, you probably would not be reading this book if you thought there were no principles underlying team success. Our experience leads us to conclude that there are principles to follow if teams are to succeed, but their implementation may vary, according to each organization's culture.

We also have noticed that the effectiveness of teams falls off dramatically if the essential principles are ignored. Although it is true that not every detail of team implementation can be successfully duplicated from one site to another, the essential principles are a different matter. Although there is no agreed-upon list of basic principles of team implementation, we think the cases in this book suggest the following five principles that are common to successful teams.

- Where feasible, redesign the work to focus on the customer and make team members interdependent.
- Make a significant investment in innovative training, especially for team leaders and coaches.
- Plan team implementation as a culture change that is likely to meet stiff resistance.
- Build grassroots support for teams among employees.
- Tie teams to the business strategy through team performance measurement and by encouraging teams to see themselves as business partners. Reinforce this connection through team-based pay.

Job and Work Process Redesign

The first basic principle in team implementation requires strong consideration of redesigning jobs and work processes to focus on the customer and to make team members more interdependent. The result of this redesign may be one of the better win-win solutions in business today: The customer gets service that is more responsive, the organization aligns teams with its business strategy, and teams get an elevating purpose. Accordingly, this book of case studies includes Blue Cross and Blue Shield of South Carolina and describes how it redesigned a large claims-processing unit into cross-functional teams that focus on the customer. The cases from Mobil Oil and the U.S. Navy describe the major focus both organizations place on job redesign. The tearing down of functional silos to improve customer service through teams is a theme throughout these cases. We see this principle applied in organizations that have high-performance teams. Some organizations, unfortunately, fail to capitalize on the powerful combination of redesigning the work to simultaneously focus on the customer and to increase the interdependence of the team members. We think that these three cases make a strong argument for doing both.

Training

The second basic principle concerns the training that is needed for team implementation. Team members and leaders must make a significant investment in training. This training typically addresses such skills as problem solving, conflict resolution, group dynamics, conducting and participating in team meetings, performance management, building customer relationships, and business literacy. In addition to these skills, leadership training is necessary for supervisors, managers, coaches, facilitators, and team leaders. Leadership training covers such skills as facilitation, setting boundaries, encouraging participation, assessing team strengths and weaknesses, and transitioning responsibilities to teams. Organizations frequently underestimate the amount of training teams require, particularly leadership training. The cases from Ethicon Endo-Surgery, Inc., a Johnson & Johnson company, Advanced Micro Devices, and the Ohio manufacturers provide valuable insights into how these companies are deploying their team member and team leadership training.

A number of training innovations have emerged over the past 10 years that have greatly benefited high-performance teams. The Johnson & Johnson and the Advanced Micro Devices cases, for instance, show the influence of the learning organization concepts at work as these organizations explore new ways to increase their capacity to learn. Much of the success of high-performance teams is due to their capacity to learn. Whether teams are endeavoring to improve work processes, develop business literacy, engage in cross training, problem solve, or interface with customers, they are increasing their capacity to learn. The more the teams learn, the more they can do. Knowledgeable teams can help to market the product or service because they make powerful impressions on the customer. As such, teams may become part of the marketing strategy.

Further innovations in learning have been necessary because of the learning demands placed on team leaders. The level of skill necessary for the team leader and coach positions sets a new standard in learning requirements. So much is expected from these people from themselves, team members, and upper management that a deeper level of learning has to occur than has historically been the case. For instance, newly learned skills simultaneously face challenges from team members who resist assuming more responsibility and from upper managers who do not fully support the team concept. However, team leaders and coaches are expected to develop high-performance teams sooner rather than later. Challenges such as this force innovations in training. Thus, we find more in-depth training and new paradigms for learning. By themselves, the classic half-day training sessions built around video role models and inspiring lectures may not be up to the challenges. Training built around insights achieved through experiential learning, such as that presented in the Advanced Micro Devices case, gives us a glimpse into the type of learning solutions required for team leader and coach training.

Culture Change

The third principle requires an understanding that the implementation of teams in most organizations is a culture change. If we just look at what most organizations reward, at who gets the media attention in sporting events, and at who solves the problem in the movies, we can clearly see that the emphasis is on the individual in our culture. Organizational cultures typically amplify this emphasis, such that the implementation of teams is a culture change greater than that of most other interventions. The degree of culture change requires a long-term commitment, a clear structure, and decisive leadership at the top. Fortunately, we have several cases with an emphasis on culture change. The cases from Mobil Oil, the U.S. Navy, Pall Gelman Sciences, Sydney Water, and Fernco present their efforts to implement teams as a culture change.

A common denominator that emerges from these cases is that team implementations require a tremendous amount of new structures. In fact, some team experts believe that teams require more structure than a traditionally managed organization. This sounds counterintuitive, unless we truly understand how much of a culture change is required for teams to flourish. The Fernco case is an excellent example of the changes in structure that made this successful team implementation possible. Steering committees, a new pay system, survey feedback, and elimination of executive perks are all strategic changes in the organizational systems. Without these systemic changes, the culture of this organization would not have changed, and teams would probably have failed.

Grassroots Support

Closely related to culture change is the fourth essential principle for successful team deployment: building grassroots support among the employees. High-performance teams consist of members who are genuinely excited about their team's progress. This kind of excitement cannot be mandated; it must be built. We are fortunate to have three cases that demonstrate how support for teams was successfully established in union environments. Even nonunion companies can learn a lot by studying these cases. Unions place tough requirements on team implementation. This creates a sort of stress test that reveals the most critical factors in obtaining employee support for the team concept. The cases from Sydney Water in Australia, Malden Mills in the United States, and Chemainus Sawmill in Canada may help us to foresee possible flaws in our efforts to gain employee support.

Each of these three cases has a procedure for representing employees in making decisions about team design and deployment. Additionally, there is a clear channel for employee complaints about the team process. Certainly, these committees take time, but they also improve communication. In addition, they signal a commitment to involving employees in the team implementation process and to taking employee concerns seriously. This investment in time eventually pays off because it takes employee buy-in to help make teams successful. We suspect that many organizations have learned this lesson the hard way.

Link Teams to Business Strategy

For the fifth basic principle of team implementation, we suggest linking the teams to the business strategy. Teams need to be a business asset, rather than another expense. The members of the very best high-performance teams operate like business partners, rather than employees. The best method for tying teams to the business is to have high-quality systems for measuring team performance. What we mean by *high quality* is that the teams fully understand their performance measures and regularly use them as a basis for problem solving, and that the measures are aligned with the business strategy. The cases from Pall Gelman Sciences, Sydney Water, and Malden Mills include a description of their team's performance measures. A second method for tying teams to the business strategy is through a team-based pay system that is linked to business measures.

The Malden Mills case makes a strong connection between progress on the business goals and team implementation. This connection would be nearly impossible without team performance measures that relate to the business goals. In addition, Malden Mills has a cross-functional team that develops a three-year business strategy. A well-developed business strategy will not only contain the expected financial results but will also detail how these results will be achieved. The how-to section of the business strategy links the teams to the plan. For instance, in this case, members of the cross-functional team discuss the importance of on-time delivery and the need for teams to help with this effort. Teams may develop their own strategy for contributing to the on-time delivery solution, and, in this way, all the teams will link their team strategy to the overall business strategy. This linkage makes them partners in the business, especially when the linkage has corresponding performance measures.

If teams are to be linked to the business strategy, then human resources activities should likewise reinforce this linkage. The Pall Gelman Sciences case demonstrates how it tied team training to business strategy. If we examine their training topics of "(1) why the company wanted to develop teams and change the plant culture; (2) how to ensure team success (meeting management, supportive paperwork, resource justification); (3) problem solving; (4) quality tools; (5) communication including listening, idea presentation, and feedback; (6) conflict resolution; (7) continuous improvement; and (8) goal setting and measurement," we can see the connection to the business strategy. The how to of the business strategy was to transform "a traditional, hierarchical, corporate culture, which stifled ingenuity and contribution, to one of high-performing cells in which people run their manufacturing areas almost as small businesses."

The case studies in this book demonstrate the five essential principles. Although the companies implement the principles in different ways, the cases teach us that there are principles to successful team implementation. All of these principles may not be necessary in all situations, but careful decisions should be made when trading off one principle over another. For instance, can an organization offer less team training if it has high-quality measurement and incentive systems for teams? If the jobs are redesigned to focus on the customer and make team members more interdependent, is training still needed on the team concept? Some organizations make these trade-offs, but we think doing so should be a conscious decision. We hope that this book of case studies will help to maximize these kinds of decisions and help the reader gain more insight and knowledge into implementing successful teams.

Transforming Teams: A Personal and Team Development Approach

Mobil Oil Corporation

Peg Howell, Sharon Lamm, Stacey Philpot, and Michael Quick

In August 1995, Mobil Oil Corporation's Lubes Customer Support Center began its reorganization from a multidepartment, functional organization to a single, team-based organization. The strategic goal of this restructuring was to improve service while reducing costs by using an organizational model of self-directed work teams. As a first step, the Customer Support Center began an innovative team-building initiative that emphasized personal development and self-awareness in addition to classic team skills. This case describes how the company achieved high-performing teams in only 18 months and outlines the unique aspects of the program as well as the consequent results.

The Setting
A Typical Day

The light indicating that calls are waiting in queue seemed to be glowing all morning. Sarah, an order process owner (OPO), had a feeling that it would be a tough day from the start. Lori and Jerry, two of her team members, arrived 10 minutes late that morning. Sarah decided it wasn't worth confronting them, especially Lori. She figured this would only increase the tension in an already strained relationship. Lori had been very defensive last week when Sarah had confronted her about socializing while the calls in queue light had been on for over an hour. She had seemed offended to receive such commentary, especially from Sarah, who was a relatively new OPO

This case was prepared to serve as a basis for discussion rather than to illustrate either effective or ineffective administrative and management practices.

compared to Lori, a 10-year veteran of the organization. "Besides," Sarah thought, "shouldn't the team lead say something to the two latecomers?"

Sarah waited for her team lead to speak to Lori or Jerry all day and was surprised that she said nothing. She wrestled with whether to approach her with her observations and ultimately decided to refrain from saying anything. She didn't want to be the person to tattle on her team members.

Later that day, as Sarah finished up her last call, she glanced toward the fax machine to see how many more orders remained for her team to process before they left for the day. When she turned around, she noticed Lori, the only other OPO from her team, in her office quickly packing her bags. Lori innocently offered a passing, "Good night, Sarah," as she left the office. Although she assumed all fax orders must have been completed, Sarah decided that she would take one last pass by the fax machine just to make sure no outstanding orders remained. Eight orders sat on the tray. "Some team we are," she thought.

This incident was typical of those at a Customer Support Center soon after it went through a major restructuring. Although some aspects of the case are unique to this organization, its problems and difficulties are common to many modern organizations following a restructuring into teams.

In this particular case, the organization moved from a functional, multidepartment organization to one that was arranged into nine regional or customer-segment-focused cross-functional teams and an administrative support services team. This new team-based structure posed many challenges and difficulties for the approximately 80 employees involved. With the new structure came new roles—roles that were created by combining activities that had formerly been done by people in six different departments. Under the new structure, no single person had the expertise to do every task, and many employees, if not most, were unclear about their roles and responsibilities. They were also having difficulty interacting with each other; communication was indirect, feedback was rarely given, and meetings were frequently lengthy and poorly organized.

In addition to these difficulties, the center was not achieving its business goals. For example, phone response time was slow with only 57 percent of calls being answered in 30 seconds. Invoicing and pricing errors were frequent. Overall the center was underperforming in several key areas.

The Intervention
An Initial Approach

Faced with this current situation and wanting to improve their business results, the center's leadership group discussed how best to handle the organization's training needs. The leadership group was made up of Mike Quick, the center's manager; five team leads; four process specialists; and a three-member implementation team. This implementation team, which was the first self-directed work team (SDWT) at the support center, was formed to find ways to close the 275 performance gaps between current skills and newly required job and team skills. Known as the Gap Busters, this team consisted of three Mobil employees.

The leadership group agreed that it would be best to first offer employees training on actual job skills, such as order taking, payment collection, and pricing, and then provide classic team-skills training in a separate program. A team of external consultants and Mobil employees selected a company that could offer team-skills training for the organization's nine customer support teams and leadership training for their four team leads. It was thought that the administrative support team and team lead would not need training.

Identification of the 275 gaps began in March 1994. The following list shows the process that identified the gaps, how the teaming gap was determined to be the most important, and the overall history of the team-building initiative:

- *March 1994: Reengineering study initiated.* Under the leadership of George Madden, general manager, the U.S. Lube Division of Mobil Oil Corporation completes a study that concludes that in order to leapfrog competition and become best in class, the entire Order Fulfillment process needs to be reengineered.

- *October 1994: Team-based organization recommended.* On the recommendation of the Reengineering Team, the Customer Support Design Team (CSDT) is formed to review the order management process and make necessary recommendations to management. On the basis of research, the involvement of individuals currently working in these processes, and the results of a three-month pilot, the CSDT recommends creating a team-based organization.

- *August 1995: Customer Support Center created.* Functions from six different departments combine to form the Lubes Customer Support Center (LCSC). Mike Quick, team lead of the CSDT, is named customer support manager.

- *August 1995: Regional teams are created.* Nine cross-functional teams are created and organized by region or customer segments. Each team varies in size from five to 20 people (depending on the size of the segment) and is made up of four roles: OPO, field marketing consultant (FMC), account administrator (AA), and team lead. Additionally, a tenth team with its own team lead was later created of individuals who provided administrative support services, such as budgeting and computer systems, to the customer and sales support teams.

- *Fall 1995: Problems surface.* The organization realizes that new skills are needed as a result of the restructuring. Management launches a team to identify and remedy the gaps that exist between what people know and what new job and team skills are needed. This team is made up of two external reengineering consultants and a variety of individuals from the organization.
- *Spring 1996: Team skills needed.* The team of outside consultants and Mobil employees identify 275 gaps that are put into 11 categories, such as training, teaming, structure and rules, process, organization, tools, behavior, role clarity, and quick hits. The organization votes the teaming gap as the one most needing immediate attention and creates an implementation team named the Gap Busters.
- *August 1996: Closing the teaming gap.* After going a year without any team training, the team of outside consultants and Mobil employees decides to select a consulting firm to do the training. A facilitator team from Moore-Howell Associates (MHA) begins the process of designing, developing, and providing the needed team training.

An Informal Assessment

In August 1996, that team selected the facilitator team of Peg Howell, Sharon Lamm, and Stacey Philpot from MHA to help the center close its "teaming gap" and offer team skills to its employees. It selected MHA because of its previous experience working with Mobil as well as its unique approach to team building. As a first step in developing an appropriate intervention, the facilitators listened to the leadership group describe the current situation at the center, their various problems, and their ultimate vision of moving to self-directed work teams.

Figures 1 through 3 show the leadership group's depiction of the evolution of the organization's structure. Figure 1, the current structure, illustrates the structure of the organization prior to any interventions. This structure is complicated, complex, and directed from the top. It also includes many external influences (consultants) and has multiple reporting relationships. One striking feature is that the Administrative Support Team stands apart from the regional or customer-segment-focused cross-functional teams. Figure 2, stage one of the process, shows the intermediate step of moving to high-performance teams. By providing teams with new skills, the organization would be able to eliminate its reliance on external consultants, simplify reporting relationships, and begin to work across teams. At this stage, the administrative team is connected to the other teams, but not integrated with them. Figure 3, stage two, illustrates the leadership group's vision of self-directed work teams. The most notable changes in this model are the elimination of team leads and a clearer focus on the processes. In this stage, teams are more tightly integrated, and team members take on the responsibilities that team leads formerly performed. Teams manage their external relationships directly, and the manager becomes a supporter and resource provider for all teams.

As the facilitators gained an understanding of what the leadership group wanted to accomplish, it became apparent to them that although the organization was looking for classic team skills training, it also needed a shift in organizational culture.

To be a successful organization made up of SDWTs, the Customer Support Center would have to replace its blaming culture with one of personal responsibility. If the leadership group wanted employees who would take initiative, actively participate, and take ownership of the business, it first would have to examine its own performance, behaviors, and interactions. In addition, the rest of the leadership group needed to articulate more clearly its vision for the future of the Customer Support Center. It also needed to indicate how the team training program would be a critical step in achieving the end goal of SDWTs. Only after articulating their vision and participating in their own training would they be able to offer a similar type of training to the rest of the organization.

Based on this assessment, the leadership group together with the facilitators revised the deliverables for the teaming project and agreed to participate in a unique program that would combine both team and personal development components.

A Unique Process

The goal of the teaming initiative was defined as "achieving a measurable improvement in the performance of the Customer Support Teams and Team Leads" by creating "a fundamental shift in mindset from a group of individuals with separate roles and responsibilities to a team-based organization with broader goals and accountability." To accomplish

Figure 1. Vision for the evolution of Lubes Customer Support Center—the current structure.

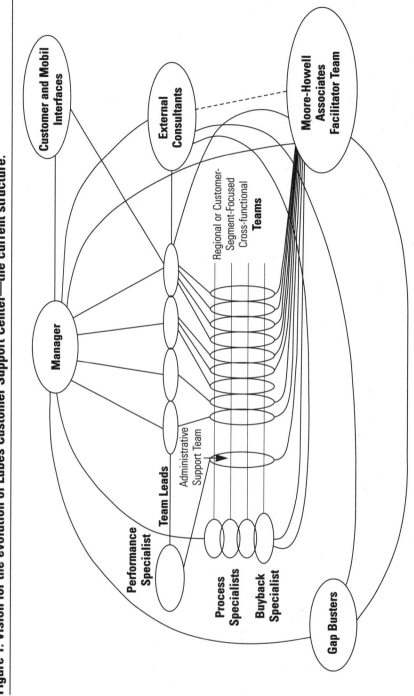

Figure 2. Vision for the evolution of Lubes Customer Support Center—Stage 1, high-performance teams.

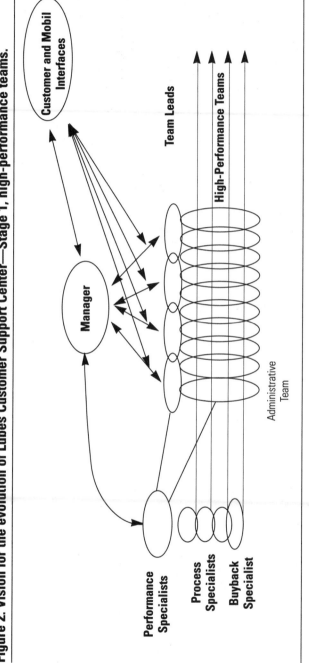

Figure 3. Vision for the evolution of Lubes Customer Support Center—Stage 2, self-directed work teams.

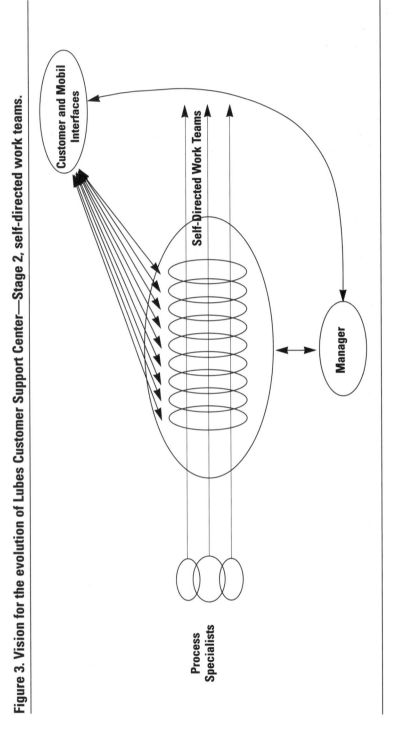

this goal, the facilitator team used an innovative process in designing the program. Instead of listing or dictating the program's objectives to the leadership group, the facilitator team began to model how the leadership group could take ownership of its own training. The facilitators met with each of the members of the leadership group individually and observed several of the leadership group's meetings. They fed their observations of these back to the leadership group so its members could use them to create the objectives for their program.

Figure 4 demonstrates how the objectives were formulated from the facilitator's observations.

After reviewing the observations and data, the leadership group selected the following objectives: trust building, communication improvement, consensus decision making, conflict resolution, feedback, and coaching. They also came up with three personal goals: (1) to create a safe learning environment, (2) to increase personal awareness, and (3) to improve self-esteem.

A Unique Design: The Leadership Team's Program, Part 1

With these objectives in mind, the facilitators designed a three-and-a-half-day program that would move the leadership group through the stages of team development—forming, storming, norming, and performing (Tuckman, 1965). The first day focused on personal awareness and development, the second day transitioned from personal awareness to interpersonal relationships and team development, and the remainder

Figure 4. Formation of objectives for leadership group off-site.

Observation ⟶	Objective
The manager was perceived as isolated, not responsive to teams' needs and not trustworthy.	To trust each other more, especially the manager.
Group members talked over one another and frequently interrupted each other.	To communicate better, especially to listen better.
Sensitive issues were ignored or sidestepped.	To give each other feedback and coaching to resolve conflicts and minimize defensiveness with each other.
The leadership group had difficulty making decisions (simple decisions took as much time and energy as larger ones).	To set goals and make decisions more effectively.

of the program provided opportunities to improve the intergroup dynamic between different roles. The facilitators intentionally selected a combination of elements that would accommodate a variety of different learning styles and personality types. These elements included:

- challenging personal assumptions using Kegan's (1996) four-column "big assumption" exercise
- communication tools, such as Argyris's (1990) ladder of inference
- one-on-one feedback sessions with each team member
- a high ropes course
- reflection time and journal writing
- information on personality types (namely, the Myers-Briggs Type Indicator [MBTI]; Myers & McCaulley, 1985) and the group's team type (also using the MBTI)
- indoor and outdoor experiential initiatives for team development
- exercises on how to make requests rooted in personal responsibility instead of blame
- creating shared team values
- conflict resolution of actual team and role conflicts
- in-the-moment process observations including personality type and gender differences
- optional body massage for relaxation and to better understand how bodies respond to stress.

Another key component was how the facilitator team interacted with the leadership group. First, the facilitator team chose to be learners along with the participants in the program. They modeled what the Customer Support Center needed most—to let go of the traditional paradigm that experts have all the answers and to begin to continuously learn and innovate in an ever-changing world. The facilitators also modeled taking personal responsibility and openly shared their own lessons and emotions. Second, prior to the program, the facilitators contracted with the leadership team to be able to coach them (individually and collectively) in the moment and offer skills training on a just-in-time (JIT) basis. Many times they also abandoned the planned agenda so the participants could address a critical issue.

Also important to the design of the program was the setting for the training. Rooted in the concept that learning requires a certain amount of risk taking and discomfort, the facilitators selected a location that would move the leadership group out of their comfort zone. The training was held on a rustic farm in rural Pennsylvania where the leadership group shared modest accommodations. The location was beautiful yet isolated, with very limited access to phones, computers, TV, and other distractions.

The leadership group training was successful on several accounts: (1) The training evaluations consistently indicated that both personal and team learning occurred, (2) their meetings immediately became more effective, (3) interactions within the group and with others outside the group were significantly improved, (4) members started referring to themselves as the leadership team instead of the leadership group, and (5) they decided to provide this same program to all their employees. In a meeting one week after the training, the team was asked, "What has it been like since you've been back (from the off-site)?" Their responses included comments such as:

- It was a wonderful experience—we created new relationships on the leadership team and can use this to fulfill our objectives.
- I feel a lot of support from the leadership team.
- I'm taking more risks and encouraging others to take more risks.
- I feel and act more confident.
- I'm utilizing my time better.

The Leadership Team's Program, Part 2

Following the first training, the leadership team was eager to create a plan to implement SDWTs. The members decided to quickly hold a second off-site meeting with the following objectives: (1) review and use the tools learned at the first training, (2) increase understanding about SDWTs, and (3) create an implementation plan for SDWTs. To accomplish these objectives, the facilitators designed a two-day program that included an exercise to review past and present mistakes, lessons, and successes; a visioning exercise to create the new self-directed organization; and an open space (Owen, 1992) exercise to plan the next steps. Additionally, as prework for the meeting, each leadership team member, with the help of a teammate, prepared a small presentation about an aspect of SDWTs. This intragroup training, or "each one, teach one approach," reinforced the concept of the leadership team's taking responsibility for its own learning and decreasing its dependence on outside experts.

The leadership team left its second program with a plan for moving forward to an organization comprised of SDWTs and with an understanding about what had prevented it from being successful in the past. The team also successfully resolved several residual interpersonal issues that arose during the course of the meeting.

Moving Forward—The 10 Team Development Programs

After the leadership team program, the facilitators joined forces with the Gap Busters to form a Program Development Team (PDT) to design and deliver each of the training programs. The team programs were modeled after the leadership team's first training and included all of the elements described above, such as personal awareness exercises, a high ropes course, one-on-one feedback sessions, and conflict resolution skills. The programs were reduced to three days; therefore, some of the material, such as information on personality types, was incorporated into introductory meetings that were held before each off-site meeting.

To ensure that the unique needs of each team were met, the PDT spent a total of one and a half days with each team prior to their training. One day was for observation. It included observation of a one-hour team meeting, a one-hour review of the MBTI, including the current team type, and a one-on-one interview with each team member. Following the observation day, the PDT synthesized the data into themes. These themes were reported back and validated with each team, and then the PDT and the team used them to create the team's training objectives.

The PDT were colearners during the intervention and continuously improved the design. First, an introduction to training day was added because the personal and team development program was substantially different from the traditional training programs that the organization was accustomed to. During this meeting, teams were given information about the training and had the opportunity to make decisions about their own program. Some of the decisions they made were the type of activities the team would do on its team night, whether they would bring alcohol, and whether the entire team would stay overnight. Also during this meeting, a panel of past participants discussed their experiences and answered questions. Their participation reinforced the idea that the PDT and facilitators were not the experts, and encouraged the organization to support its own learning.

Follow-Up

After each team program, the PDT used participant feedback to make improvements to the next program. In addition, each team participated in a final Observe/Coach Day three to four months after its program. During this day, the facilitator team did the following:
- helped the team review personal assumptions and tools from the program
- observed a team meeting

- made process observations
- heard feedback from team members on team progress
- delivered just-in-time training based on needs identified via observations and the team's self-assessment.

Following is a detailed summary of the steps of the intervention by date:

- *August 1996: Deliverables established.* The leadership group gives the facilitator team a list of expected deliverables, which include: (1) design and deliver team improvement training and support for eight customer support teams, (2) design and deliver facilitative leadership training and coaching for four team leads, (3) develop and deliver a team effectiveness measurement instrument and process, and (4) provide general support to the Customer Support Center leadership and external consultants during the team improvement process.

- *August-September 1996: Initial assessment conducted.* Findings included: (1) meetings are poorly run and ineffective, (2) there is difficulty in making decisions, (3) there is a lack of role clarity, (4) the manager is having difficulties with the group, and (5) members feel that they lack needed skills for the team environment they have created.

- *August-September 1996: Past research reviewed.* Facilitator team reviews gap research and information. Findings included: (1) employees did not know about SDWTs or why the organization is organized around teams, (2) there is a lack of role clarity between team members, (3) team members are not taking personal responsibility for their team relationships or work.

- *September 1996: Deliverables revised.* Based on the above findings, the deliverables are changed as follows: (1) to include nine customer teams and an administrative support team in the program, (2) to include a personal awareness and coaching aspect in the program, and (3) to have the entire leadership group instead of just the team leads participate in the team program.

- *September 1996: Intervention planned.* Using the revised deliverables, the facilitator team maps out an organizational development plan that includes seven basic steps: (1) strategy articulation meetings; (2) initial leadership group training; (3) follow-up leadership team training and planning session; (4) baseline team observation and feedback; (5) team programs; (6) follow-up team observations, feedback, and JIT training; and (7) leadership team coaching.

- *October 1996: Strategy meetings held.* In an attempt to have everyone at the support center understand the strategy and the manager's vision of moving to SDWTs, a series of four meetings (each attended by a portion of the LCSC) are held. The manager commits to supporting the organization in achieving a level of high performance for all teams by the end of 1997 and becoming self-directed by 1999.

- *October 1996: Prepare the leadership group.* The facilitator team prepares the leadership group by reviewing the MBTI, examining the group's team type, and asking the members to evaluate how they feel they are doing as a team through the use of several outdoor experiential activities.
- *November 1996: The leadership group's team program.* The facilitator team meets with the leadership group to verify that it bought into the manager's vision of moving to SDWTs and prepares the members for the off-site meeting. The leadership group's transformation from a group to a team is accomplished in two parts. Part 1 combines both personal development and team skills. Part 2 applies the learning from the first part and creates the next steps in strategy implementation.
- *December 1996 to April 1997: The 10 Team Programs.* The leadership group requests that all the team programs last three days and be similar in design to the one it had. The programs are held from mid-December 1996 through April 1997.
- *March-June 1997: Follow-up, the observe/coach days.* The facilitator team observes team meetings individually, offers feedback, and reviews the tools learned during the team programs. Additional tools are taught on a JIT basis according to each team's needs.
- *June 1997: Closure with the leadership team.* As the final step of the intervention, the facilitator team conducts a participative final presentation. A celebration luncheon follows.

Lessons Learned
Learning From Mistakes

Throughout the intervention, the facilitators struggled with how directive to be during the team programs. A directive approach would have perpetuated the blaming culture that the intervention was trying to change. For example, when the facilitators used a directive approach and told the participants that they were required to stay overnight, participants responded with anger and resentment toward the facilitators. However, when the facilitators allowed the team to make this decision themselves, the team responded by accommodating their team members' needs. As a result, only two out of 80 people declined to stay overnight. This experience also provided a first lesson in group decision making.

Another difficulty faced during the intervention was how to respond to the few participants who felt the training was not worthwhile.

Although the facilitators told participants that they were always free to leave the team programs, several members questioned the freedom of that choice because the program was sponsored by their employer. Comments from just one passively cynical or openly critical participant impeded the team's development and hampered the learning of the other participants. The facilitators dealt with uncooperative participants by focusing on the tools and objectives of the program and by supporting those team members who wanted to participate. They also helped turn around some cynical participants by helping them connect with the commitments that were underlying their complaints, such as their commitment to their team's success.

A third issue the facilitators faced was not overloading the program. Each program had very ambitious objectives, and the PDT routinely attempted to tackle them all. After receiving feedback from participants that the days ran too long and that there were not enough breaks, the facilitators modified the design to provide longer breaks. However, the issue of overloading was never successfully resolved.

Finally, another lesson was about balancing the need for the teams to keep their training experience confidential yet share what they learned with the rest of the organization. The facilitators let the teams determine how they wanted to talk about their experiences when they returned from their team programs and most preferred to say very little. The net effect was that very little cross-team learning occurred. The facilitators might have been able to increase the shared learning if they had included an all-team intervention after the team programs were completed. By not encouraging cross-team communication, the facilitators lost an opportunity to create a mechanism for teams to support each other in keeping their program alive and to reinforce their personal and team lessons.

Key Success Factors

One of the most significant factors contributing to the success of the program was the approach of the facilitators and leadership team, which emphasized walking the talk. Two important aspects of this approach were the facilitators' position as colearners throughout the program and the patience and courage of the leadership group. The leadership group took a risk by deciding to offer this unusual training program. Its members managed the organization's initial concerns about the program by first clarifying the support center's strategy and then linking that strategy to the training. They also were willing to go through their own training first.

Another key success factor was the program's innovative design. First, it included a personal development component. The facilitators felt it was essential to start with self-awareness before moving to interpersonal or team development. They believe that many team-building attempts fail because the sometimes difficult work of personal change is not tackled and therefore does not occur in traditional team-skills training. Second, the training was designed to incorporate a variety of learning styles. Having different types of activities modeled an appreciation of diversity and helped reach different types of participants. Third, the use of a rustic unconventional site was critical to creating a unique and safe learning experience.

A third factor for success was the manager's leadership. During the intervention, he took great risks within his organization and with his superiors. He also provided the facilitators freedom to do what the organization needed and was open to their coaching. He was willing to examine his own behaviors, interactions, and assumptions. The manager also took the time and made the effort to articulate his organizational vision clearly and outline how the team training programs were consistent with that vision.

The fourth success factor was the use of a group of three Mobil Lubes employees (the Gap Busters) to work with the facilitators as the PDT. Having Mobil employees assist in all aspects of the program ensured that each program was customized, relevant, and useful for the organization. The Gap Busters offered insider knowledge that the facilitators would have not otherwise known. Working together with internal employees was also consistent with the facilitator's colearner approach, and discouraged the organization from viewing the facilitators as experts. In addition, these people remain in the organization as key change agents and continue to be informal facilitators and instructors.

Table 1 summarizes the lessons learned.

Results

Since the intervention, the Lubes Customer Support Center's business results have improved dramatically, as the following changes show:
- Phone response time has improved, from 57 percent to 95 percent of calls being answered within 30 seconds.
- Mobil's cash flow has been improved by $8 million through reducing Days Sales Outstanding the equivalent of two days.
- Pricing errors have declined by 500 percent.
- Invoice errors have been reduced from 4 percent to 1.2 percent of total invoices (on 50,000 invoices monthly).

Table 1. Lessons learned.

	Manager and Leadership Team	Facilitator Team
Organizational Change Process	• Be open, willing, and able to take risks. • Have the support of higher management. • Clearly articulate and communicate vision and why change process is necessary to organization. • Be comfortable with uncertainty of the outcome. • Be willing to go through self-assessment and understand there is a relationship between one's own change and development and the organization's change. • Remember change is not an event but a process.	• Have the leadership team go through their own training first. • Act as colearners throughout the process and be interdependent and vulnerable. • Be sensitive to the unique needs of the organization. • Recognize that internal employees (e.g., Gap Busters) on program design team are invaluable. • Have full support of management. • Remember change is a nonlinear process. • Do not insert facilitator team as member of organization.
Team-Training Programs	• Be willing to finance the project. • Trust facilitators and let them design program. • Respect participants' confidentiality. • Reinforce learning by modeling use of tools and lessons learned in the program. • Support teams' constant learning by sharing personal learning and leadership team's learning on an ongoing basis. • Be willing to support team decisions, even those that are contrary to the leadership team's thinking.	• Have team members set the objectives for the training (in response to feedback from observation days). • Be willing to use a unique design. Combine a variety of elements to reach all personality types and learning styles. • Debrief and continuously improve; use evaluations to make changes to program. • Facilitators should be colearners and model different learning styles. • Program should be off site to create a "safe place" for learning. • Do not overpack schedule. Allow time to reflect on what has been learned.

Conclusion

Things look different now when you enter the Mobil Lubes Customer Support Center. Team meetings are much more productive, and team members have far more autonomy. Teams are hiring their own team members, managing their own budgets, making decisions about how to change the role structure within their teams and across teams, and conducting new member transition sessions. Communication is more direct and honest, and problems are more quickly resolved. Team members are voluntarily soliciting feedback from one another, and teams are less isolated from each other as they ask each other for help in solving their problems.

The leadership team is working on sustaining the gains they have made. They and the other members of the Lubes Customer Support Center continue to face the day-to-day challenges of their organization and strive to maintain the trust, open communication, and enthusiasm that was generated during the teaming initiative.

Currently, they are implementing a new computer system that has a significant impact on every job in the center. The teams have demonstrated remarkable skill and resilience while undergoing this major change. In addition, Mike Quick left LCSC in December 1998 to begin a new position with Mobil. A selection committee consisting of LCSC employees, his supervisor, and other Mobil employees selected his replacement, utilizing a process that LCSC team members designed. The committee promoted John Pleasant, one of the original Gap Busters, to the LCSC manager position because of his demonstrated leadership and commitment to the center during these changes. This decision is noteworthy because in Mobil it is rare for someone from within the organization to be promoted to a manager position such as this. This decision and the process from which it was made ensure the continuity and sustainability of the new LCSC culture.

LCSC has become a showcase for effective teamwork, and is frequently asked to tell their story to other organizations, both inside and outside Mobil. Its employees continue to successfully meet or exceed annual goals and take on additional responsibilities on their path to becoming fully self-directed work teams.

A Typical Day, Revisited

Sarah had to hurry into work this morning because she was facilitating her team meeting. The main topic on the agenda was how the team was going to complete a huge project involving incorrect billings and pricing errors, most of which were caused by people outside the team.

Her team lead was not going to be there, but she was confident that her team could address the issues anyway. This was a big change from a year ago when she was first hired onto the team. Certainly, her knowledge and understanding of the job had changed, but there was more. People around her were more willing to discuss things and take everyone's view into account. Her team lead appeared to be helping the team rather than ignoring their problems. Sarah truly enjoyed working with the people around her.

As the meeting began, Sarah reviewed why they had agreed to meet, what the time contract was, and what the desired outcome of the meeting was. Lori brought up the fact that it really wasn't the team's problem because they didn't cause the majority of the errors. Another team member countered by saying that it didn't make a difference who caused the error, the team should take ownership of fixing it. Jerry said this was an awfully big project and that the only way he could see accomplishing it would be to work on the weekend. To that everyone let out a groan.

Sarah asked if anyone knew what the work would actually entail, and everyone admitted they hadn't really taken the time to understand the many issues involved. The team spent the first part of the meeting identifying what work would need to be done. Then, knowing what the project involved, they divided up tasks and took responsibility for accomplishing specific pieces.

Sarah reminded them they also needed to set some due dates. Because their time contract for the meeting was up, they agreed to list their ideas via e-mail and vote electronically on the top three. A short morning meeting would be held to decide, by consensus, what the completion time frame would look like. In addition, the team volunteered to help the entire department learn the correct procedures to prevent this from happening again. Sarah was very happy; her team had made great progress in just a two-hour meeting and without the team lead.

Questions for Discussion

1. What are the key assumptions that underlie this intervention?
2. What kind of support did management provide in this initiative? What should be the role of management in a team-based organization?
3. What did the manager, leadership group, and facilitators do in this initiative that will contribute to the future development of self-directed work teams? What could they have done differently that might have contributed further?
4. What will team members and management need to do in order to sustain this organizational change? What support systems do you think they will need to put into place to sustain this change?
5. How can some of the principles in this case be applied to your organization?

The Authors

Peg Howell, formerly of Moore-Howell Associates, is president of Howell Consulting Group, L.C., an organizational change management firm specializing in the human side of strategy implementation and team building. In the past, she's been national marketing manager for Outward Bound's professional development programs, director of business development for Cabot Corporation, assistant dean of M.B.A. Program Administration at Harvard Business School, and offshore drilling engineer for Chevron USA. She holds an M.B.A. from the Harvard University Graduate School of Business Administration and a B.S. in petroleum engineering from Marietta College. Howell can be reached at phowell914@aol.com or 2033 Wethersfield Court, Reston, VA 20191-3627.

Sharon Lamm is president of Lamm Associates, Ltd., an adult learning and organization development firm. She has experience as an internal and external consultant, and has worked with several organizations in a variety of industries. Her work spans across the United States, Europe, Beijing, Hong Kong, and Singapore. Lamm holds a B.S. in management, B.A. in psychology, and master's degree in industrial and labor relations from Cornell University, and she is currently completing her doctoral dissertation in adult education at Teachers College, Columbia University. She has written and presented papers at several professional and academic conferences.

Stacey Philpot is a doctoral candidate in organizational psychology at Rutgers University. She has experience administering a variety of organizational, team, and individual assessments, and is a certified consultant for Team Management Systems and the Myers-Briggs Type Indicator. Philpot graduated from Dickinson College with a B.A. in social psychology.

Michael Quick has worked for Mobil Oil Corporation since 1985. He has held various positions in sales and operations including marketing team manager, territory manager, and production supervisor. He was appointed lube customer support manager in 1995 and currently holds that position. Quick graduated from Iowa State with a B.S. in chemical engineering and distributed studies.

References

Argyris, C. (1990). *Overcoming Organizational Defenses*. Needham, MA: Allyn and Bacon.

Kegan, R. (1996, July 12). Lecture for the Institute of Workplace Learning. Teacher's College, Columbia University, New York.

Myers, I., and M. McCaulley. (1985).*Manual: A Guide to the Development and Use of the Myers-Briggs Type Indicator.* Palo Alto, CA: Consulting Psychologists Press.

Owen, H. (1992). *Open Space Technology: A User's Guide.* Potomac, MD: Abbot.

Tuckman, B. (1965). "Developmental Sequence in Small Groups." *Psychological Bulletin 6396,* 384–399.

Transforming a Traditional Manufacturing Organization

Pall Gelman Sciences

Greg Scheessele and Susan Heathfield

Gelman Sciences, a division of the Pall Corporation, has undergone a trans-formational change that revolutionized the relationship of the company with the people it employs. At the same time, the company has revolutionized its manufacturing and distribution processes and transformed the corporate cul-ture in the operations group. This case study explores the journey under-taken by company members since 1993; it highlights both the successes and the steps company leaders would do differently, from a four-year retrospec-tive. This journey transformed a traditional, hierarchical, corporate culture, which stifled ingenuity and contribution, to one of high-performing cells in which people run their manufacturing areas almost as small businesses.

Gelman Sciences has several manufacturing facilities. This case study highlights the progress of plant 1, Cartridge/Capsule manufacturing in Ann Arbor, Michigan, and its relationship with corporate leadership.

Background

In 1993, Charles Gelman, founder and CEO of Gelman Sciences, a leading manufacturer of microporous membrane filtration prod-ucts, recognized the need to change the culture of his company. His concern evolved from awareness of industry competition, the desire to grow in sales and profitability, and the conviction that the com-pany was underutilizing the people it employed. He also wanted a workplace that fostered "happy" people.

This case was prepared to serve as a basis for discussion rather than to illustrate either effective or in-effective administrative and management practices.

Gelman also recognized, in the face of several failed employee participation efforts, that he needed to do something differently this time. He was convinced that tapping the ability of the people in the company to contribute more than their production capabilities was the key to the future of the company. Unfortunately, at the time this story begins, company employees viewed these efforts as the flavor of the month and were disenfranchised and reluctant to participate in the next program.

At the same time, the Gelman Sciences culture was one of fear, in which managers concerned themselves with their own areas only, and vice presidents and midlevel managers hoarded power. These individuals micromanaged the work of others and operated an old-time manufacturing company, in a modern industry.

Industry Profile

The microfiltration and separation industry services many industries. The primary industries include industrial process (for example, pharmaceutical and electronics), laboratory, research, quality control, and the medical device field (for example, IV therapy and blood filtration). It is a highly regulated industry (including, for example, the Food and Drug Administration, Good Manufacturing Practices, CE mark, and ISO certification).

The key players in the marketplace were Pall, Millipore, Gelman Sciences, Whatman, and Sartorious plus many smaller niche contenders. Pall and Millipore are the two largest competitors with annual sales near $1 billion and $600 million, respectively. Gelman Sciences had annual sales of $120 million in recent history.

In February 1997, Pall acquired Gelman Sciences in order to expand its own product portfolio in the areas of lab and membrane products. This expansion was in response to the ever-increasing demand by customers to be a full-service supplier and to compete more directly with Millipore in all markets. (Millipore is a large supplier to the lab and analytical marketplace.)

In general, product development and marketing have driven the industry, with minimal attention to customer service, responsiveness, and supply chain management. Margins are high due to the nature of industry pricing. However, this has started to change in the past four to six years. Customers are becoming more supply chain cost conscious; regulations and governing bodies are beginning to challenge health-care costs. Practices common to other market arenas are influencing the industry.

Leadership Is Key

Concerned about prior failures, Charles Gelman hired a consultant, Susan Heathfield, in 1993, to work with company management to design a participation process.

Greg Scheessele, the newly hired associate director of manufacturing for plant 1, firmly believed in the concepts of employee participation and lean manufacturing, as exemplified by the Toyota Production System. He believes people are an organization's greatest and most flexible resource of knowledge, skill, and capacity.

The key change that led to an environmental shift was Scheessele's promotion to vice president of operations, with responsibility for two plants and the warehousing and distribution activities of Ann Arbor. He determined that the group could not succeed in leading Gelman Sciences to growth and profitability if it did not revise its culture and establish direction and focus.

Thus, Scheessele and key operations' staff members developed a mission statement to focus operations' efforts and supporting measurement systems to guide resource allocation and ensure ownership. The group recognized that all employees would need to be involved as team members and would be required or encouraged to assume control and leadership over their work processes if progress were to be sustained. This was the beginning of the change process.

Under Scheessele's guidance, and in this environment, a plan for continuous improvement teams, formed around work processes, was initiated in the plant. Simultaneously, two University of Michigan graduate students were hired to map the process flow of the plant with the long-term goal of streamlining and refining process and product flow and to create the opportunity for manufacturing cells and lean manufacturing practices.

In June 1993, the plan moved forward. Doug Broughman, formerly in finance, was promoted to manufacturing manager. This change resulted in the two key managers responsible for the plant sharing a vision and a direction that has not faltered.

Changes in Management Philosophy and Vision

At the time of the implementation discussions, the operations' management (and entire organization, for that matter) did not consider a team-based culture and structure to be very productive. Also, very little effort was spent developing and communicating vision and direction because most of the leadership came from, and was expected to come from, two senior people within the company. One of these individuals was the founder and CEO. The other person was the president and chief operating officer (COO). The team-building efforts prior to 1994 included very focused product market and development teams and a few teams oriented to business processes. In all cases, the teams were managed very closely with minimal resources provided and little direction and vision provided as guiding lights. As a result, the teams failed.

In the beginning of the change process, the manager or supervisor set the pace and direction (most likely received from above). The manager determined if progress was under way and, if it wasn't, changed course with little communication to the workers. As a result, the employees had little or no insight into the overall game plan.

At this point, motivation was low. People would not take ownership of their work processes because of lack of knowledge and fear of reprisal. Absenteeism was high. People believed the only opportunity to advance within the company was to achieve managerial status. This environment was exemplified by a sign a manager posted on a machine: "1,250 per shift, Just Do It."

Evidence of overall morale issues cropped up at management brown bag lunches with the CEO or in messages left for the CEO on the voice mail system. When employees complained, the CEO took their input as fact, and either management was disciplined, up to and including termination, or direction was changed on the basis of a single piece of information.

The position a person held within the organization was a major influence on the lower morale. Senior management didn't always seriously consider employee input, taking the view that, "How could an employee know enough to improve the business?" Also, the fear of being fired for any reason was high. This concern stifled most involvement and risk taking.

A changed message began to emanate from the corporate offices. Today, management's role has changed considerably with the implementation of work teams.

On the basis of the identified culture and the plans for the future, managers and supervisors who were planning the implementation of teams determined that the training must be both a conversion process and a training process. Thus, managers, supervisors, engineers, and other managerial and support personnel participated in six months of training before teams were implemented.

Topics of the training included participatory management, that is, the Toyota Production System methods of Tiachii Ohno for continuous improvement, fourth-generation management from Joiner Associates, philosophy of management, the supervisor's changing role, and communication. Managerial and support personnel viewed films and held discussions, first biweekly and then weekly, before other employees were included. Participants read books and articles and familiarized themselves with the new philosophies. These meetings also established the framework for teams within plant 1.

Work Teams Planned

An informal assessment of organizational culture and structure was made while the plans for teams were developed. Operations' management determined employees' capabilities and their ability to grow, and identified necessary training to overcome the areas of weakness. The organizational structure and capability assessment identified the following features:

- The materials planner, purchasing group, and materials group associated with the plant's product lines did not report directly to the plant and had their own objectives.
- The manufacturing engineering organization reported to a separate manager within the operations' group. The manager did not believe in progressive technical methods and did not support employee ownership and involvement. The manager's belief was that people should be replaced with automation. He also believed that the production unit should be protected from the influence of outside groups such as marketing, planning, and research and development (R&D). Also, over 50 percent of the engineering staff did not have the formal technical preparation necessary to perform their responsibilities, and 90 percent of them did not think in terms of process. Instead, they thought of and addressed opportunities as components and did not understand basic continuous improvement concepts.
- The entire production area was segregated into four walled-in areas in separate parts of the building. Communication was impeded.
- Plant Quality Control did not understand the concept of continuous improvement or variation reduction. Quality staff members also reported to a separate functional group with separate objectives.
- The production and maintenance employees did not have basic team building, problem solving, and resource management skills.
- The supervisors and managers had never coached teams or led organizational improvement efforts. Their direction had focused them on two areas of responsibility: completing projects that senior management gave to them and getting daily production through the plant

and over to the warehouse. They were skeptical about employees' ability to help with continuous improvement or their willingness to do so.

- Plant production employees were recovering from the failure of a variety of programs implemented over the years. Most were skeptical about anything different happening this time. Some people were also comfortable doing jobs that did not require them to think.
- The larger organization, with its political and fear-driven culture, and its lack of shared values, beliefs, direction, and vision, had had a significant impact on prior efforts for change in the plant.

Operations management addressed each of these issues over four years.

Work Teams Implemented

The plant's management group met with the consultant to plan how to create a culture in which employees worked to improve the plant's processes. Operations' management gave clear direction to the plant management that the current culture would not support the improvements necessary for the future.

Once the plant management team developed an implementation plan, which included team structure, the purpose for the teams, the timing for team rollout, and so on, it informed the employees of the change in operating structure. During meetings with each shift, the plant management asked all employees to become committed to and involved in the changes. Each session provided time for questions and answers. At times, the managers had to say they didn't know exactly how the changes would turn out, but they consistently communicated that they expected to make progress.

The entire process was difficult for the plant management team, which was facing doing something it had never done before. At this time, the plant manager was new to his position. The organization was on the verge of radically changing its structure and culture. There were diverse feelings in the management group about involving hourly employees in teams. However, the management team provided the leadership necessary for the team process.

After the meetings, in October 1993, approximately 15 process-driven teams were established. Team sizes ranged from four to approximately 12 production operators. There were some difficulties in keeping teams communicating across three shifts, so some teams combined across shifts, making them too large for effective participation. To solve this problem, teams met by shift, and occasionally met across shifts to discuss mutual issues. Teams were provided an hour per week for continuous improvement activities, and an engineer was assigned to each team to support their efforts. Communication was expanded and, simultaneously, the Operations Group worked to measure process performance, so teams would know how they were doing.

An external consultant offered initial training in two-hour blocks once a month for 18 months. At the time, this was a risky strategy both for management and employees because former change efforts at Gelman Sciences experienced brief support before management discarded them as failures. In order for the current training to be effective and lasting, it needed to be provided over an extended time frame. However, the employees felt the training would never be completed because management would not commit to the extended time. Instead, the employees felt management would drop this approach and pursue another theme of the day before the initial training was completed.

Initially, the training was scheduled for 12 months, but it was extended to 18 months because the plant manager wanted to ensure longer term support for the fledgling groups. While the groups became more supportive of the process and the training was provided, supervisors and engineers were expected to attend and work closely with the teams so they would experience success.

Training topics included the following:
- why the company wanted to develop teams and change the plant culture
- how to ensure team success (meeting management, supportive paperwork, resource justification)
- problem solving
- quality tools
- communication including listening, idea presentation, and feedback
- conflict resolution
- continuous improvement
- goal setting and measurement.

A comment that a production operator made to the consultant during the first class session demonstrates the amount of progress the team members needed to make. This operator glared at the consultant, folded her arms, and said, "We don't have to do a thing. You'll be out of here in six months, and everything will get back to normal." She was brave to speak up, but others felt the same way. (Twelve months later, this individual was the recorder on her team, and regularly asked when the next training class was scheduled.)

Shortly after this, and important for the evolution of the teams, the plant layout was revised to include one open production area that had a process-driven layout with open communication between production and quality control.

These teams have been continuously evolving, under the direction of Doug Broughman, and the plant supervisors, Luanne Ignasiak and Doug Fett, who were recently joined by Kevin Smith.

The Evolution of the Plant and the Teams

While the teams were receiving their training, managers and supervisors continued to meet with the consultant to redesign their roles. As an example of how this role was redefined, during the first year, based on the corporate direction established by Greg Scheessele and his team, Doug Broughman created the strategic plan and the measurables for the plant by himself. The next year he included supervisors and others in his planning retreat. In 1997, Broughman included supervisors and representatives of the teams in the planning retreat.

By the end of 1994, it was evident that although the teams had made progress and were contributing to continuous improvement, more education was needed for everyone. The management group also needed to determine a more effective method for managing and leading the teams. Successes were receiving attention from management, but few others in the company were learning from the successes.

Teams had a tendency to complete a project and then drift without direction. The most successful teams were those in which an engineer or a supervisor played an active role. During this time, the teams were asked to begin measuring their work and setting improvement goals. Managers hoped that the groups would take ownership of their measurements and begin to focus on scrap reduction, productivity, and quality to a greater degree. During the first year, many, but not all, team projects focused on housekeeping and other comfort and safety-related issues.

In 1994, a lean-manufacturing and quality assurance consultant, Walton Hancock, a professor from the University of Michigan, was engaged to assist with scrap reduction in the plant. After familiarizing himself with the plant's work processes, he provided training in methods of lean manufacturing to operations management, the engineers, and representatives from quality and finance. The class met once per week for two hours, and Hancock gave homework assignments that related specifically to the plant's process improvement plans. He also provided weekly follow-up and interim guidance. The major focus of his assignments was on reducing waste, especially scrap reduction, within the operations.

This training provided members of the plant with additional tools with which they could attack problems and a better understanding of lean thinking.

Personnel Changes

Everyone associated with continuous improvement and teams received at least 18 months of training, coaching, and encouragement to participate wholeheartedly in the emerging, changing culture. At the end of that time, three groups continued to put up roadblocks to progress, necessitating the following personnel changes:

- The engineering manager was released. Teams had experienced support from engineering only when an individual engineer was personally motivated and interested in providing support. The larger organization, under the leadership of this individual, did not support the team process. Additionally, several engineers who could not make the transition from a project to a process orientation and were not motivated to improve current processes were urged to leave the company. Teams went to great lengths to develop positive relationships with these engineers. (One team even sent its photograph to its assigned engineer to remind him of its existence and need for his help.)

  The engineering manager was not replaced immediately (the group now reports to the plant manager), and the company filled the open engineering positions with process-oriented, analytical, degreed engineers. Several of the new engineers were industrial engineers who were able to work closely with the teams.

- The materials group was reorganized to report directly to the plant manager, and its objectives were aligned with the plant's plans. Employees received team training and lean-manufacturing training. Doug Scheessele asked Bryon Marks, the leader of the group, to develop the plant's relationships with suppliers and bring lean thinking to purchasing and material management.

- Reporting in an isolated quality organization, quality control employees were unable to make the transition from their traditional quality role to the new role that teams require. The quality control organization was reorganized to report directly to the plant manager. Members received training and were challenged to become involved with solving and preventing process problems, rather than inspecting for and reporting errors. Human resource staff members became involved with these changes to ensure equitable compensation, to act as sounding boards for anxious employees, and to assist with the process of improvement.

- Finally, a group of hourly employees, known as group leaders, needed to change their role. The supervisor who led them asked the group leaders to redesign their role to align more appropriately with the evolution of high-performance work teams. The longer the operations group worked with teams, the more confident they became that teams could evolve to self-direction. The group leaders knew the building was evolving into cells dictated by product flow and away from the old process orientation, wherein one group leader led all of the people who worked on a pleating machine, for example. The group did not make much progress in the first several months, but eventually recognized and met the challenge. This slow progress was primarily because they perceived the changes as a loss to themselves. By 1997, members of this group were serving as cell facilitators in a completely redesigned role reporting to production supervisors.

Human Resource Systems

Over the past four years, significant changes have been made in all human resource support systems, including compensation, the recognition system, the appraisal system, and job descriptions.

Prior to the formation of teams, the company had implemented a program in which employees who suggested cost-saving measures that were implemented received up to 10 percent of the savings their plan generated during the first year. Once teams were formed, it became clear that the program was breeding competition, ill will, and conflict. Employees would not freely offer an idea in a team meeting if they then had to share the award with team members. The suggestion program was changed to demonstrate a bias in favor of team suggestions and for implementation of the ideas, rather than idea origination. This change also caused teams to become active in data collection and measurement following the implementation of their ideas. (Since becoming part of the Pall Corporation in February 1997, this system has been phased out; it is likely it would have been eliminated in any case. The suggestion program generated unhealthy competition and created a climate in which people felt they must receive payment for anything extra they did or for any idea they generated. As an example, in one Gelman facility, a group wanted an award for suggesting an ice cream vending machine in the lunchroom.)

Over the next couple of years, with the assistance of Gary Yezbick, the vice president of human resources, and the human resources staff, the company adopted a gainsharing system. The gainsharing system has had three years to evolve, and the measurements have become more closely tied, each year, to what plant employees actually control. The system focuses employee effort on productivity improvement, scrap reduction and reliable, timely customer delivery performance. The program has the potential to increase each employee's gross compensation by 10 percent.

Early in the process, the company changed its performance appraisal system to provide support for the continuous improvement process. Fifty percent of the review was dedicated to recognizing people who performed well with their team, in the training activities, and in leadership activities with the teams. Plant management informed the entire group a year in advance that the performance review process would change. The new format was introduced and explained at length. Because employees were worried about the new and higher expectations, the management group developed methods for employees to "recover" if an individual did not meet the standards expressed in the review format. (Unfortunately, the company has not eliminated the annual performance review, but because of the creation of team measures, employees do know how they are doing on a daily basis.) The next step in the evolution of the groups will be a peer review system.

The job description of every position within the plant changed significantly over the past couple of years. The descriptions now include team involvement responsibilities and encourage creativity and involvement. Employees were significantly involved in creating the new job descriptions.

Additionally, Greg Scheessele holds quarterly communication meetings with everyone who works for Pall Gelman Sciences. These meetings update staff on the business and provide an opportunity for questions and discussion. Frequent plant meetings provide even more opportunities for communication.

The Steering Committee

As teams progressed, in late 1994, the management group sought a way to support them more closely. The consultant encouraged Doug Broughman to assign an internal employee to the role of training and teams. Because no one was available, she encouraged the start of a steering committee to supplement the management group that already supported the teams. Broughman founded the Continuous Improvement Steering Committee in July 1995, and it has met weekly ever since to more closely support the teams. A cross-functional group of people from operations management, quality, materials, and engineering make up this group. Each member also serves as the sponsor to one or more teams. The role of the sponsor is support, communication, and training. In 1997, the group was expanded even further to include several cell facilitators.

The steering committee reviews projects, team mission statements, meeting minutes, and team objectives. The group defined its purpose or mission as, "to foster, encourage, and build a continuous team environment in Building #1 Operations by providing direction, resources, training, and feedback to the continuous improvement teams in a consistent and regular manner."

The group meets at least annually with each team. At first, teams that were scheduled to meet with the steering committee put together elaborate presentations that took weeks to prepare. To encourage more attention to improvements and less attention to the presentation, the steering committee established guidelines for length and content. The committee has a rotating leader and meets weekly on an alternating day, so sponsors have the opportunity to meet with their teams regularly. During the weekly meeting, the group recognizes staff and team accomplishments by posting items to what it calls a good news board.

The steering committee has recently redesigned itself to meet with a different purpose each week. One week the group meets to assign short-term Kaizen (that is, continuous improvement) projects or problems to solve; the next week it meets with the operations group for the building. In another week, it meets with scheduled teams. In the final week, it reviews the progress on the Kaizen projects. The steering committee has been a highly successful team that has worked well to provide leadership for the other teams.

The Past Year: Evolution Continues

In late 1995, the operations staff began to think about cellular manufacturing to further incorporate principles of lean manufacturing, to redesign teams around product flow, and to give people control over a whole product or process where possible. The group experimented with several approaches to designing cells and went on field trips to other companies with operating cells. The operations group moved some machines closer together and limited the number of tubs of work in progress (WIP). Encouraged by the small successes even this limited approach to cells afforded, Broughman sent two supervisors, Luanne Ignasiak and Doug Fett, and two industrial engineers, Matt Zayko and Sarah (Neill) Deiner, to a cellular manufacturing seminar sponsored by the Society of Manufacturing Engineers (SME).

During 1996, this group designed a weeklong class to bring all plant employees up to speed about the advantages and benefits of cellular manufacturing. At this point, the 15 teams in the building were completely reorganized by the operations group into eight product-based cell teams. Their training, which Ignasiak, Fett, Zayko, and Deiner provided for each cell individually, covered the advantages and difficulties of switching to cells, how to draw a process flow chart for a product moving through the cell, and the difference between value-added and non–value-added steps to the customer in the operation. Training also taught quality control procedures, capacity analysis, line balancing, task times, and the use of visual display boards as well as how to compute cell capacity, how to run the line when understaffed, and how to organize work areas through the use of tool boards.

Following training, Ignasiak, Fett, Zayko, and Deiner assisted each cell to design several layouts. Since then, team members have grown in their ability to manage their own work area every day. The teams are making changes in their cells, tracking their own measurements, setting goals, making and following their own schedule, releasing their own material, solving downtime problems, and serving on the steering committee and in planning sessions. Team meetings, for the most part, have moved from conference rooms to the plant floor. More meetings are occurring in real-time problem solving and between shifts.

Currently, the former group leaders are transitioning into the role of cell facilitators. They are meeting with the consultant to redesign their role and receive coaching in the leadership role they designed for themselves to play. (The major stumbling blocks have been that the cell facilitators are expected to run machines and teach their own roles and responsibilities to all members of the cell.) Plans for the next year include peer evaluation, further integration of cell facilitators as team members, and other high-level work-team skills.

Performance Improvement

Pall Gelman Sciences has accomplished much through the continuous improvement process. Supervisors are now coaches and advisors. The boss mentality is diminishing as employees accept ownership. Supervisors are learning and developing skills that allow them to communicate business information to the teams. They redirect teams that have wavered from the expected path, and they have become resource providers. Within cells, communication has strengthened, thereby paving the way for less machine downtime, lower scrap and customer complaints, and less WIP. The teams communicate status between shifts and to suppliers. They are becoming more responsible for addressing supplier quality and delivery issues and have started to interact with customers to resolve mutual problems and eliminate shared waste. As a result, product flow cell teams or project teams are addressing delivery, cost, and quality issues with significant success. Specific results since the implementation of teams include:

- the reduction of product lead times from 10 days to six days on standard products and from 30 days to 14 days on nonstandard, which means 30 percent of products can go out the same day they are ordered.
- improvement in delivery performance from 76.3 percent to 91.2 percent
- increase in inventory turns from 3.5 to 6.5
- reduction in scrap from $1.45 per unit to $.92 per unit
- reduction in cycle time between 25 percent and 45 percent
- increase in throughput from 10.5 units per hour in 1996 to 12.7 units per hour in 1997
- reduction in utilized floor space by 25 percent
- involvement of the entire plant's staff, both hourly and salaried, in managing the plant's future.

Although the progress has been substantial, the most significant accomplishment has been the growth of the people involved with the process. The employees own the business processes and are motivated to continuously improve.

Lessons Learned

Many lessons have been learned during this cultural change. The key lesson is how important communication and the timing of the communication is to the success of this process. A second key opportunity for improvement during the next significant organizational and cultural change will be to involve other functional groups at an earlier point in the change process.

The relationship between operations and the rest of the organization has been strained due to the two very different cultures clashing over the past four years. (As an example, sales and product development staff want to speak with the plant manager about customer or product issues; the plant manager wants them to speak with the team.) Although there were valid reasons to nurture the high-performance teams in isolation from the rest of the company at the beginning of the process, this separation also created rework, a necessity to constantly educate, and fights with other areas of the organization to receive their support for the changes. Earlier communication that would have provided an opportunity for discussion about the impending improvements and organizational growth could have prevented the cultural clashes.

Human resources staff should have been involved earlier in the transition. Human resources department staff members, who supported the plant and organization, wanted to be significantly involved from the beginning. This was in part due to their belief that they should be involved in all changes related to employees. Also, the group did not fully understand the whole concept of employee involvement, decision making, and ownership. In many ways, their lack of early involvement can be defined as a control issue. The human resources group wanted to control the changes; operations management wanted to control the changes. Negotiation over the years brought about more of a partnership.

The control mechanisms (obstacles) used throughout the process by some human resources staff members were job descriptions, lack of career path planning, multiple reviews and approval levels, and slow documentation response time. The other internal obstacle the human resources group had to overcome was that of functional thinking. They hadn't converted to process thinking. This way of thinking had an impact on setting new job expectations, the support required by the operations' management when disciplinary actions were taken, and cooperation between departments.

Recommended future actions include the following:

- Involve the human resources group in the planning and training from the beginning. Never assume the human resources department understands the benefit of employee involvement or ownership or will support the concept. Revise job descriptions to reflect process ownership and continual improvement rather than silo, functional responsibilities, and doing established tasks. Because the continuous improvement process is dynamic, revise the human resource approval processes (that is, reviews, merit increases, promotions, hiring) to become more responsive and flexible to support the environment of improvement.

- Release those who cannot or will not grasp the concepts of continual improvement and employee involvement and ownership earlier in the change process. Examples of these employees in this plant include the engineering manager and several of the engineers. It is noble to make an effort to convert these people, but, at some point, there is no return on the investment of time. This needs to be recognized sooner and acted upon. It will minimize the negative impact of their actions on the success of the rest of the people in the teams.

- It is impossible to overcommunicate. Frequent communication from the vice president of operations and at the plant level is critical for changing the culture, expectations, and roles. Quarterly shift meetings with the vice president should have been implemented earlier in the process. Supervisors should communicate progress, especially praise and recognition for positive progress, more regularly to the cell team members. Communication about the cultural change should have been distributed outside the plant and with interacting groups throughout the organization sooner. This would have reduced the misunderstandings and hurt feelings generated by the cultural difference between the plant and the rest of the organization.

- The teams should have been product-flow driven from the beginning. Although the teams improved the original manufacturing process areas, the nature of process-driven teams impeded communication and measurable progress. Also, process-driven teams were strategically in conflict with the philosophy of lean thinking, and, thus, created undue stress and insufficient progress for the teams. The teams should have been organized in this way originally, even though the company would have had to bite the bullet and invest the money in redesigning the plant. This cannot be stressed enough. Teams must be able to experience progress early in the whole cultural change in order to become absorbed by the change. Team members must become believers.

- Various human resource support, reward, and recognition systems should have been redesigned earlier. Eliminating the suggestion program earlier would have saved some wear and tear on team members. Implementing gainsharing more quickly would have helped people to see what was in it for them earlier in the process.

- Although the group took field trips to other companies later in the process, earlier trips might have helped the supervisors and group leaders see the opportunities differently, and initially, in ways that films, training, books, and articles could not articulate.

- The role of the group leader was the most difficult to change. Plant management should have made a concerted effort to address this role earlier in the process. Because the expectations changed so dramatically, several group leaders eventually decided to leave or move to operator roles. Others resisted, and much training, coaching, and time has been invested in helping them adopt a peer role in their teams.

Conclusion

The transformation of the traditional mass production, batch-and-queue, make-to-order, make-to-stock, top-down directed manufacturing environment to a team-oriented, continuously improving, lean manufacturing environment was possible because of the company's adherence to the following six key areas of philosophical support and actions:
- clear expectations and vision communicated consistently and frequently throughout the operations group
- unwavering commitment and support, with a willingness to experiment, to devote time, and, potentially, to allow failure, from executive and plant management
- supportive consulting and training, both internally and externally provided, as needed, to assist change and knowledge development
- early involvement of appropriate people in honest dialogue
- changing functional responsibilities, management style, and expectations of contribution in all employee groups
- redesigning and creating human resource systems to support progress.

The journey has been both difficult and rewarding. People experienced and created change they could not have visualized in 1993. Changes were introduced steadily and consistently, but everything did not change at once. Changes were made with great concern for people. This allowed most of the people to come with the plant leadership on the journey. No one's job is the same as it was in 1993, and more changes continue to be made every day. Because the people leading and guiding the changes have grown in their roles and the people participating in the teams have grown in their roles, nothing will ever be the same again. The plant progresses on an upward path that is not stoppable given the employees' knowledge, experience, and willingness to keep experimenting.

Questions for Discussion

1. The conclusion to this case study lists six key areas of philosophical support and actions taken to transform the company from a traditional manufacturing environment to a team-based, continuously im-

proving, lean-manufacturing environment. What are these steps and what was done to achieve each of these steps? Why are these areas key to cultural transformation?

2. What were some of the initial obstacles the company faced in its team-implementation process? How did the company deal with these obstacles?

3. Managers had six months of training prior to team implementation. What types of training did they receive? How would you change this stage of the process if you were in charge of the management training?

4. Communication plays a key role in the process of implementing teams. Cite some of the ways communication occurred within this company. Did the company communicate effectively? Why or why not? How could communication have been improved?

5. The group leaders had difficulty transitioning their role to team member and cell facilitator. Why do you think this was such a difficult transition?

6. What lessons did the company learn for making the next improvement evolution or cultural change more effectively?

The Authors

Greg Scheessele is the senior vice president for Gelman Sciences' manufacturing company, a division of the Pall Corporation that specializes in the manufacture of filtration and separation devices for the laboratory, health-care, and industrial process markets. Direct responsibilities include establishing and managing corporate supply chain strategy from order management through manufacturing and distribution. Scheessele has 15 years of industrial experience with 10 years of progressive assignments in quality, engineering, and production at General Motors. He graduated from Purdue University with a Bachelor of Science degree in mechanical engineering and a Master of Science in industrial and systems engineering from the University of Michigan. Scheessele can be reached at Pall Gelman Sciences, 600 S. Wagner Road, Ann Arbor, MI; phone: 734.913.6335; e-mail: gkm-scheessele@worldnet.att.net.

Susan Heathfield is president of Heathfield Consulting Associates, a management consulting, training, and organization development company specializing in the human side of implementing continuous improvement and employee involvement and empowerment through planned change processes. She has worked with more than 100 clients since 1988. Prior to founding her company, Heath-field worked in training and organization development at several General Motors locations and managed the largest community college extension center in Michigan. She earned bachelor's and master's degrees at the University of Michigan. She completed advanced graduate studies at Michigan State University in labor and industrial relations, management, and education. Heathfield can be reached at Heathfield Consulting Associates, 1831 Haslett Road, Williamston, MI 48895; phone: 517.655.3320; e-mail: s.heathfield@tsc.techsmith.com.

Notes

Many thanks to Doug Broughman, Matt Zayko, and Walt Hancock for information about cell formation and lean manufacturing. They highlighted some of this information in an upcoming book chapter on lean manufacturing.

The Learning Council

ETHICON Endo-Surgery, Inc., a Johnson & Johnson Company

Phyllis Saltzman and Amy Meyer

This case study explains the solution employees in one company found to a disorganized learning process. The employees created the Learning Council, a team of associates who volunteered to work together to align organizational training with the company's strategic objectives. This high-performance work team began in 1994 and has already shown measurable results in increasing the company's commitment to training and development and saved the company substantial amounts of money.

Background

The Learning Council is a cross-functional team representing all sites and divisions of ETHICON Endo-Surgery, Inc. (EES), a Johnson & Johnson (J&J) Company. Johnson & Johnson has $22.6 billion in sales and is the world's most comprehensive and broadly based manufacturer of health-care products. EES is one of the fastest-growing companies in the J&J family and produces mechanical and videoscopic surgical products. Its employees firmly believe in the importance of quality and constantly strive to achieve higher levels of quality as a company.

The Learning Council is a self-sustaining team of 15 volunteers, which includes the authors. Each volunteer has a busy, full-time position in his or her own part of the EES world. We come together because of our passion for learning. We have just completed our fourth year as a team.

This case was prepared to serve as a basis for discussion rather than to illustrate either effective or ineffective administrative and management practices.

The Learning Council is the following:

- a team that is driving the learning of the "learning organization"
- a team that hangs together and continues to exist, in spite of being part of an organization in flux
- a team that outproduces and outlives other teams
- a team of professionals that squeeze and reorganize their schedules to attend meetings because the meetings are so productive and so much fun
- a team that shares information rather than hoards it
- a team that holds as a basic tenet the development of its members
- a team that does its share to drive the business.

It focuses on business results through the following:

- building educational networks within the EES community that maximize learning-resource utilization
- establishing new educational platforms to have an impact on business performance
- providing a forum for associates to learn about business and themselves to enhance their ability to contribute to the bottom line.

The Process

Because members of the Learning Council don't work side-by-side in their full-time positions and because members don't attend all council meetings, the clarity of its process becomes essential for its success. Figure 1 illustrates this process.

The process begins and ends with the trainee customer. From an analysis of customer evaluations and upon examination of the business objectives that EES's board of directors sets, we set our goals. We generate alternative, plausible solutions to achievement of these goals. We select solutions, prioritize goals, set time frames, and make team assignments.

Our established group norms and modus operandi allow us to function in a constantly changing environment. We meet as a team every other Wednesday afternoon at a regular time in a regular location. Attendance varies depending upon members' workloads and schedules. The predictability of the meetings makes it feasible to block time and to attend most of the meetings. An agenda is usually sent out before the meeting. At each meeting, a different member volunteers to keep notes. Within 48 hours of the meeting, the volunteer mails out the notes via e-mail to all members. This practice supports active participation by those who were not able to attend that particular meeting.

Figure 1. The Learning Council process.

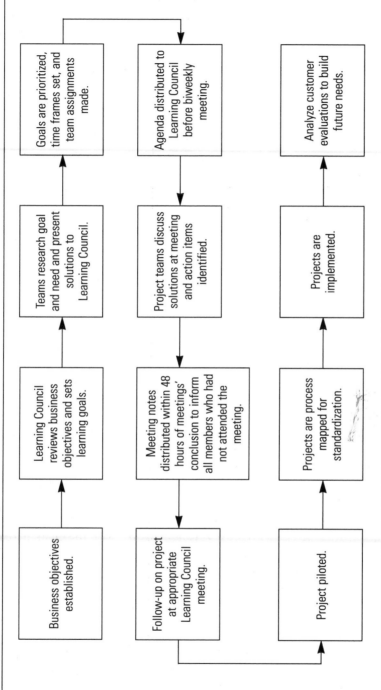

Why is working as a team crucial? Why not organize ourselves as a traditional training department? A decentralized membership ensures we know the organization. We have our feet deeply entrenched in our own parts of the company. This dual "loyalty" keeps us accountable to the business objectives.

Teams work. Thirteen heads are better than one. We feed off each other to stretch the imagination of the organization around learning. Members are fully empowered to contribute at a maximal level. The stress and responsibility of project leadership are shared.

Because there is no direct reporting structure for most of us, we have more freedom to risk. Because there is no direct reporting structure, it is feasible for us to bring relevant information to the council that will influence the success of the company from our own divisions. The team structure is fundamental in allowing us to do our work.

Our projects are linked to the Learning Council's prioritized list of goals and objectives. The council sets the goals and objectives at a yearly session in which we reevaluate our foci and ensure that they are linked to the business objectives. Usually, a project is piloted somewhere in the company before we make a major investment of financial and human resources. Once the Learning Council adopts a project, we map the process so that any Learning Council member can manage it. This interchangeability is critical because of the nature of our corporate environment: We have to be able to cover for each other. The process maps allow us to do so without cross training. They act as a performance support tool for our jobs on the Learning Council. The process maps detail what has to be done, step by step. A process map can be a checklist or it can be a flow chart, depending on the need.

For example, the Learning Council sponsors approximately 10 business literacy workshops yearly at all plant sites. Their stated purpose is to raise our employees business literacy with specific reference to the corporate business objectives, particularly to the sales and marketing plan. If the company's business focus is on gynecology, for example, we offer workshops on this topic. The topics vary from year to year as our business's objectives vary. On occasion, a specific plant site has a business need that is different from that in the rest of the company. When that happens, the Learning Council designs and delivers a course tailored for it.

Another example is our use of the J&J satellite learning series to address a corporate objective around developing leadership skills at all levels of the organization. The Learning Council selects the year's broadcasts on the basis of our strategic direction. In this way, we link the learning activities to the business objectives. Evaluations help us to stay on track so that we can ensure we are meeting the objectives.

After implementation of the Learning Council's projects, we gather feedback from our customers, of course, and the process begins again.

Generally, each year, the Learning Council goes through a regular renewal activity. In January, we go off-site to meet and revisit our vision, mission, and objectives and reexamine the organizational and divisional objectives. From this work, we prioritize our projects for the year.

Midyear, we do a reality check to make sure we are on target. We meet to review the projects selected in January and to reevaluate them to fit in our ever-changing environment.

In the third quarter, we build in a Learning Council development activity, which will stretch our horizons and shake up our own thinking and learning. This is our commitment to practicing what we preach. Examples from the last few years include off-site, intense study sessions on learning organizations, chaos mathematics, and a new paradigm of psychology for corporate effectiveness.

Finally, at the end of the year, we review our lessons learned, successes, and customer evaluations. We take a moment to reflect, to pause.

Examples of customer evaluations include trainee reaction (Kirkpatrick's Level 1) response sheets used at every J&J sponsored event, trainee learning (Level 2) testing of business literacy workshops, trainee behavioral change (Level 3) by certified production trainers on the manufacturing floor, and results (Level 4) for the operations schools regarding cost reduction.

To ensure standardization throughout the company, we implement an ongoing system of checks, balances, and revision mechanisms. We proactively gather the needs of our respective divisions for formal course development. We solicit feedback from customer groups. To increase creativity and innovation, we seek outside expertise and literature in support of learning opportunities. By using electronic media, we change course content and communication strategies in a timely and cost-effective manner.

To be more effective, we commit to each other to:
- honor and celebrate diversity of team members (beyond race and gender)
- allow members to flow in and out of the team
- have a clear vision and mission
- select the appropriate media (that is, inherently flexible, easily updated)

- recognize that leadership can make a difference
- constantly seek new members
- make membership voluntary.

To complete our definition of the Learning Council, let us address what we are not. We are not the human resources division. They are accountable for team building and formal management training throughout the organization. We are not the traditional nuts-and-bolts training developers. We import finished training products and tweak them to meet our objectives.

Why the Learning Council Shouldn't Work

What if you had an environment of constant change, including frequent reorganization, frequent changes of direct management, and frequent change of direction and prioritization from management? What if you knew your job was secure because you knew you were making a contribution, but many of the folks around you were moving, being promoted, leaving? What if walls literally came up and down in the physical facility around you? What if some team members took on heavy new responsibilities prohibiting them from team participation? What if the team was geographically separated across nations? What if there was a high turnover rate among top management? What if the basic technologies of the organization were changing with mind-boggling speed?

The Learning Council has more reasons that it shouldn't work than it should. But we are still here.

What Difference Does the Learning Council Make?

More than three years ago, no process was in place to manage corporate learning. Each corporate division financed its own training with little alignment to company strategic goals. There was much duplication and little sharing of resources among divisions. Figure 2 on page 56 reflects this lack of process.

After establishment of the Learning Council, the divisions could work together to align training with the organization's strategic objectives. Because of the communication facilitated among Learning Council members, we identified synergies and shared resources, as figure 3 shows.

Looking back on our progress, we believe that the following are critical to the success of the Learning Council:
- Hold a shared vision.

- Have fun by scheduling quality time together, taking time to get to know one another, celebrating humor, laughing, and including all of this in our regular work.
- Establish camaraderie based on trust and communication, inclusion, and a sense of belonging.
- Hold regularly scheduled meetings with a published agenda and expected outcomes, providing a sense of purpose and accomplishment.
- Complete process maps.
- Debrief at the end of each meeting.
- Apply what is learned in development classes to the way our team functions.
- Use lessons-learned strategies.

The Learning Council has found that we are successful year after year because we intuitively and collectively pay attention to the individual, the team, the company, and our working processes. Members have the opportunity to work cross-functionally, work on corporate-wide initiatives, make a difference in changing the environment, and be involved in innovative efforts. The icing on the cake is having such high-quality colleagues with whom to work across the organization. For each of us, the Learning Council is the best meeting of the work week. We can't wait to get there.

Questions to Consider if You Head Down This Path

If the Learning Council concept makes sense to you, you might want to consider the following questions:
- How will Learning Council members be selected?
- How will the council be organized?
- How will you facilitate team communication?
- How will you market your Learning Council within your organization?
- How will you support team development and renewal? How will you walk the talk, ensuring the development of the team members?
- How will you measure your work?
- How will you stay in touch with your customer?

At EES, our Learning Council members are selected because they
- have some responsibility for training, education, learning, or development in their division
- have a personal interest in learning or commitment to it
- are people of influence within their division or the company
- have the ability to make a time commitment
- have beneficial skills (for example, balancing the number of strategic thinkers and idea generators with the number of doer-implementers).

Figure 2. Before the Learning Council.

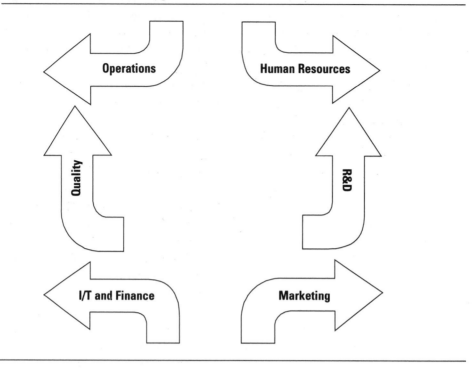

Figure 3. After the Learning Council.

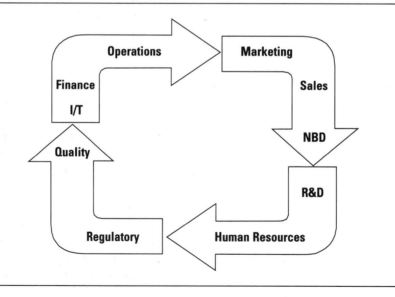

We have a team leader, and each of us makes a yearly commitment to the council. Within the council, we have subteams responsible for projects. We facilitate communication by religiously sticking to our predictable schedule and predictable processes. We market the council within the organization in the following way:

- *Using Learning Council verbiage.* This is true in our introductions of events and in our companywide electronic bulletin board announcements.
- *Introducing all council events.* A Learning Council member introduces all the council's events, thus establishing a clear presence.
- *Including council work in status reports.* Each team member includes Learning Council work in the respective divisional monthly status report.
- *Reporting about opportunities for staff.* Team members talk to their respective management about the council and development opportunities for their people.
- *Using an established network to get out information on events.* The council member in charge sends e-mail to all council members describing the event. The council members bounce this message to the management of their respective divisions. This personalized announcement comes from the divisional Learning Council representative and seems to have a greater impact.

The EES Learning Council handles team development and renewal using a model of team performance. The Learning Council also commits to holding a yearly event for council member personal development. Finally, during every meeting, new ideas seem to sneak in because each of us is a minilearning machine, and we can't help ourselves.

We measure our work using standard qualitative and quantitative training measures. Examples are trainee comments and ratings, paper and pencil testing graded on computer using electronic scoring sheets, trainer observation of trainee behavior, and financial statement analysis.

The EES Learning Council stays in touch with its customers by paying attention to the measurement data we collect and by being our own customers (there is often a Learning Council member or two in the role of learner at our events).

The Impact

The EES Learning Council has had an impact on the organization. Specific quantifiable results include the following:

- 10 percent improvement in company commitment to associate training and development

- 43 percent increase in participation in the reimbursement program for higher education work done by employees on their own time
- establishment of a train-the-trainer program, which, thus far, 56 of our internal trainers have attended
- through work in concert with the Johnson & Johnson Learning Services division, elimination of 15 duplicate courses
- increased internal training capacity to reduce costs, resulting in an estimated $38,000 savings per class, or, approximately, $76,000 savings per year.

Becoming a learning organization is of value. The Learning Council, a high-performance work team, is helping ETHICON Endo-Surgery, a Johnson & Johnson company, move in the direction of becoming a learning organization. We have fun on this very highly productive and business-objectives focused team. We are compelled and energized to be part of the team. What could be better? It's a win-win deal.

Questions for Discussion

1. In your personal or professional experience, have you been on a team or working group that has the characteristics of Learning Council? Discuss.
2. If you could ask questions of the Learning Council, what would they be? Direct them to your fellow discussion group members. Can you predict the way Learning Council would answer them?
3. What is missing in the approach outlined by the Learning Council?
4. What are the main elements that make the Learning Council work?
5. What elements of what the Learning Council does could you apply to your own situation?

The Authors

Phyllis Saltzman is responsible for educational strategy and evaluation at ETHICON Endo-Surgery, a Johnson & Johnson company. She focuses on, among other things, participation on the Learning Council, a high-performance work team which manages the learning organization elements of the company, consultation to the Professional Education Council, a consortium of professional education directors from the Johnson & Johnson professional-sector companies, and leadership on electronic educational initiatives. Before joining Johnson & Johnson, Saltzman spent 10 years abroad doing similar work in the high-tech industry, training international customers and working in the public education domain. Her department is team based. Saltzman received her doctoral degree at The Ohio State University in teacher education and curriculum theory, specializing in innovation and creativity. She can be contacted by e-mail at psaltzma@eesus.jnj.com.

Amy Meyer was the manager of Employee Development and Learning Systems. She created the Learning Council and led the team. She was also responsible for corporate employee development. She has work experience in both the computer and health-care industries. She sees her ability to contribute to the organization as unique in that her theory of work and management differs from the norm. She is particularly interested in empowerment and practical implementation of new ideas. She has found ways to make this work in a team-based corporate world. She focuses on bringing the right resources to the task and creating an environment where ideas come out. Her line is to help people to become the best they can be. She is currently responsible for recruiting.

Dynamic Team Leadership Development for Managers: Integrating Reflective Learning and Experiential Training

Advanced Micro Devices

Garry McDaniel

The 1990s are being labeled the decade of the "learning organization" (Senge and Fulmer, 1993). Peter Senge, author of The Fifth Discipline, *defines a learning organization as one that continually expands its capacity to create its future (1990, p. 14). The ability of an organization to learn and share what it learns quickly is viewed as a competitive advantage in a high-tech, high-change business world. Organizations recognize that managers play a critical role in an organization's ability to meet its strategic business objectives, maintain daily operations, and facilitate positive change and learning. Many researchers believe that for organizations to compete effectively they need to reexamine traditional assumptions that inform how managers learn and apply the team leadership skills and knowledge needed to excel in both tactical and strategic issues on the job (Argyris, 1993; Sayles, 1993). Advanced Micro Devices (AMD), a world-class manufacturer of integrated circuits, has begun such an examination. This case study describes a collaborative effort of AMD and one of its vendors to customize and implement a powerful experiential learning program designed to improve managers' ability to think and act in ways that will enhance the company's goal of becoming a learning organization.*

Problem Statement

AMD competes in a global business environment characterized by highly skilled competitors, evolving employee roles and relationships, increasingly flat organizational structures, demands for com-

This case was prepared to serve as a basis for discussion rather than to illustrate either effective or ineffective administrative and management practices.

plex, quality products, shorter product or service cycle times, and the need to continuously improve employee personal, professional, and technical skills. This new work environment expands the traditional role of managers in areas such as strategic thinking, coaching, facilitating continuous improvement, and alignment of work to support the organization's goals (Bennis, 1989; Kouzes and Posner, 1993, 1995; Sayles, 1993).

Learning professionals have generally employed traditional training delivery methods for conducting management development (Marsick, 1987). These methods have consisted of providing knowledge and skill training primarily through classroom lecture, guided discussion, role plays, and media presentations of so-called good and bad behavior. Traditional training methods do have advantages in terms of cost and ease of design and development time, and they are useful for fulfilling some learning requirements for management training at AMD. However, research indicates that these methods rarely result in long-term knowledge retention and behavioral change (Fisher, Merron, and Tolbert, 1987; Laird, 1985). Marsick and Watkins (1990, p. 4) observe, "Employees may demonstrate that they have learned new knowledge and skills at the end of a training activity, but they find it difficult to transfer this learning to their normal work environment."

To examine methods for enhancing managerial learning transfer in the workplace, this paper explores the following questions:
1. What does research indicate the most effective method or methods are for skill retention and transfer in the workplace?
2. How has this method or methods been integrated into one specific learning program to enhance management team leadership skill retention and transfer to the workplace at AMD?

Significance

In the 1980s, American business discovered that viewing the role of management as planning, organizing, controlling, coordinating, and commanding was too narrow an interpretation if organizations were to compete effectively in the world market of the 1990s (Sayles, 1993). Although these traditional management roles are important, additional competencies are needed in the workplace including team building and team leadership skills, knowledge of systems thinking, and the ability to reflect critically and share mental models with others (Senge, 1990; Champy, 1995). Managers now have responsibility for building an environment of integrity, trust, openness, and shared vision. They are being expected to shift from a role in which they act as transactional managers, charged with maintaining the status quo, to transformational managers, charged with encouraging and leading dynamic change through empowered teams (Spreitzer and Quinn, 1996).

The inability to perform these new roles can be damaging to the long- and short-term efficiency and effectiveness of an organization. Clemmer (1991) observes that poor management training may lead to unsatisfactory results in areas such as providing high-quality personal service, product quality, interactions with team members and employees, decision making, and the ability to develop others. Researchers note that individuals who are unsuccessful as managers are often unable to assume these new roles, incorporate new and more productive knowledge, face their own shortcomings, challenge their mental models, share insights, accept constructive feedback, or view their work and the work of the business systemically (Deming, 1986; Clemmer, 1991; Schön, 1987; Senge, 1990; Simons, 1995). Management training that does not achieve intended results has negative long- and short-term effects on the organization, and training participants and senior management often view it as a waste of valuable time, funding, and resources (Robinson and Robinson, 1989).

Theoretical Framework

If current methods of preparing managers for their roles are not resulting in sufficient long-term knowledge retention and behavioral change, what does research suggest are effective methods for skill retention and transfer in the workplace? Albert Einstein observed, "The significant problems we face today cannot be solved at the same level of thinking we were at when we created them" (cited in Covey, 1989, p. 42). Accordingly, a manager cannot be expected to exhibit radical changes in knowledge or behaviors if prompted by the same traditional training methods. Spreitzer and Quinn (1996) agree, noting that traditional approaches to management training have limited ability to achieve behavioral change. In an extensive research effort with 3,000 Ford Motor Company managers, Spreitzer and Quinn found that an effective transformational management program would need to be designed on a new set of assumptions. Results clearly indicated that a successful program would go beyond informing managers; it would provide them with opportunities to transform themselves—to challenge traditional assumptions, roles, and organizational practices (Spreitzer and Quinn, 1996).

Other research supports the view that individuals learn new knowledge, skills, and behavior more effectively when they are deeply involved as participants in the development and practical implementation of the skills and knowledge to be learned. John Dewey (cited in Schön, 1987, p. 17) noted that a learner "...has to see on his own behalf and in his own way the relationship between means and methods employed and results achieved. Nobody else can see for him, and he can't see just by being 'told,' although the right kind of telling may guide his seeing and thus help him see what he needs to see." Schön (1987) and others (Argyris and Schön, 1974; Brookfield, 1986; Mezirow, 1990) also note that learning and behavioral change can be enhanced by having learners go beyond simply doing to consciously deliberating on the thinking that shapes their actions. This process, characterized by Schön as reflection-in-action, is one wherein the learner reflects on the thinking that led to a result and how strategies of action or ways of framing problems might be restructured (1987).

Argyris and Schön (1974) have shown that there is often a gap or difference between what organizations and individuals intend to do and what actually happens. This dynamic is what they call the difference between an espoused theory (what organizations and individuals say they do when asked) and a theory-in-use (what organizations and individuals do when observed). Argyris and Schön also note that the gap between espoused theory and theory-in-use is often unconscious.

Methodology

In 1994, an internal needs assessment indicated that managers at AMD needed to enhance their knowledge and practice in areas such as developing team leadership, strategic focus, alignment of operations with organizational goals, and communication skills. An advisory group that comprised representatives from the Department of Human Resources, Organization Development, Learning and Development, and representatives from management determined that conventional training techniques could be used to present some basic foundational knowledge in areas such as project planning, business knowledge, personnel, meeting management, and interpersonal skills. However, advisory group members also felt that conventional methods would not offer participants the opportunity to view and practice these varied skill sets in an integrated manner, nor did they allow managers to reflect on the congruence between their espoused theories and theories-in-use.

The advisory group determined that adding a reflective component to a highly learner-driven experience might provide managers with the opportunity to rethink current practices and develop new insights, skills, and behaviors. Members felt it was important to select a learning experience that would allow participants to practice, reflect upon, and develop action plans around knowledge and skills identified as crucial to their evolving roles on the job.

To begin to address these concerns, AMD began a collaborative effort with one of its vendors, Eagle's Flight Creative Training Excellence, Inc. (Eagle's Flight) to customize an existing proprietary simulation called Gold of the Desert Kings. The objective of this collaboration was to provide newly promoted and incumbent AMD managers with an opportunity to participate in a dynamic, highly interactive simulation that would serve as a transformational catalyst for learning to surface and reflect on their own deeply held mental models, share insights, and conduct on-the-job action planning on the basis of personal, interpersonal, business, and environmental dynamics.

The program was an interactive and participant-driven simulation to assist managers with exploring the conflicting dynamics that help or hinder the maximization of team productivity in a competitive environment. Alex Somos, president of Eagle's Flight observed, "Our programs prompt learning by guiding participants through experiences using simulations which prompt self-discovery. The high level of self-discovery is achieved by taking the same pressures and challenges that teams face every day on the job and disguising them as fun, unusual, and nonthreatening simulations." In its original form, the four-hour simulation called for teams of three to six people to be pitted against each other in a setting that duplicated the individual and team dynamics of the participants' actual work environment. The context for the simulation was a race from home base across the desert to the mountains to mine gold, and then back to home base, as figure 1 shows. The simulation prompts each team of managers to plan their strategy and goals, obtain needed resources, and determine roles and responsibilities in order to mine as much gold as possible.

The map, rules, hazards, and opportunities in the simulation are metaphors for the realities within organizations that teams and individuals face every day on the job. For example, work teams begin the simulation from a safe area represented by home base in the lower right-hand corner of the map. At home base, each team must make decisions regarding information and resources at their disposal and hazards (known and unknown) that lie in their path, and they must

Figure 1. Gold of the Desert Kings map.

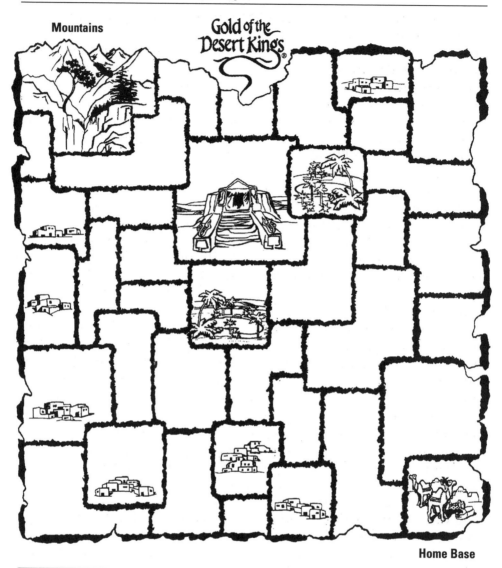

Reprinted with permission of Eagle's Flight™.

develop a strategy under time-limited conditions to reach the mountains and mine for gold. But reaching the mountains and mining for gold is only half the battle—the teams must survive the journey home under the same unknown, hazardous, and time-limited conditions. Although many simulations always conclude with a happy ending, Gold of the Desert Kings closely mirrors the harsh realities of today's competitive business environment. Vendor research and AMD's experience indicate that approximately 25 percent of the teams that begin the simulation die in the desert. How effectively teams communicate, plan, set goals, utilize resources, strategize, and share roles and responsibilities has a significant impact on both their ability to survive the undertaking and on the level of reward at the end of the simulation. This message is not lost on the participants who readily grasp the connection between the simulation and the real world in which they work.

Much of the simulation's success derives from its design as a microworld or transitional object, which Senge describes as "... a microcosm of reality where it is safe to play" (Senge, 1990, p. 314). In essence, the exciting, fast-paced, fun ambiance of the simulation allows participants to forgo posturing, or acting a part, which they might normally demonstrate during a role-playing exercise. Instead, they act as they normally would on the job. The real impact of the experience is vividly illustrated to the participants following the simulation during the debrief.

The vendor designed the debrief discussion so team members would see the parallels between their behavior in the real world and their behavior as individuals and as team members during the simulation. As team members and individuals, participants consider how they might modify their actions or behaviors on the job. To achieve a higher level of insight and impetus for change, AMD worked closely with the vendor to develop activities and graphics to further prompt participants to take personal responsibility for exposing, reflecting on, and testing the mental models they relied upon when making decisions and taking actions during the simulation. On the basis of their experience, team members then are led through a discussion focusing on the extent their behavior and actions during the simulation mirror their behavior, goal setting, planning, communication, and on-the-job actions. This approach enables them to become the catalyst for relating their own learning to their daily work environment, their personal work habits, and interpersonal, management, and team leadership styles. Team members conclude the debrief by developing action plans for personal improvement or organizational improvement, or both.

Managers participating in the simulation often are surprised at the gap between what they said their team goals and strategy were at the beginning of the simulation, and the actions they took. The gaps that users or facilitators identify through Schön's reflection-in-action process can be mapped in writing or speech through the method that Argyris, Putnam, and Smith (1985) described to illustrate how an individual or organization might move from a faulty espoused theory to a congruent theory-in-use.

Mapping Reflective Learning

Mapping displays values and assumptions, actions and strategies, and outcomes and consequences. The power of the mapping process lies in its ability to raise users' awareness of conflicts between what teams said were their values and assumptions and the actions they took. Users can explore the disparity between the two to determine actual and intended outcomes and consequences. Facilitators and users can obtain the information needed to construct maps through observations, interviews, focus groups, critical incidents, or, as in this simulation, written exercises, group discussion, and reflection on intentions and actions. An example of the mapping process based on typical team dynamics during the simulation appears in table 1.

The table illustrates typical espoused theories that teams hold when the simulation begins. The first column of values and assumptions indicates that during the simulation team members say that having a clear mission, strategy, and goals, good information, and thoughtful planning will help them achieve their desired outcomes. In the second column, teams say that their strategy or plan of action is to develop a clear, shared mission, strategy, and goals, and to gather rel-

Table 1. Team's espoused theory map.

Values and assumptions	Actions and strategies	Outcomes and consequences
A clear mission, strategy, and goals are important.	Develop a clear understanding and commitment to a shared mission, strategy, and goals.	Achieve mission, strategy, and goals.
Information is important for achieving high outcomes.	Gather all relevant data; publicly test data for accuracy.	Decisions implemented on the basis of data.
Planning is important for achieving high outcomes.	Plan and align resource needs, data, roles, and responsibilities to support achievement of the desired strategy and goals.	Achieve strategy and goals through efficient and effective planning.

evant data and conduct thorough planning based on resource needs, data, and their roles and responsibilities. In the third column, teams say they expect that the outcome will be to achieve their mission, strategy, and goals by basing their decisions on data and effective action plan implementation.

Assume that each team member had good intentions during the activity—that each one really did believe and intend to act as though a shared, well-understood direction and plan were critical to success. Despite good intentions, teams frequently act quite differently. Table 2 displays the values and assumptions most teams convey through their performance during the simulation. Note that although teams say in column one that a mission, strategy, and goals are important, they enact a short-term strategy with minimal data collection and planning. Further, column two illustrates that the team unconsciously acts as if it can ignore the misalignment between clear direction, valid information, and effective planning without any negative repercussions. As a result, teams launch into the simulation with poorly conceived strategies, invalid data, and poor plans and, consequently, they perform much less effectively than they expected.

As this mapping process illustrates, team members who can visualize their espoused theory and their theory-in-use can help them see that what they are doing is counterproductive to their stated goals.

Table 2. Team's theory-in-use map.

Values and assumptions	Actions and strategies	Outcomes and consequences
Mission, strategy, and goals are important, but activity is more important.	Develop a vague mission, strategy, and goals that may be interpreted in any way; superficially check with each other for shared understanding.	Teams launch into the simulation with little or no clear direction or strategy.
Information is important, but activity is more important.	Collect only basic information needed to begin the activity as soon as possible.	Decisions are made and actions taken based on assumptions and untested data.
Long-term planning is important, but short-term planning is easier and what is rewarded.	Conduct minimal planning and don't test the plan against resource needs, data, or roles and responsibilities.	Short-term planning and the rush to begin activity leads to low performance levels or death in the desert.

If the team members are sincere, open, and honest in the debrief, they can use Schön's mapping process to understand the incongruence between what they say and what they do. Through this reflective process, team members then can see how their behavior on the job might follow the same pattern, and they can redesign action plans to achieve higher performance levels.

Redesigning to Avoid and Minimize Incongruent Theories-in-Use

To address an incongruent process once discovered, Argyris and Schön's (1974) recommendations for increasing individual and organizational congruence could be helpful. These include:

- *Maximize valid information.* Organizations and individuals should seek and provide information based on directly observable data that have been publicly tested with others for accuracy.
- *Maximize free and informed choice.* Organizations and individuals should be aware of all the information possible that is pertinent to making decisions or taking action.
- *Maximize commitment to decisions made.* Organizations and individuals should hold themselves responsible and accountable for the choices they have made.
- *Combine advocacy and inquiry.* Organizations and individuals should express their opinions and views, and ask for feedback and reactions to elicit productive dialogue.
- *Protect self and others appropriately.* Organizations and individuals should protect themselves and others when feeling defensive or emotionally threatened, but they should do so in ways that allow them and others to continue learning (this is quite difficult to do).

The author suggests three additional recommendations on the basis of research, needs assessment data, and experience with this simulation:

- *Think systemically.* Organizations and individuals who can think in more interconnected and consequential ways will have a greater likelihood for avoiding unintended outcomes in the design and implementation of their strategies.
- *Look for problems and try to fix them.* Organizations and individuals who actively seek out problems and attempt to address them stand a much better chance of avoiding or minimizing nonproductive behaviors and actions.
- *Reflect on organizational and individual practices.* Organizations and individuals who routinely challenge their assumptions and contemplate their actions stand a better chance of avoiding unintended outcomes.

Table 3, a redesign of the team's theory-in-use map illustrates how things might be different if an organization or individual enacted the guidelines described above.

Participants often find it difficult to face the incongruence between their espoused theories and those they use. Notice that in order to minimize or avoid faulty thinking and wasted activity, team members must be willing to critically examine their individual and collective values and assumptions, actions and strategies, and outcomes and consequences. Moreover, in order to avoid future recurrences, team members must exhibit a willingness and commitment to be open, inclusive, and systemic in their thinking.

Comparing table 2 with table 3, one notices that table 2, being activity driven, is more reactive and oriented to a quick fix as team members tend to launch into their activities with little direction or strategy. The actions that the team described in table 3 tend to be more thoughtful and oriented to the big picture. In table 3, team members ensure that their mission, strategy, and goals are shared, that they are based on explicit data, and that they are periodically checked for alignment. As one might surmise, teams that take the

Table 3. Redesign of team's theory-in-use map.

Values and assumptions	Actions and strategies	Outcomes and consequences
A mission, strategy, and goal statements are important, and should be explicitly shared, understood, and committed to by all team members.	Collaboratively develop appropriate mission statement, strategy, and goals that all team members share, understand, and commit to. Periodically review the mission, strategy, and goals against the team's actions to ensure alignment.	Shared mission, strategy, and goals are collaboratively developed and implemented along with a process for checking team actions for alignment. The result is much higher performance during the simulation.
Valid, tested information is important in order to achieve high outcomes.	Collect and understand all available information.	Decisions are made and actions taken on the basis of valid, tested information.
Both long-term and short-term planning are important and need to be accomplished before activity begins.	Ensure information is used to plan short- and long-term resource use and that long- and short-term planning is aligned with the team mission, strategy, and goals.	Development of long- and short-term plans that are aligned with the team mission, strategy, and goals leads to high performance.

time to develop thoughtful, informed strategies and goals outperform those teams that leap into the simulation with little forethought.

Application on the Job

Managers who have participated in the simulation find the learning experience effective in prompting the examination of assumptions and mental models that inform decisions and action. Typical comments from participants include, "It is one of the best workshops I have attended" and "I found that the concepts introduced and the parallels to the real organizational environment were very helpful and are directly transferable to my job as a team leader." Although this Level 1 (Kirkpatrick, 1975) feedback is helpful, the purpose of the simulation is to enable participants to develop new skills, insights, and a repertoire of experiences that will have positive consequences on the job. Follow-up interviews with managers indicate that the simulation is achieving the desired results.

One participant was Bill Sedenberg, automation section manager in AMD's advanced manufacturing facility in Austin, Texas. He noted that the rapid pace of change and demand for quick results often led him to react to team-related issues from a "firefighting" mode of thinking. "After participating in the simulation, I became much more conscious of planning to seek out and consider inputs of team members, long-term business needs and to develop contingency plans to deal with unplanned occurrences," he said. Sedenberg observed that as a result of the workshop, he developed a plan for developing internal team members to fill a projected job vacancy. When the job became available, he was able to promote a team member into it with a minimum of disruption in productivity. "Having a contingency plan that allowed me to react quickly to the staff vacancy was not only good for the team as a whole, but for the individual who was promoted," Sedenberg stated.

Sharon Shaw, manager of AMD's Technical Library Services, observed that the competitive and time-pressured format of the activity closely matched that of her work environment. "Because our work environment demands a fast turnaround, our team has a perceived sense of urgency. As a result, we tend to become task oriented rather than 'begin with the end in mind' planners." Shaw noted that this reactive orientation led to her team being less productive than desired. To address this issue, she began scheduling time for the team to plan and reflect on how well plans integrate with customer demands and long-term goals. As a result of this planning time, Shaw observed that unit productivity has increased: "Because we focus on our priorities and mission, our use of time has become more productive. We review our schedules by long-term results rather than daily completed tasks in mind. This orientation still requires a balance between customer needs and the proactive posture to accomplish long-term goals. However, in the 'big picture,' this approach definitely results in better service to our customers."

A third example comes from Maggie Rausch, a production planner in AMD's Planning and Logistics Section. Rausch observed that prior to the training, she felt overwhelmed with some of the data gathering and reporting tasks for which she was responsible. Another team member in her unit appeared to have some free time, but Rausch assumed that the team member would not be receptive to taking on some of this important task. During the simulation, Rausch recognized that without verifying the team member's willingness and interest in assisting her, the situation would not change. Upon her return to the workplace, Rausch noted, "I was surprised to find that not only was my teammate willing to help me out, but she saw the expanded role as one of providing more challenge to her job. It was a real 'win-win' outcome for both of us!" Rausch stated that the sharing of responsibilities provided a more challenging role for her teammate, and it has freed up three to four hours per week that Rausch can use to focus on higher leverage activities.

As these three examples indicate, integrating reflection into a microworld activity assisted participants in improving their mental models, and, consequently, on-the-job productivity. The reflective process that led these individuals to improve their on-the-job performance can be mapped in the same manner as the team thought process during Gold of the Desert Kings. Table 4 illustrates the espoused theories for the examples. It shows that the three individuals had espoused theories that rationally indicate how success in their jobs should be achieved.

However what they said and what they actually did on the job were not always aligned, as table 5 shows.

That table illustrates that in actual practice the participants were operating in contradiction to their espoused theories, as we all do from time to time. Bill Sedenberg knew that involvement from team members and accurate data would lead to better decisions. But taking the time to gain the perspectives of those team members, obtain their buy-in and support, and gather accurate data were time-consuming tasks that he avoided. As a result, he made decisions and took actions

Table 4. Participants' espoused theory map.

Values and assumptions	Actions and strategies	Outcomes and consequences
Sedenberg: Professional expertise, skill, and planning will lead to rapid and effective problem solving.	Gather the opinions and insights of others; obtain all relevant data prior to making decisions and taking action.	Resolve problems quickly, effectively, and for the long term.
Shaw: Planning is important for achievement of high performance.	Take time to plan; gather all relevant data and test for accuracy.	Time for planning is allotted and action plans based on relevant, correct data are implemented with great success.
Rausch: Open, honest communication about one's workload needs leads to a healthy, productive work environment.	Share workload needs with others.	Workload is distributed efficiently, which allows for more effective use of everyone's time and expertise.

Table 5. Participants' theory-in-use map.

Values and assumptions	Actions and strategies	Outcomes and consequences
Sedenberg: Involving others and gathering data are important, but responding quickly to problems is much easier.	React quickly to "fires" without gaining adequate consultation from others or appropriate data.	Less-effective decisions, hurt feelings from those not consulted, long-term problems not solved.
Shaw: Long-term planning is important, but short-term planning is easier and what is rewarded.	Collect only basic information needed to begin the activity as soon as possible.	Short-term planning and the rush to begin activity lead to lower performance levels.
Rausch: Sharing information about workload needs is good, but one risks being told "no."	Continue to do more work in the same amount of time.	Less time to focus on quality, personal stress, and frustration.

that did not have the desired support or insights of his team members, and did not always resolve problems over the long term. Sharon Shaw's team believed that long-term planning was important, but it operated in a reactive, activity-driven mode. Maggie Rausch intuitively knew that it would be beneficial to her to be open about workload needs, but she assumed that others would not help and continued to persevere even when quality might slip. As a result of the learning process, all three individuals were able to reframe their mental models and improve personal and team productivity on the job, as table 6 shows. As this table suggests, the ability of individuals to stop and reflect critically on their behavior and mental models can improve their productivity on the job.

Conclusion

This case study has explored two questions: What does research indicate the most effective methods are for skill retention and transfer in the workplace? and How have these methods been integrated into one specific learning program to enhance management team leadership skill retention and transfer to the workplace at AMD?

In addressing the first question, this case study has submitted that effective working environments encourage and provide opportuni-

Table 6. Redesigning the theory-in-use maps.

Values and assumptions	Actions and strategies	Outcomes and consequences
Sedenberg: Reacting quickly, gathering data, and obtaining input and buy-in from the team are also important.	Develop contingency plans for making decisions, involving team members, and based on data.	More effective decisions and actions taken that are supported by team members and have a longer-lasting effect.
Shaw: Both long- and short-term planning are important and need to be accomplished before activity begins.	Plan to plan, and reflect twice a day so information is used to align long- and short-term resource use with the unit mission, strategy, and goals.	Development of effective long- and short-term plans that are aligned with the unit mission, strategy, and goals leads to high performance.
Rausch: Sharing work with teammates is important and may benefit everyone.	Share workload needs and advantages with teammates.	Tasks are shared with teammates providing time to ensure quality and customer service.

ties for the surfacing of mental models and an awareness and understanding of their implications. Organizations recognize that managers play an important role in an organization's ability to meet its strategic business objectives, maintain daily operations, and facilitate positive change and learning. Research indicates that to compete effectively organizations need to reexamine traditional assumptions that inform how managers learn and apply the team leadership skills and knowledge needed to excel in both tactical and strategic issues on the job (Argyris, 1993; Sayles, 1993). Scholars have shown that learning methods that comprehensively involve participants in the development and processing of the content and reflect on the assumptions that undergird both their personal and organizational mental models are effective for achieving learning transfer in the workplace (Mezirow, 1990). Mezirow notes that this reflective component enhances each individual's ability to explore, challenge, and change his or her perspective. This process enables people to restructure their distortions, false assumptions, and incorrect perceptions and, therefore, to make conscious choices and decisions on the basis of their new perspectives. This constant state of inquiry, reflection, testing, and reformulation of perspective and mental models is important to AMD's quest to become a learning organization.

Working in partnership with the talented staff at Eagle's Flight, AMD integrated these learning methods into Gold of the Desert Kings to enhance the retention and transfer of team leadership skills to the workplace at AMD. Through written activities, graphic illustrations, and reflective discussion, participants in Gold of the Desert Kings achieve a high level of participation and reflection. Additional opportunities to develop workable action plans support learning transfer to the workplace. Evaluation results and interviews with managers indicate that this effort has been an important factor for assisting managers to learn and transfer that learning to the workplace.

High-technology organizations are increasingly aware that their ability to learn and share learning is a competitive advantage in a business world characterized by rapid change. AMD has responded by developing learning opportunities for its management staff that assist them in examining the impact of their mental models on the decisions and actions of work teams. Creating work environments and continual learning opportunities that foster sharing of information, reflection in action, and appropriate redesign of behaviors or processes is a proactive step toward ensuring that AMD managers learn to foster a high-performing team environment that will help AMD learn faster than its competitors.

Questions for Discussion

1. Take a minute to think about the two or three learning events that had the greatest positive impact on you. Describe what significant learning each conveyed to you. Review what you described for each event and see if there are any common characteristics. What does this tell you about how you learn?

2. Take a minute to think about the two or three learning events that had the greatest negative impact on you. Describe what significant learning each conveyed to you. Review what you described for each event and see if there are any common characteristics. What does this tell you about how you learn compared to the type of learning that had a positive impact on you?

3. What barriers do you see to the transfer of learning from a classroom setting to the workplace? Why are these barriers? What can you suggest to overcome these barriers?

4. In many business or team simulations, everything works out okay for the participants. What value do you see in having a simulation in which teams fail to finish the simulation (for example, they "die" in the desert)?

The Author

Garry McDaniel is currently manager of Advanced Micro Devices' Corporate Leadership Design Center. His degrees include an Ed.D. in human resource development leadership from the University of Texas, an M.Ed. in counseling from Southwest Texas State University in 1978, and a B.S. in environmental management in 1976. McDaniel served in the United States Air Force and has worked in the field of adult learning and organizational change for over 20 years. He has published widely in a number of magazines, journals, and books and serves on the executive board for the Center for the Study of Work Teams and the editorial board for *Infrastructure Electronic Journal*. McDaniel can be contacted at 11506 Charred Oak Drive, Austin, Texas 78759; e-mail: garry.mcdaniel@amd.com.

References

Argyris, C. (1993). *Knowledge for Action: A Guide to Overcoming Barriers to Organizational Change*. San Francisco: Jossey-Bass.

Argyris, C., and D. Schön. (1974). *Theory in Practice: Increasing Professional Effectiveness*. San Francisco: Jossey-Bass.

Argyris, C., R. Putnam, and D. Smith. (1985). *Action Science: Concepts, Methods and Skills for Research and Intervention*. San Francisco: Jossey-Bass.

Bennis, W. (1989). *Why Leaders Can't Lead: The Unconscious Conspiracy Continues*. San Francisco: Jossey-Bass.

Brookfield, S. (1986). *Understanding and Facilitating Adult Learning*. San Francisco: Jossey-Bass.

Champy, J. (1995). *Reengineering Management: The Mandate for New Leadership* (pp. 129–148). New York: Harper Business.

Clemmer, J. (1991). *Firing on All Cylinders: The Service/Quality System for High Powered Corporate Performance*. Toronto: Macmillan of Canada.

Covey, S. (1989). *The Seven Habits of Highly Effective People: Powerful Lessons in Personal Change*. New York: Simon and Schuster.

Deming, E. (1986). *Out of the Crisis* (p. 23). Cambridge: Massachusetts Institute of Technology, Center for Advanced Engineering Study.

Fisher, D., R. Merron, and W. Tolbert. (1987). "Human Development and Managerial Effectiveness." *Group and Organizational Studies, 12,* 257–273.

Kirkpatrick, D. (ed.). (1975). *Evaluating Training Programs*. Madison, WI: American Society for Training & Development.

Kouzes, J., and B. Posner. (1993). *Credibility: How Leaders Gain and Lose It, Why People Demand It*. San Francisco: Jossey-Bass.

Kouzes, J., and B. Posner. (1995). *The Leadership Challenge*. San Francisco: Jossey-Bass.

Laird, D. (1985). *Approaches to Training and Development*. Reading, MA: Addison-Wesley.

Marsick, V. (ed.). (1987). *Learning in the Workplace*. London: Croom Helm.

Marsick, V., and K. Watkins. (1990). *Informal and Incidental Learning in the Workplace*. New York: Routledge.

Mezirow, J., and Associates. (1990). *Fostering Critical Reflection in Adulthood: A Guide to Transformative and Emancipatory Learning*. San Francisco: Jossey-Bass.

Robinson, D., and J. Robinson. (1989). *Training for Impact: How to Link Training to Business Needs and Measure the Results*. San Francisco: Jossey Bass.

Sayles, L. (1993). *The Working Leader: The Triumph of High Performance Over Conventional Management Principles*. New York: The Free Press.

Schön, D. (1987). *Educating the Reflective Practitioner*. San Francisco: Jossey-Bass.

Senge, P. (1990). *The Fifth Discipline: The Art and Practice of the Learning Organization*. New York: Doubleday.

Senge, P., and R. Fulmer. (1993). "Simulations, Systems Thinking and Anticipatory Learning." *Journal of Management Development, 12*(6), 21–33.

Simons, R. (1995). *Levers of Control: How Managers Use Innovative Control Systems to Drive Strategic Renewal.* Cambridge: Harvard Business School Press.

Spreitzer, G., and R. Quinn. (1996). "Empowering Middle Managers to Be Transformational Leaders." *Journal of Applied Behavioral Science, 32*, 237–261.

The Team Development Continuum

Ohio State Manufacturers

Karen Just

This study is a summary of best practices from a recent statewide project designed to help Ohio manufacturers in their journey to teams. The results yielded a generic team-building model and continuum, pitfalls to avoid, development of effective team-performance-management systems, and a multirater 360 feedback instrument. All the information is easily adaptable to other organizations because it ranges from beginner to more advanced team concepts. Because this was a statewide project conducted by a group of two-year colleges, all company names have been omitted.

Introduction

Ten Ohio manufacturers agreed to participate in a two-year pilot study of work teams. They ranged from small companies of fewer than 50 employees to medium-sized companies with up to 350 employees. Each of the companies was hoping to create a high-performance, high-commitment organization as the result of this project. The goal of the project was to create work systems that provided greater autonomy and greater empowerment for employees. Although each company was moving toward a team concept, some planned on going all the way to self-direction, whereas others had no such intention.

The reasons each company chose to use a team concept varied greatly, but each company developed specific performance or behavioral outcomes it wished to achieve. One of our strong premises was that companies should never "do teams" just for the sake of "doing teams"

This case was prepared to serve as a basis for discussion rather than to illustrate either effective or ineffective administrative and management practices. All names and organization have been disguised at the request of the author or organization.

or because some other company is doing them. Rather, they should have solid business reasons. Teams are a vehicle by which to achieve some end result. They are not an end in themselves.

Most of the companies cited the need for major improvements in productivity due to competition as the number one reason for implementing a team-based culture. The need to significantly improve quality while reducing costs and reducing lead times and becoming more customer focused were the underlying factors needed to ensure future success.

Implementation Process

We began the team-development journey by outlining a three-step process that each company would follow. The process included the following steps:

- Provide education and training.
- Create a steering team.
- Create a design team.

Provide Education and Training

For each company, we organized a series of educational experiences. These experiences included general informational sessions, videos, books and articles, plant visits, discussion groups, and readiness assessments. We spent a great deal of time examining what other companies had done successfully and what seemed not to work as well.

One tool, the team-development continuum, which appears in table 1, provided everyone with a clear idea that teams are an evolutionary process. They can keep growing with the addition of new skills, and each company would decide how far along the continuum it wished to move. In addition, we had each company complete a group of readiness assessments so it could see exactly where there were gaps between what it hoped to achieve and where it was at the time. The gap analysis gave a clear picture of some of the types of training that each company would need as well as which nontraining interventions needed to be put in place. This analysis laid the foundation for each organization to determine how it thought its teams should look and what they should do.

Each company spent time creating the vision of what it hoped to accomplish. The companies examined what they were doing well, what they needed to be doing differently, and how they would begin to move toward the vision. Much of our work in this area was based

Table 1. Team development continuum.

Problem-Solving Team	Process Improvement Team	Functional Work Team	Semi-autonomous Work Team	Cross-functional Work Team	Self-directed Work Team

on the front-end analysis model by Joe Harless (1973). We created a working draft of the vision and circulated it throughout the organization for input and suggested revisions. After several drafts, each organization approved the final vision, and it was ready to be put into action. At this point, several of the organizations had copies of their vision statements printed and posted throughout their facilities. Most companies followed that with a statement of their organizational values, which was one important outcome of the visioning process.

Next, each organization outlined the specific performance and behavioral outcomes needed to achieve their vision. These performance and behavioral outcomes became the basis of their transition plan. From the data, we determined which were training interventions and which were not. Our decisions stemmed from the Mager model (1970) and had their basis in whether people were unable but willing to perform the task (training intervention) or if the people were able but unwilling to perform the task at hand (a motivational or environmental issue). Where training was not the answer, the consultants instituted a variety of interventions. Where training was an issue, curriculum designers developed a training module using the performance and behavioral outcomes as the basis for the session.

Follow-up was designed to ensure transfer of training back to the job. The follow-up and evaluation model was based on the Kirkpatrick four levels of evaluation model. Each organization took performance improvement measurements after several weeks and again after several months on the job. The team revised training as needed from the actual performance data. Team members in every organization participated in a planned training sequence that included the following workshops and topics :

- Phase one, interpersonal skills
  —Introduction to team concept, four to 8 hours
  —Dealing with change, two to four hours
  —Trust building, two to four hours
  —Personal style awareness, four to six hours
  —Workplace communications, six to eight hours
  —Conducting effective meetings, two to three hours
  —Dealing with conflict in teams, four to eight hours
  —Time and stress management, four to six hours
- Phase two, general technical skills
  —Customer satisfaction, six to eight hours
  —Quality basics, eight to 16 hours

—Problem solving and decision making, 16 to 20 hours
—Analyzing and improving work processes, six to eight hours
—Team specific cross training in technical skills, varies
- Phase three, toward self-direction
—Clarifying vision, mission, roles, and goals, four to eight hours
—Establishing a team performance management system, six to 10 hours
—Peer feedback using multirater 360 feedback, eight to 16 hours
—Team performance and compensation for teams, four to eight hours
—Team specific training in self-management skills, varies

In addition to the above training, supervisors and managers participated in 40 to 60 hours of training in understanding their new roles and developing the skills to make them successful. We titled the course The Changing Role of Management: From Cop to Coach. The training included modules on building the team, facilitation skills, training skills, and becoming what we called a people developer. The transition was relatively easy for some and unbearably difficult for others. There were some casualties, mostly of their own choosing. A few supervisors chose to return to their former roles as team members. Some of them moved to other areas in the plant. Others made the transition very successfully and now can't imagine going back to the old way!

We also offered a few sessions that were open to the supervisors and managers from all of the participating companies. This gave them a chance to share their thoughts and concerns with the larger group. It was great therapy to hear that most of the others were having the same concerns and difficulties, but even better to get some new ideas about how they all handled the transition.

Create a Steering Team

Each company selected a steering team of from six to 12 members, consisting of senior managers, labor leaders, key staff managers, and a vertical slice of the organization. The Steering Team establishes the vision for the redesigned organization. Usually, the team developed the vision in partnership with the Design Team, described below, and with a great deal of input from everyone in the organization, but the final vision emerges from the Steering Team. The vision should explain the team concept as that team sees it at this point in time, understanding it will most likely change along the way. At the very least, the vision will continue to evolve as the teams grow and mature. This evolving vision is a critical concept to explain to everyone in the organization, because it is often a source of contention. The Steering Team's overall mission is to:

- decide policy issues
- provide resources
- clarify constraints
- provide sanctions to experiment.

The major functions of the Steering Team include:

- communicating information about the change
- providing the needed resources
- planning and managing the overall process
- dealing with policy and systems issues.

One of the Steering Team's first tasks was to select the Design Team members. Together the teams clarified decisions about the general framework, which rules were not to be violated, which areas teams could not get involved with, and which organization-wide goals they needed to achieve.

In most of the companies, while the Steering Team and Design Team were busy learning about their tasks, employees who soon would become team members began the interpersonal skills training outlined above.

Create a Design Team

The major functions of the Design Team are to do the following:

- assess the current system
- create the vision of the new system
- develop the transition plan
- conduct a design review
- manage the implementation of the transition plan.

The Design Team should consist of managers, supervisors, labor leaders, and employees from all key areas of the organization to be redesigned.

Some of the companies used one design team for the entire organization, whereas others created new design teams for each area as it was redesigned. Both methods worked equally well for the companies. No matter how the team is organized, one of the most critical issues to remember is that it must work hard to gather input from everyone who is not serving on it. The information the Design Team uses to make its decisions should have been gathered from as many people as possible.

Training for the team includes all the work team training outlined in the previous section plus a session on the specifics of work redesign and reengineering principles. The Design Team also is charged with developing a library of as many books on redesign as possible so its members can learn about what has and has not worked for other companies. The team members then begin to assemble their own plan of action.

Often, a design team begins by completing a thorough analysis of the current work system, including a detailed flow chart of all core work processes. These flow charts, which detail the current work process, are often referred to as *is* maps because they document the process the way it is currently. Once the detailed flow charts are completed, the group begins its analysis of the processes. Ways to reduce and eliminate non–value-added work are suggested and implemented. Soon after, the task of reducing time spent on the value-added tasks is also undertaken. Each of these areas is important to examine because they improve both the effectiveness and efficiency of processes.

In their redesign work, most of the design teams used some variation of the original Job Diagnostic Survey. This model stresses the importance of skill variety, task identity, task significance, autonomy, and feedback from the job. Input is gathered from all team members and close-in support people about how everyone thinks the work could best be done. Consensus should be reached about how to design the new process. This may sound simple enough, but is often the most difficult task in the entire redesign process. Spending a great deal of time here until everyone can support the end result will pay off significantly in the future. If everyone does not understood and support a new process at this point, there can be problems once implementation begins.

Next the Design Team creates the *should* maps for each core process. These process maps chart out how the process should look after the redesign work. They should incorporate the information from the vision that has already been created. It is the everyday working of these new processes that will lead the organization toward its mission. It is important to mention here that these should maps are not cast in stone, but may change continually to incorporate the best thinking of the group as its information continues to grow. Even after the new processes are in place, it will be critical to keep the teams working on continuous improvements to their processes. Improvement to core work processes is one of the most effective methods by which teams can improve their productivity and their bottom line.

Once the new processes were designed, each team conducted a gap analysis to identify what technical training would be needed to run the new process efficiently. A training matrix was developed. It listed each team member and the specific training each person would need as well as who would provide the training and when.

After sufficient time passed and the team members were able to demonstrate that their multiskilling was working, the teams decided when they were ready to begin the journey toward self-direction. Several teams chose not to pursue self-direction. For their purposes, high-performance, multiskilled technical teams were as far as they hoped to go. For the teams that chose the self-directed path, the phase 3 training and development sequence was started at this point.

Toward Self-Direction

The critical issue for the teams headed toward self-direction was whether they felt ready to become empowered to take on management responsibilities. When they thought they were ready, they spent time deciding which of the many management tasks made the most sense for them to take on. To help make the decision easier, team members were asked to think of their team as a business within a business and consider the following question: "If this were our own business, what would we need to manage in order to be a successful business?" This may sound like a very simple question, but it is a critical one because its answer will serve as the foundation for the teams' soon-to-be-created team performance management system. Each team will uncover the areas for which it will be held accountable—the areas that need to be monitored, controlled, and improved to ensure business success. How the companies handled this task varied somewhat. A few of the companies had the supervisors and managers choose which tasks seemed most appropriate to transfer to the team. Most of the companies used a joint approach in which the team, in cooperation with supervisors and managers, agreed on which tasks to transfer to the team and in what order to transfer those tasks. This approach took more time, but was well worth it. There was considerably more buy-in from the teams that had a key role in choosing which management tasks to take on. Although the areas of accountability varied somewhat from team to team, some of the most common areas of accountability included the following:

- quality
- customer satisfaction
- production
- safety
- cost

- maintenance
- housekeeping
- team relations
- human resources.

Determining the areas of accountability helps the teams to prioritize which tasks they will begin to manage. For example, in the area of team relations, teams might choose to help set up vacation schedules, assign overtime, participate in hiring decisions, give peer feedback, participate in team performance reviews, and so on. Teams determine for themselves which areas make the most sense for them at this time. These areas of accountability are the foundation of the team performance management system that will now be established.

Once the areas of accountability are determined, the teams need to determine how they will measure each of the areas. Several key measures should be established for each area of accountability. It is important that the measures focus on outcomes and on customers and that each measure have a goal that gives the teams something to reach for. The goals should be SMART—Specific, Measurable and Observable, Attainable (but provide a real stretch), Realistic (within the power of the team), and Time bound. One example is to reduce scrap in a department by 4 percent over the next three months.

The goals should be the basis for a feedback system that provides accurate, timely information to the team about its performance. The feedback system should serve as a tool for the team to develop its problem-solving and process-improvement strategies. It is important that there is really a system in place that incorporates several types of data as feedback, not just one or two pieces of information, or the team may get a skewed view of its performance.

One useful tool is a responsibility matrix. It is a simple tool that outlines who does what and within what time frame. It is, in a sense, the action plan for the accomplishment of the goals. Figure 1 shows an example of one piece of a team performance management system that lists the area of accountability, measures, goals, and feedback the team will have.

As the team continues to mature, new responsibilities can be added as appropriate. Responsibilities should be added only when previous tasks are well in hand. One caution is not to add too many responsibilities too quickly, or the team may feel overwhelmed rather than challenged.

A few of the teams were able to integrate their team performance systems with their compensation package. By doing so, they created a

Figure 1. One piece of a team performance management plan.

Area of Accountability:	Quality
Measures:	First-time pass rate Number of customer complaints
Goals:	To achieve a 99% first-time pass rate over the next six months To reduce customer complaints by 10% within two months
Feedback:	First-time pass report (daily) Customer complaint records (weekly)

sense of accountability because their performance was tied directly to their compensation. Each company handled the integration a bit differently.

The most successful integrations occurred when the team had helped to establish the areas of accountability, measures, goals, and feedback system. In these cases, it was much easier for them to tie their performance to their compensation. Several used a quarterly point system. Each range of points earned gave the team a specific percentage of its base pay as a quarterly bonus. It is critical that only goals that are within the team's control should contribute to their compensation or take away from it. Some groups did not offer team-specific bonuses but compiled the results of all their teams and awarded the same percentage bonus to all of them. Each method has distinct advantages and disadvantages, and each company must decide which method makes the most sense for it.

Some of the teams decided to institute a peer feedback system to help them continue to develop and improve their quarterly point goals. Several teams developed their own assessment instrument that they use semiannually. Each team member rates his or her teammates on a variety of predetermined criteria. Examples are given for each statement to help all team members understand why they received the rating. After examining the data, each team member develops specific short-range and long-range goals for his or her own development. Team members share their goals with the team so they can have the support of all their team members. As you can imagine, a great deal of trust is required for the system to work effectively. A good deal of training was provided before using the instrument to prevent its misuse. The following implementation process was used by each of the teams who developed their own multirater 360 feedback instrument:

1. Team meeting to discuss the developmental purpose of multirater 360 feedback
2a. Management team determines key criteria for assessment
2b. Team members determine key criteria for assessment
3. Final selection, by consensus, of key criteria
4a. Team members develop specific questions for feedback instrument
4b. Management develops specific questions for feedback instrument
5. Final selection of specific questions is made by team relations team members
6. Feedback form is developed and revised from team and management feedback
7. Refresher training in feedback, the 360 process, and use of the instrument
8. Administer pilot instrument
9. Evaluate pilot form
10. Revise instrument as needed
11. Discuss personal development plans at team meetings
12. Track progress of personal development plans
13. Continue to improve the instrument with each use
14. Develop and implement support group instrument

After a year, a companion support group instrument was created. All close-in support people complete the assessment annually for the team. This has expanded the peer feedback system extensively. The feedback has proven to be an invaluable resource for both personal and team growth.

Lessons Learned

Throughout the project, a list was kept of what worked well and what did not work well for each company. To this point, we have focused on what did work well, but we want to share some ideas that did not work—pitfalls, if you will—so you might avoid them on your team journey.

- Don't move too quickly. This is a major change, and people need a chance to get used to some of the new ideas.
- Get everyone's input throughout the process. This will allow for greater buy-in.
- Never say never! Those who say, "It could never be done here," should get out of the way of the people who are already doing it!
- Nothing is cast in stone, rather it is cast in Jell-O so it can be reconfigured as needed.

- Everyone in the organization should participate in the training sequence—no exceptions!
- Effective team performance management systems are based on goals that are within the control of the team to accomplish. They are closely linked to team compensation.
- Compensation should come after performance improvements have been demonstrated, not as an incentive to create improvements. Compensation must be tied to team performance management.
- Compensation should be influenced to a great extent by the actual performance of the teams, and all team members should understand how they affect their compensation plan.

Following are general implementation guidelines. Some of the steps overlap. This is not a linear process.

1. Provide education and training and consulting about teams.
2. Decide to develop a team-based environment.
3. Select a steering team.
4. Select a design team.
5. Create the vision.
6. Conduct a front-end analysis.
7. Clarify the constraints.
8. Communicate the vision and the constraints.
9. Create is process maps.
10. Create should process maps.
11. Conduct a gap analysis.
12. Develop the transition plan.
13. Implement and oversee the transition plan.
14. Provide phase one team training.
15. Functional teams are in place.
16. Provide phase two team training.
17. One or more of the following teams are in place: multiskilled functional, problem solving, process improvement, semiautonomous, or cross functional.
18. Provide phase three team training.
19. Develop team performance management system.
20. Self-directed teams are in place.
21. Teams continue to mature and take on added responsibilities.

As part of a front-end analysis and throughout the team development process, organizations should ask themselves a variety of strategic and tactical questions. Following are some of the critical questions to consider during the transition.

Strategic Questions

1. Why do you think you want teams?
2. What do you hope to accomplish?
3. Specifically, how will people be working differently?
4. Current reality check...What is going well for the organization right now?
5. What should the organization be doing differently?
6. How will the organization measure progress so you *know* if things are really working as planned?
7. What are the boundaries as you see them right now? (That is, what won't the team do?)
8. How fully is the organization able to integrate all critical functions to provide seamless customer-driven order fulfillment? (That is, can we integrate sales, manufacturing, marketing, and accounting?)
9. Is the current work system fair game for possible redesign, or must the work system remain as is?
10. If the work system must remain as is, why? Please be specific.
11. How will you design the new structure?
12. When do you hope to have this new process up and running?
13. When should you begin to develop a team performance management system?
14. How will you determine when the team is ready to accept additional responsibility and accountability for its area?

Tactical Questions

1. How many people should be on each team?
2. What is their current skill level on technical issues? On interpersonal issues?
3. What training is needed, and when is it needed?
4. How will the design team work?
5. How will the design team share its information with the rest of the team?
6. Can you establish a time line (approximate) and distribute or post it so everyone can stay tuned to the progress being made and what is coming next?
7. When should you start working on a team compensation plan? (Note: Do not begin to compensate for improved performance before it has been demonstrated!)
8. How can you be sure to focus the compensation plan on accomplishments, not on activity?

Additional Considerations

1. What is the competition doing?
2. Do any of your newer associates have team experience from other places they have worked?
3. Have you built a circulating library of some of the best books or videos on effective teams?
4. Do you use the information to consider if the concepts learned could work for us in some modified form?
5. How open minded is your organization being about these changes?
6. How often do you hear words such as "That would never work around here," or "But that's the way we have always done it around here!"

Summary

To ensure the most successful team development intervention, companies should follow each of the guidelines, although they might not complete them in the exact order presented. Under ideal circumstances, companies would follow them to the letter. However, most of us do not live in a perfect world. My recommendation is to follow them to the best of your ability. Leaving out steps or rushing through them will create problems for you down the road. This should not come as any surprise, because it is true in our business operations daily. We sometimes choose to take shortcuts, usually to find ourselves taking more time to make corrections after the fact!

How an organization implements each step will vary greatly on the basis of its needs, vision, and situation. There are no cookie-cutter approaches to team development. You must experiment to find out what works best for your organization. These guidelines are not the answer to everything; they are simply guidelines.

Spend plenty of time in the planning stages. Gather input from everyone in the organization, often. Lay out a specific, detailed plan, but remember it is not cast in stone. Let the plan change as it goes along. At any given time, you can only see as far as the horizon, but as you keep moving toward the horizon, your view continues to expand. Things that seemed impossible to do in the past now seem like the right things to do. That is what continuous improvement is all about. Do your research, trust your instincts, get some professional assistance, and then go forward knowing you will have both successes and failures. Work hard to have huge successes and small failures. Learn from the failures so they don't recur. Spread the word about the successes so you are creating an internal team of champions.

If you are headed toward self-direction, be sure that your team performance plan specifies what is important for the team to manage. Reward accomplishments that are valuable. Provide the team with all the resources it needs to move at the rate at which its members feel comfortable. Do not pile on too much too soon, especially in taking on management tasks, or the team will feel overwhelmed and will not be very successful. Keep in mind that some skills, such as managing costs and establishing peer feedback, may take longer than some easier tasks like managing quality and safety, which the team may feel more comfortable with. Don't push it. If the team doesn't seem ready for the new skill, it probably isn't ready for it yet.

The teams you create, no matter where you choose to stop along the team development continuum, should help your organization to become an even more high-performance, high-commitment organization than it has ever been before.

Questions for Discussion

1. Is our organization interested in making the journey to teams?
2. Where is our organization on the team development continuum?
3. Have we begun to use any of the guidelines described in this article?
4. What pitfalls will we face during the team development journey?
5. What do we have to do to get started?

The Author

Karen Just is the owner and senior consultant of K & D Consulting, a training and consulting company specializing in team development, interpersonal skills, and process improvement. She previously worked with North Central Technical College in Mansfield, Ohio. She works with client companies to help them improve their work processes through team development. Her work ranges from the basics of team development to team performance management and integrating performance and compensation for teams. Just is a frequent presenter at conferences on a variety of topics related to team development. She is active in several professional organizations including The Association for Quality and Participation (AQP) and the American Society for Training & Development (ASTD). She holds a master's degree in training and organization development from The Ohio State University. She can be contacted at 7 Clay Lane, Rowley, MA 01969; phone: 978.948.0826; e-mail: Ka_just@yahoo.com.

References

Harless, J.H. (1973). "An Analysis of Front-End Analysis." *Improving Human Performance: A Research Quarterly, 4,* 229–244.

Mager, R., and P. Pipe. (1970). *Analyzing Performance Problems.* Belmont, CA: Fearon Publishers.

The Implementation
of Self-Managing Teams

Sydney Water Corporation Pty Ltd.

Brett M. Wright and John L. Cordery

This case study describes the steps the Sydney Water Corporation took in undertaking a major work redesign-based reform, involving the introduction of flexible self-managing production teams within 29 wastewater treatment plants. The case study explores the various internal and external factors that provided the impetus for change and the processes that gave rise to a highly successful organizational transition. Finally, this case describes the implications for strategic human resource management generally.

A dominant feature of human resource practice over recent years has been the widespread adoption of team-based approaches to work organization, particularly self-managing teams (Lawler, 1990; Lawler, Mohrman, and Ledford, 1992; Macduffie, 1995; Osterman, 1994). From a human resource management perspective, the implementation of self-managing teams is frequently portrayed as an effective strategic response to increased competitiveness and uncertainty in the business environment, giving rise to improved productivity while contributing toward a better quality of work life for employees (Cordery, 1996).

The impact of self-managing teamwork on both organizational and employee outcomes in a variety of industry sectors has been fairly well studied over recent times (Campion, Medsker, and Higgs, 1993; Cohen and Ledford, 1994; Cordery, Mueller, and Smith, 1991; Pearson, 1992; Wall, Kemp, Jackson, and Clegg, 1986). What emerges from much of this research, however, is a somewhat inconsistent picture.

This case was prepared to serve as a basis for discussion rather than to illustrate either effective or ineffective administrative and management practices.

In some cases, work attitudes or performance or both appear to improve as a result of this approach to work design, and sometimes they don't (Goodman, Devadas, and Hughson, 1988; Kelly, 1992). One reason for these findings lies in the failure of mainstream job-design theory to adequately consider the organizational context within which job redesign occurs (Oldham and Hackman, 1980; Roberts and Glick, 1981), thereby providing insufficient guidance to human resource practitioners who wish to use work redesign as a vehicle for productivity improvement. For example, it would appear that moderate to high process uncertainty or variability, task interdependence, and employee desires for autonomy are among a number of contingency variables determining the likely effectiveness of autonomous and team-based work designs (Pearce and Ravlin, 1987; Wall and Jackson, 1995). This contingency perspective is in stark contrast to the strong prescriptive orientation toward self-managing teams that is evident within the human resource management literature and in practice (Osterman, 1994; Walton, 1985; Wellins, Byham, and Wilson, 1991).

There is, however, another frequently ignored contextual factor that is critical to the success of work redesign. A significant proportion of the literature describing the operation of self-managing teams reports on their operation in new, or greenfield, sites. Frequently, however, implementation occurs at established, or brownfield, sites. To be successful in these sites, the new form of work organization must supplant existing work structures and associated management systems and practices. In addition, changes must be successfully negotiated within the context of a tradition of management-employee relations, which has been defined by the existing systems and practices and which creates political barriers to the reform process (Storey, 1992). In the context of historically poor management-employee relations, the difficulty of this transition is magnified. Thus, in many instances of workplace reform, the integrity of the work design that is eventually put into practice will be dependent on the success of the transition process. It is through this process that the theoretical, or planned, work design is operationalized in the context of the existing organization, elements of the existing human resource management system unfrozen, and a new strategic fit between these elements cemented in place.

The Organizational Setting

The setting for this case study is the wastewater treatment plants in the TransWater subsidiary of the Sydney Water Corporation, a state-owned corporation that provides water and sewerage services to the Sydney Basin, in New South Wales, Australia. These services are provided to a population estimated at 3,757,000 in an area of operation totaling almost 13,000 square kilometers. The 29 plants in the study are very much like factories in the process industry, producing a specified product in a continuous manner. All operate 24 hours per day, with three plants staffed on a 24-hour basis with a rotating shift pattern, and the remaining 26 plants staffed on a day-work basis only. Prior to the implementation of self-managing production teams, there were 500 employees in wastewater treatment, approximately 300 employed in day-to-day operation or production, and the remaining 200 employees provided technical-engineering and administrative support.

At the time of the study, the organization was hierarchical with a strong engineering-based culture, a large number of job classifications, and corresponding demarcations. Operation of the plants was regarded as a relatively low-skilled blue-collar function supported by high levels of white-collar technical-engineering and administrative support employees. The strong blue-collar focus in the operating area of the business, coupled with heightened environmental awareness and community intolerance to plant by-passes or performance failures, contributed to the development of a strong industrial bargaining base for the unionized workforce. In practice, the workforce consistently used the threat of releasing untreated sewage from the wastewater treatment plants through the withdrawal of their labor as a bargaining device. Management-employee relations were best described as adversarial, with a history of mistrust, intolerance, and high levels of industrial disputation in the business. Much of the disputation centered on reinforcing demarcations between the work that blue-collar employees performed and that of the technical and engineering staff.

Generally at the time of this study, attempts to introduce new technology (often with the express aim of replacing employees in what was perceived as a hostile and recalcitrant workforce) were the force behind introduction of change within the organization, and the adversarial management-employee relations climate meant that this change typically involved very little consultation with the workforce and their representatives. The off-line technical and engineering support groups drove technical change, and it was common, given the lack of consultation with operations staff, for very expensive capital and operating solutions to fail. In many cases, the equipment either did not work at all, or, because of the difficulties experienced in getting it to work, operations employees refused to operate the new technology and it sat idle until removed.

Pressure for Change

Within this organizational setting, pressure for change derived from two external sources: the drive to introduce competition in the water sector and the need to operate higher levels of automation and introduce technology to meet increasingly stringent environmental standards.

The drive to introduce competition into the water sector in Australia is a consequence of the increasing globalization of the water industry coupled with government pressures for competition-based reform in monopolistic industries across the country. The water industry in Australia has been a monopoly, which the public sector has operated. The result of increased competition has been the emergence of private-sector participation in areas previously regarded as core public-sector functions. In the wastewater treatment plants this translates into competition from foreign water companies to operate the plants that Sydney Water currently operates. Their presence has contributed to a growing perception by employees, unions, and management that the status-quo, business survival, and as an adjunct job security are all under threat, and hence the three groups have shown a willingness to address change.

In addition to the increasing market and political pressure on organizations (such as Sydney Water) to reform in the wastewater treatment plant area, there also have been rapid technological advances in wastewater treatment. In response to growing environmental awareness and corresponding community concern for the impact of plant discharges on inland river systems and the ocean, wastewater treatment processes have become increasingly complex to meet increasing environmental discharge standards. Advanced computer-based automation and control systems are available to replace traditional manually operated technology. These developments in treatment complexity and plant control are radically changing the traditional competencies that have been required to operate wastewater treatment plants, lifting and transforming the skill level required (Majchrzak, 1988a, 1988b). Traditional manual crisis-oriented competencies are increasingly seen as no longer appropriate within the operating focus of continuous production and process control that is necessary for the reliable production of a specified effluent from a highly automated or computer-controlled wastewater treatment plant. Thus the traditional skill requirements to operate wastewater treatment plants have changed.

Finally, an international benchmarking study that the organization conducted yielded a number of reported best practice labor metrics in terms of the size of the operational and technical-engineering-administrative support workforces in the business relative to production capacity. Allowing for differences across countries, plant types, ages, and the like, it was readily apparent that the organization appeared to be overstaffed in both the operational and the technical-engineering-administrative support areas.

The Design Process

The development of the reform proposal was a direct response to these change imperatives facing the water industry globally and locally. This provided the necessary impetus to challenge and breach the existing approaches to wastewater treatment plant operation and generated a willingness on the part of key stakeholders to consider reform.

The approach used to identify the nature of work organization reform needed was grounded in sociotechnical systems (STS) theory (Pasmore, 1988; Susman and Chase, 1986). STS theory focuses on the "joint optimization" of the operation of the technical and social systems of production through the organization of work. STS approaches stress the need to control the key production variances at source while providing job roles that enable employees to satisfy valued social and psychological needs, such as autonomy, variety, learning opportunities, and feedback (Cherns, 1976).

As one of the key features of STS designs is the attempt to control variance at source (that is, to have the control of variations to the production process as close to the workplace as possible), the organization determined that this form of design presented a number of significant prospects for the wastewater treatment plants. In controlling variance at source, an STS design therefore has the potential to vest control in the operations workforce and, hence, reduce the need for much of the technical-engineering and administrative support, which as a consequence would improve the organization on the benchmarking best practice labor metrics.

The STS approach involved a strategic analysis that identified a number of the key business processes in the wastewater treatment plants as a focus to develop the reform proposal. This analysis viewed wastewater treatment as a number of key business processes, or as a horizontal organization (Jacob, 1992; Porter, 1985). One of the key business processes the analysis identified was production, reinforcing the central theme of the wastewater treatment business. From this analysis, a team of production managers and the organizational development manager determines subprocesses for the key process of production wherein each subprocess represented one component of the total production process in a wastewater treatment plant. For each of these subprocesses, the team identified lead and lag indicators of subprocess performance.

The team then constructed a process influence matrix, which appears in figure 1, that showed an assessment of the influence of the lead indicators for each subprocess on the plant performance parameters. This information then was manipulated within the context of wastewater treatment plant performance objectives. In simplistic terms, this is to control the discharge of pollutants to the environment. This corresponds to controlling the average level of pollutants discharged and the variation in the level of discharge. Within this performance framework, the team compiled the lead indicators together with their relative influence on plant performance measures from the process influence matrix in figure 1 in a performance indicator evaluation matrix (see figure 2). This performance indicator evaluation matrix classified the following:

- the variables in the subprocess that had an impact on the variability of process performance
- the fixed components of the subprocess affecting average performance that could be changed only by a change in the subprocess operating parameters.

Thus the two key factors that had the potential to be influenced by a production team were:

- the ability to control the existing production process and, in doing so, reduce the variability in effluent performance
- the ability to modify the existing parameters of the various subprocesses to achieve an improvement in the average value of effluent performance.

It was readily apparent from this analysis that the nature of the lead indicators was such that without the responsibility and skills in the production team to influence those indicators, improvements would be difficult to achieve. In addition, the nature of the production process on a wastewater treatment plant is such that there is a critical time effect. Delays in changing plant process parameters as a consequence of the need to access remote technical and engineering support adversely contributes to variability and average value of plant effluent.

Figure 1. Process influence matrix.

Subprocess

Parameter	Screenings	Sedimentation and Grit	Anoxic	Aeration	Clarification	Chemical Dosing	Tertiary Treatment	Sludge Handling	Chlorination
Non-filterable Residue	■	■		▶	■	■	■		
Biological Oxygen Demand	▶	▶	▶	■	▶		■		
Phosphorus			▶	■	▶	■	■	▶	▶
Ammonia				■					
Total Nitrogen			■		▶				
Fecal Coliforms									■
Chlorine Residual									■

Legend: ■ Strong influence
▶ Weak influence
Blank No Influence

Figure 2. Performance indicator evaluation matrix.

		Contribution to Variability	
		Low	**High**
Contribution to Average	**Low**	• Dissolved Air Flotation (DAF) operating effectiveness.	• RBCOD (food) level in anoxic/aerobic zone.
	High	• Grit removal frequency. • Anoxic zone pH level. • Return Activated Sludge (RAS) recycle volume to anoxic zone. • Chemical dosing rate for alkalinity in aeration zone. • Polyelectrolyte dosing rate for sludge dewatering. • Alkalinity level in aeration zone. • Backwash frequency in tertiary filters.	• Screen cleaning frequency. • Primary sludge wastage frequency/rate. • Dissolved oxygen level in anoxic zone. • Aeration rate in aeration zone. • Mixed liquor recycle volume to anoxic zone. • Wastage rate from RAS or mixed liquor. • Operator competency in aeration, chemical dosing, and sludge handling. • Chemical dosing rate for phosphorus removal in aeration zone. • Flow rate and strength of influent in dosing area. • Dosing rate of disinfectant. • Sludge blanket level in clarifiers.

Therefore, following this analysis, it was deemed that the responsibility and skills for controlling those factors that had high contributions to variability and average value of plant effluent should reside with operating or production personnel, not with a remote technical and engineering support group.

Significant process variability is one of the preconditions for the design and activation of self-managing teams identified by Pearce and Ravlin (1987). A further precondition is the degree to which there is a collective aspect to tasks, such that group members must coordinate their activities in order to complete a task. The high level of interdependence that characterizes the subprocesses in the total production process within wastewater treatment plants, as highlighted in the subprocess influence matrix in figure 1, suggested that effective control over process variances would require the exercise of a substantial degree of collective responsibility on the part of the plant operations or production workforce. On this basis and in accordance with Hackman's (1977) proposed criteria for the use of group-based work design, the organizational development manager considered a team-based approach to work design the most appropriate vehicle for future work design in wastewater treatment plants. The business's management team decided that each plant would be operated by a self-managing team (several in the case of shift plants) with responsibility for the following:

- operating a wastewater treatment plant
- controlling all key variances
- solving problems to do with plant operation or performance
- deciding on methods of work, task schedules, and assignment of members to different tasks
- scheduling and approving planned leave
- arranging cover for absences
- managing the plant operational budget
- developing plant plans and budgets
- ordering goods and services within procurement guidelines
- managing the interface with customers.

The full scope of the responsibilities of the teams has developed over time, as is evident from table 1, a team generated list of responsibilities one year after implementation.

The design of the new team member or production officer roles was based an operator upgrading strategy (Susman and Chase, 1986). The new production officer roles incorporated many of the technical and engineering and administrative competencies integral to the operation of a wastewater treatment plant. Coupled with this, the lower skilled nonproduction support competencies traditionally performed by the production roles was outsourced to a group called Facility Services.

The Negotiation of the Change Process

Despite the pressures for change, the sheer magnitude of the change program to self-managing teams, directly affecting the 294 employees engaged in wastewater treatment or production in an area characterized by industrial hostility, required that management take a different approach. The traditional approach had been characterized by management directive and subsequent industrial unrest.

The new approach involved a series of consultative processes previously unknown within the organization. Recognizing the external and internal pressures for change described earlier, both management and the union agreed at the outset on the vision for the future of the business, but recognized that each party would potentially have a different view of the path to that outcome. To resolve the issue, management selected a team of four to represent it, and the union se-

Table 1. Responsibilities of production teams.

Production

- Producing plant effluent that meets EPA license in the most cost-effective manner
- Producing biosolids that can be beneficially reused, wherever possible
- Producing screenings and grit that can be disposed of to landfill
- Maximizing the reuse of treated effluent on the plant
- Determining the capacity and capability of each unit process on the plant.

Assets

- Managing the maintenance of plant and equipment to ensure system availability targets are met
- Specifying operational and performance requirements for the creation of new assets
- Managing the creation of minor assets, modifications, projects, and overhauls
- Taking over new assets and ensuring they meet operational, maintenance, and safety requirements
- Ensuring that the scope of work for maintenance of each item of equipment matches the plant's needs
- Managing all housekeeping required by the plant.

Reporting

- Cost-period performance analysis and reporting to the business management teams
- License reporting to the EPA

The Team Members Themselves

- Managing all aspects of safety on the plant
- Ensuring effective communication between team members and cooperating with support teams
- Scheduling rosters, annual leave, and overtime while maintaining effective plant operations
- Developing a learning agreement for each team member on the basis of identified competency gaps
- Cross training so that all team members know how to complete essential production tasks
- Scheduling other training including statutory training, team skills training, and production training
- Handling all administration functions once given the appropriate training and resources
- Assessing team and individual performance.

continued on page 107

lected nine representatives, consisting of the senior assistant secretary, four white-collar (salaried) union delegates, and four blue-collar (wages) union delegates.

The initial agreement that both parties reached on the end point or business vision, which said, "A production focused Waste Water Treatment Business achieving best practice in meeting regulatory requirements at least cost," provided the team with a much easier task than had been anticipated. The consultative process was, therefore, primarily concerned with the how of transition, or reaching agree-

Table 1. Responsibilities of production teams (continued).

Planning

- Developing and implementing plant plans to meet the needs of the plant and the business
- Developing and implementing budget plans
- Developing, reviewing, and updating Incident Management Plans.

Suppliers

- Procuring goods and services in accordance with guidelines and financial delegations
- Negotiating service agreements and managing suppliers to ensure quality, quantity, and timeliness of goods and services ordered.

Customers

- Working with regional partners (customers) to provide integrated wastewater system management
- Managing the interface with the local community through plant tours, open days, and effective complaint handling procedures.

Quality

- Developing and implementing the process management program (PMP), including standard operating procedures (SOPs) and unit process guidelines (UPGs), to minimize variation in plant products
- Continually improving SOPs and UPGs to ensure they represent best practice at any point in time
- Focusing on reducing operational costs and deferring capital investment through process optimization
- Identifying where automation of the process will enable team resources to be better utilized
- Implementing an accredited quality system for the plant.

Budgeting

- Preparing and meeting annual operational budgets
- Providing input into annual capital budgets
- Allocating all costs to processes using the process costing system.

---

ment on a joint road map. The goodwill between the parties and the level of trust that developed during this negotiation process was unheard of in the business. In recognition of this step, the team issued a number of joint communiqués, under both the organization's and union's letterheads, which gave support to its cooperative nature and helped to garner employees' support before they held a mass meeting to vote on acceptance of the reform proposal.

Agreement on the path to reform took approximately six weeks for the negotiating team to resolve, during which time not a single day was lost due to industrial disputation. Essentially this was possible because both parties approached the negotiations as negotiations, rather than each party attempting to impose its views on the other. Following agreement in principle between the management and union representatives on the team, a mass meeting of all employees in the business was called to consider the agreed means of achieving the business vision. As a result of the goodwill developed in the negotiation process and through the positive feedback to the workforce as to the true consultative nature of that process, the mass meeting unanimously endorsed the business vision and the negotiated process of achieving that vision.

The Agreed Reform Process

The agreed reform process was essentially an enormous "spill and fill" exercise with all 294 employees affected required to do the following:

- apply for one of the new production officer positions
- apply for voluntary redundancy (voluntary separation from the organization) or redeployment (placement elsewhere in the organization if a role existed)
- or apply for a transfer to a new Facility Services Group.

Three key design features of the reform proposal facilitated the workforce's acceptance of the reform proposal. The first was the creation of what was called a train-on-production-officer position. This enabled those employees who just failed to meet the base competency level a period of six months' breathing space to overcome their deficiencies and be reevaluated. There were many long-serving employees in the business that had given good service over many years, but the organization was now saying those skills were inappropriate. Management believed there was an obligation to provide these employees with the opportunity to acquire and demonstrate these skills which management had not previously required or actively developed. Upon reevaluation, they would secure a production officer position if successful or, if unsuccessful, would have the options of redundancy or redeployment or transfer to the Facility Services Group. The facility services business provided a safety net for those who were unable or unwilling to take on the new production officer roles, but who wished to remain with the organization.

Thus the reform proposal satisfied management's aims of moving to a new high-skilled production workforce, and it also met the union's requirements. All employees had an option of staying with the organization if they so wished, and those employees who may not have had the opportunity to acquire production officer skills had a six-month window of opportunity to do so.

The final feature in the negotiation process was an agreement that stated that although only 186 new production officer positions were required (with specified numbers at each level), the numbers would be fluid for the transfer and accreditation process of the existing employees. In effect, this meant that if all 294 existing employees applied and were successful, the organization would appoint all 294 applicants and use natural attrition to achieve the 186 required. Both management and the union knew that this was highly unlikely, based on their knowledge of employee skills and of the significant numbers who wished to accept voluntary redundancy. It did, however, provide a major selling point for the reform proposal to the workforce and was a major ingredient in the proposal's acceptance with no industrial action. Such an outcome is rare in such a large-scale reform involving a blue-collar workforce.

Key Features of the Implementation Process

The successful implementation of job redesign is dependent on far more than the appropriateness of the job design. The implementation process must be carefully planned to ensure a smooth transition to the new job design, and this case study is no different. A number of key features of the implementation process outlined below contributed to the successful implementation.

The Smoothing Team

With such a major reform, the issues facing employees, unions, and management were enormous. Previous experience of change in the organization suggested that implementation of the reform would be extremely problematic. It was recognized that a strategy needed to be put in place to address the multitude of issues that arise with such a large-scale implementation, such as communication and the impact of the reform on individuals. A strategy was necessary because for many employees, the outcomes were uncertain.

To address these issues and to facilitate the successful implementation of the reform, the organizational development manager established a Smoothing Team. It comprised the two senior union delegates who participated in the negotiation process, and, as per the name, their role was to smooth out all the potential day-to-day hurdles that were to arise throughout the implementation process. The stated objectives of this team were as follows:

- to support line management in the presentation, dissemination, and communication of the reform principles
- to facilitate solutions to implementation issues
- to develop information packages where appropriate to ensure a consistent message and common understanding of the key issues of the reform
- to document or communicate in "plain English" the reform principles
- to facilitate solutions to relocations or relief and the like
- to address individual concerns or problems throughout the implementation
- to facilitate the exiting of personnel through the Voluntary Redundancy Program.

The key attribute of this team was that they were key members of the union negotiating team for the reform. Hence, they were fully involved in the negotiations and as a consequence had an excellent knowledge of the details of what was a complex reform. In addition they had the respect of the entire workforce and in doing so were well able to assist management to mediate the day-to-day problems associated with implementation. Throughout the implementation process this team proved invaluable in addressing issues before they became major problems and in ensuring a common level of understanding for all employees. There were numerous examples of where the team was successful in averting potential industrial problems by developing innovative solutions to issues that previously would have resulted in industrial disputation. More important, most of the issues never reached management because the teams addressed them through effective communication before they escalated into major problems.

The Internal Appeals Process

The management-union negotiating team introduced another mechanism—an internal appeals process—to assist with the transition process for those employees who were unsuccessful in their application for one of the new production officer roles. The process was yet another way to ensure that the assessment of existing employees was fair and equitable. The Appeals Team consisted of management and union nominees, which reinforced the participative nature of the reform process.

Train-on Outcomes

After the original assessment, a process was put in place with each of the train-on production officers, whereby each employee developed a personal development plan or learning agreement in an attempt to overcome any competency deficiencies. These employees were provided with assistance in terms of training courses, on-the-job training, and mentoring in an attempt to gain the necessary competencies. As agreed in the workplace reform negotiations, a review of the train-on employees occurred six months after the original assessment. Approximately 75 percent of the train-on employees were successfully accredited as production officers at that time.

The Supporting Management Role

Research suggests that, once implemented, self-managing teams rely on significant modifications to other elements of the management system (for example, supervision, rewards, selection, training, performance appraisal, and information systems) for their survival and effectiveness (Oldham and Hackman, 1980; Pearce and Ravlin, 1987). Failure to generate positive outcomes through work redesign may reflect a lack of internal consistency between the work design and other elements of human resource policy and practice. Changes to the role of supervisors and managers appear particularly important in this regard (Cordery and Wall, 1985; Cummings, 1978; Manz, Keating, and Donnellon, 1990; Manz and Sims, 1987).

To support the new empowered production officer positions, the team of production managers and the organizational development manager redesigned the management role above the production officers to be more supportive of the team concept. The new management roles were retitled production facilitators/coordinators with responsibilities that included: providing support to the production teams; having a mentor or coach role in assisting the development of the teams; and assisting the production teams in boundary management issues. The change in focus of this level of management was a strategy designed to ensure that the management within the business was aligned and supportive of the front-line empowered production teams.

Implementation Problems

Implementation has not been without its difficulties as the teams have learned to operate within a system of team-based control, as opposed to the old system of managerial control (Barker, 1993). A strategic review of the reform conducted 12 months after implementation identified a number of issues or concerns that were posing difficulties.

Team Leadership and Team Hierarchy

The most significant issue to emerge related to the lack of a designated team leader. This caused concern in some teams, especially in regard to the externally imposed safety and regulatory requirements for a responsible person. These requirements are hierarchical rather than team based. The supporting management systems within the organization also reflect this lack of flexibility. Although on paper the authority to approve financial expenditures is now the responsibility of teams, in practice the delegations have continued to reside with the most senior production officer in the team. This financial responsibility reinforces the former hierarchical system, where only the superintendent and supervisor had financial delegations. This finding is consistent with the observations of Oldham and Hackman (1980, p. 248) that there is a "diminution (or even a reversal) of anticipated outcomes" of job design efforts as a consequence of the existing nonaligned organizational systems and practices. This financial power at the higher production officer levels indeed may be a factor in the reported resistance of some higher level production officers in letting go of their traditional roles. That is, those superintendents and supervisors absorbed into the teams have found it difficult to share the power they once possessed with the team as a whole. Such an outcome is not unexpected (Manz et al., 1990). These examples highlight the need to address the external environment to the organization and indeed the systems within the organization that do not support the transition to self-management.

Downskilling of Production Officers

One of the key elements of the reform package was a requirement that all production officers perform all activities for which they are competent, thus eliminating demarcations within the business. In the case of some of the higher or more competent production officers, there has been some resistance to performing some of the lower skilled, unpleasant, or manual tasks. This unwillingness has not been conducive to flexibility within the teams. Some team members have perceived it as evidence of a hierarchy within the teams. That is, some production officers only do the "good" jobs. More competent production officers perceive the need to do these lower skilled, unpleasant, or manual tasks as deskilling.

Nonperforming Team Members

Issues such as what to do with team members who fail to contribute adequately to the work of the team, or who are unable to adapt to the demands of the new work system, also have posed significant internal challenges to the fledgling teams. They are not issues restricted to the lower level production officer positions. In some cases, teams have expressed their dissatisfaction with the role being performed by the most competent production officers on the plants but have been unable to find a means to address these issues. The outcome of this has been a level of frustration within some teams as they find it difficult to pursue any course of action within the team. There also has been no formal process to raise the issue external to the team. Although some teams have contended well with resolving these issues, others uncomfortable with the lack of a designated team leader have had difficulties. Indeed teams that have found it difficult to resolve these issues have been hesitant to raise the matter outside the team for fear of giving the perception that their team was not functioning as well as other teams.

The Mix of Old and New

The influx of a number of new employees external to the existing workforce has led to some tensions within teams. The new employees' different skills mix have put pressure on some of the existing employees to change. Alternatively there are reports that in some areas there has been a tendency for some teams to fall back into old habits. This reversion has generally occurred in teams in which new members are in the minority. There also has been tension among teams and criticism of the high-performing teams, particularly because some teams that have embraced the new work organization have set benchmarks in performance, which have put pressure on other teams to catch up.

Team Composition

The challenges associated with selecting complementary team members has presented some difficulties because plants are dispersed throughout the Sydney Basin and have varying levels of production uncertainty and because individual production officers have a range of competency profiles. Although it is desirable to build a team to operate a plant with an appropriate competency mix, individuals wish to work as close to home as possible. The business also has attempted to meet its outcomes with minimum inconvenience to individuals. In practice this means that there tends to have been a high level of flexibility on location for the higher two levels of production officers and little flexibility for the two lower levels. This variation has presented some difficulties for the business, particularly for the two lower levels of production officer whose competencies tend to be more plant specific than the higher level production officers are. Thus with the wide variance in production uncertainty of plants, the rotation of production officers and the broadening of plant specific competencies present future challenges.

The Rate of Change and Team Development

The final issue for implementation has been the rate of change and the need for some team members and management to be tolerant of different change or development time frames for teams. With such a large number of geographically spread teams, with different competency mixes, and the different levels of production uncertainty of the plants, it is natural that teams will develop at their own rates. Some teams have expressed concern that management is not cognizant of these realities and has therefore put pressure on some teams it perceived to be lagging.

Nevertheless, any implementation of this scale has issues associated with it, but, perhaps more important in this instance, it has occurred without the traditional recourse to industrial action that occurs in confrontationist interventions.

Work Design Outcomes

The success of the work design can be gauged in terms of the following outcomes. This has included improvements in plant performance, unplanned absences, injury frequency, and in the structural changes as a consequence of the work design that have provided greater operational flexibility:

1. After 12 months, plant performance had increased significantly on the two primary performance measures. There was a mean reduction in the variation in the nonfilterable residue in the plant effluents of 11.23 percent and the total phosphorus load in the plant effluents was reduced by 37.26 percent. Both of these reductions were significant at $p < 0.001$.

2. Unplanned absences decreased by 27.90 percent ($p < 0.05$) and the frequency of industrial injuries by 34.63 percent ($p < 0.01$) in the 12 months after implementation compared with the 12 months prior to implementation.

3. A key feature of the reform was a reduction in job classifications from 21 to four. Four levels of production officer positions replaced the existing blue-collar and white-collar mix of some 21 job classifications that tended to be narrow, task focused, and not conducive to the business needs of a flexible workforce.

4. The industrial climate within the business prior to the reform implementing self-managing teams was one of hostility. The partnering

approach with the union to the reform driven by a consultative process raised the expectations of both parties for a more favorable industrial climate in the future. An outward sign of this goodwill is the absence of direct industrial action in the business in the 12 months following the reform. The total number of appearances before the State Industrial Commission to hear and resolve a dispute declined from 21 in the year prior to the reform to none in the year following.

5. The introduction of self-managing teams implies that a greater level of responsibility is being vested with the front-line workforce, including the absorption of many of the traditional supervisory functions into the team. A consequence of this type of change is pressure on middle-management roles in organizations, and this case was no different. The reform touched the previous supervisor and superintendent roles and absorbed them into the team. With the production officer competencies including a number of traditional technical and engineering and administrative support competencies, and the redesign of the management role above the teams, the reform had a significant impact on the levels of management in the business. The reform reduced the levels of management from as many as nine to five in both the shift and nonshift plants.

6. The higher competencies of the new production officer workforce enable the control of key variances of the production processes to be contained within the teams. This change negated the need for many of the traditional support requirements present when the downgraded operations strategy was in effect enabling a reduction of 29 percent in support personnel.

7. As a consequence of the broader and higher skill requirements of the new production officer positions in the self-managing teams, average remuneration for the production workforce increased by approximately 25 percent, whereas there was an overall reduction in total labor costs of approximately 31 percent. These impacts were direct consequences of the upgrading strategy that reduced the requirement for many of the nonproduction or support employees and refined the number of direct production staff required.

Mechanisms Underlying Achieved Outcome

To provide a greater depth of understanding to the underlying causes of the changes in wastewater treatment plant performance, the organizational development manager conducted a number of unstructured informal interviews with union officials, management, and production officers. These interviews provide the basis for the following insights into the performance improvement with the introduction of self-managing production teams in the wastewater treatment plants in the TransWater subsidiary of Sydney Water. In the following examples, a contrast is made between the old and new ways of work to account for improved performance, which generally can be traced back to the design features or theoretical predictions from self-managing team theory.

Broader Strategic View of the Plant

Wastewater treatment plants tend to be a focal point for visits or tours from schools, the public, overseas delegations, and the like. In the past these tours were conducted by white-collar employees only, not the direct production workforce. Under the new work organization, the production officers at each plant conduct the tours. Through the interview process, the production officers highlighted that through these tours they have been able to gain a greater understanding of the operating context in which their plant operates, including an awareness of what the public wants and a greater understanding of the licensing requirements of the regulator, the Environmental Protection Authority. Their more strategic knowledge of the plant operating context has led to an increase in appreciation of the external significance of the job (Kelly, 1978). The production officers say that this understanding provides them with a more complete framework in which to make operational decisions that ultimately have an impact on the plant stakeholders.

Delegations

The new way of work enables the production officers to have a financial delegation that can procure supplies and other resources when required within budgetary constraints. Previously this right was reserved for the supervisor or superintendent. This change is a result of an increase in team control or discretion (Cummings, 1978). The most significant consequence of this is that the production teams are able to organize their own equipment when required without having to refer to higher authority. This ability minimizes the cycle time to address events that cause variances in plant performance if equipment needs to be hired or the like, thus reducing the impact of these events. The reduction in cycle time to address events that cause variations in plant performance has critical implications for plant performance, especially in biological processes. Once biological processes get out of control, it takes a significant period to bring them back within operating parameters, and all the while plant performance is impaired. If the cycle time to address variances is reduced by enabling the team to take action earlier, the adverse impact of such events can be eliminated or reduced.

From another perspective, the devolution of financial authority to the production teams enables them to practice just-in-time management to minimize the overall costs of production. This means that under the old system the team would request orders for additional chemicals and the like well in advance of reaching minimal levels as there was a need to maintain sufficient buffer stocks to cater for the cycle time of the paperwork process to place new orders. With the team able to directly place the order, the team possesses greater management of its supplies and can more effectively manage its chemical stocks and practice just-in-time purchasing practices.

The Ability to Prioritize

With traditionally managed wastewater production teams, the discretion held by the team is minimal. Under the new self-managing work team organization, the production team is fully responsible for how it allocates work within the team and the order in which it is carried out. This devolution of greater control to the team is another source of cycle time reduction that contributes to the minimization of plant variances. It negates the need for the team to confer with a supervisor or superintendent whom they may not be able to contact directly, but rather the team can directly act to address the problem or alternatively anticipate an occurrence, both actions resulting in a minimization of the impact on performance.

Commitment

The philosophy engendered by the self-managing team culture is that the team is responsible for the operation of the plant. This philosophy has created a sense of ownership within the team and a sense of commitment, another theoretical outcome from a self-managing team design (Emery, 1959). This sense of commitment is new and has manifested itself in greater participation in decision making and group action in the team relative to the plant's performance. With the ability to make decisions and act on those decisions, there has been a more active involvement by team members in prioritizing areas for improvement in plant performance and a greater commitment to work toward those improvements. Under the previous supervisor- or superintendent-led regime, priorities were imposed and, hence, the level of commitment in ensuring the achievement of outcomes was far less.

Demarcations and Competency Upgrading

The elimination of demarcations and the upgrading of the production officer competencies have increased the efficiency of the production officer role markedly. For example, in the self-managing teams a production officer can decide to take a sample of the plant's processes at any time, analyze that sample, and decide on any corrective action to the plant processes to be taken. Before the reform this would have been a long and complicated process with a number of parties involved. If a sample was required outside the normal sampling timetable, the production officer would have been required to request that a sampling officer take a sample, because the production role was prohibited from taking samples. This request would be managed within the priorities of the sampling officer, not those of the production process, and, hence, a time delay could ensue. Once the sample was analyzed, the results would be provided back to the production officer, but any action to significantly change the process would have to be approved by an off-site technical expert. Thus the production officer would have to contact the off-site technical expert, relay the results, and seek approval to make changes to the process. Meanwhile the process would have been steadily deteriorating. Removal of the demarcations and the absorption of technical support competencies into the production officer role have drastically reduced the number of people involved and the cycle time for action, translating into the new production officer role being able to exert greater control over the production process. Thus, a consequence of the removal of demarcations and multiskilling (Cordery, 1996) has been greater job variety (Kelly, 1978) and increased capacity to control plant variances.

Plant Upgrades and Optimization

When plant upgrades are contemplated or the plant is to be optimized, the production officers are fully involved in the process. Under the previous organization, off-line technical support groups imposed solutions without regard to the production team's needs, and, hence, the production teams did not embrace the solutions. As a consequence, these so-called solutions were never as successful as they might have been. With the full involvement of the new production officer role in decision making (Cummings, 1978), all production officers are involved in optimization as part of normal day-to-day activities, not as a special project. Thus, optimization is ongoing and driven by the production officers, making it more successful through ownership and commitment (Emery, 1959) to the process. Plant upgrades are now addressed in a different manner. Technical support groups planning upgrades now regard the production team as their client, ensuring that the designs for plant upgrades meet the needs and address the considerations of the production team. This has reinforced the production team ownership of the plant and ensured their commitment to successfully taking over and operating plant upgrades in the future.

Internal Benchmarking

One of the significant changes with the new production teams is the active internal benchmarking across plants that the teams themselves initiated as a function of increased team control and decision making (Cummings, 1978). It was not carried out previously due to the focus on the day-to-day issues of production work. This was a function of the management-control oriented philosophy prior to the self-managing teams that restricted the role of the production workforce and impeded the supervisor and superintendent role as it became more one of supervision rather than focusing on business performance improvement. This internal benchmarking initiative is a sign of the significant shift of the production role to focus on performance improvement, rather than performing day-to-day plant operation as directed. Such internal benchmarking has achieved benefits in terms of elimination of duplication and the propagation of new ideas. Meetings to discuss improvement opportunities are open to all production officers, rather than only the most senior. These meetings are in open forums and have the potential to leverage skills and knowledge across plants, increasing the competencies of the production officers and their ability to improve and cope with process issues, and, hence, enhance performance.

Industrial Disputes

One of the more interesting comments to arise from the informal interviews was the effect of the changed industrial relations environment where issues are now resolved within the business without resort to industrial action. The Smoothing Team has been credited with much of the success in ensuring that both management and the workforce promptly deal with issues. According to the production officers, the consequence of this more stable work environment is that the plants are not put under stress. This, together with the sense of ownership of the plant teams and the corresponding increase in the level of commitment, results in greater levels of control over plant operations being exercised by the production officers, translating into improved plant performance.

Process Changes

Changes to the plant processes and the timing of those changes have a significant impact on plant performance and variation. With full team consultation prior to process changes and built-in technical support in the production officer roles, the production team is in a far better position to manage the process. Perhaps more important, the production team now understands the reasons behind the need to make process changes, rather than in the previous work organization when off-line technical support people simply told team members to "just make the change, you do not need to worry about why." This means that production team members' learning is facilitated as well as cross learning from more knowledgeable members of the team. Such a change in the role of the team leads to greater control of the plant processes and places team members in a position to enhance their learning, leading to an ability to anticipate process upsets to ensure ongoing plant performance (Wall, Corbett, Martin, Clegg, and Jackson, 1990).

Support Personnel

As a consequence of the upgrading strategy (Susman and Chase, 1986), which has led to an increased level of control and sense of ownership of the plant and processes, the production officers have taken on a more proactive role. This change has resulted in a different relationship with support personnel. Because the technical support personnel now view the production officers as their customers rather than just as operators, their "we know best" attitude has been replaced by a constructive working relationship that is centered on improved plant performance.

An example of the proactive nature of the production teams is evident in the activities of one production team to educate the 24-hour Service Center on the meaning of the out-of-hours plant alarms. For those plants only staffed during the day, any significant faults activate alarms that are relayed to a central Service Center that relays that information to a nominated production officer from the relevant plant. The Service Center staff does not know the plant or how to interpret the alarms. Thus all calls are transferred to the production officer, which results in out-of-hours calls and possibly unnecessary overtime costs. The production team at one plant educated the Service Center team on the significance of the alarms through alarm simulations that led to a changed format of alarms so that out-of-hours costs could be minimized. If a particular fault such as a pump failure occurred before four a.m., for example, it would be necessary for a member of the production team to go out and rectify the fault. If the same fault occurred after four a.m., however, it could be safely ignored and rectified by the production team when it arrived at the plant the next morning. Such education of the Service Center team by the production officers represents a new approach to plant operation that is commensurate with the new level of responsibility. In the past, the staff members' approach was either that it was not their job or that nobody asked for their opinion.

Self-Esteem

Perhaps the most significant and widespread finding from the observational and interview process was the perceived increase in the production officers' level of self-esteem or mental health (Herbst, 1974). This is best reflected in their comments, such as "now we feel like we are needed" and we are now "not just coming to work for the money as we feel like we are having an input." This is a direct result of the increased level of control (Cummings, 1978) afforded to the production officers that translates into higher levels of commitment of the production workforce.

Cross-Team Support

Before the introduction of the self-managing teams, the production workforce operated its own plants, had very little contact with other plants, and certainly would not involve itself in another plant's operations. Under the new work organization, the teams provide support to each other across plants to facilitate learning and, in simple terms, to help out. This cooperation has taken the form of assisting to cover staff shortages at one plant or providing operational support that is absent in a team. One plant, for example, was faced with a petrochemical infiltration that had the potential to drastically affect the plant processes. A team at another plant had experienced such an occurrence and sent two of its production officers to assist that plant's production team in dealing with the problem. Such cross-team support is a fundamental element in improving the overall business's performance and is a direct consequence of the increased level of control and commitment in the new work organization. Under the previous regime, operators were neither permitted to leave the plant without their supervisor's approval nor motivated to do so.

Dealing with Poor Performers

One of the major impacts of the self-managing production work team environment has been the impact of peer pressure within the teams, including dealing with poor performers. In the past, supervisors or superintendents identified poor performers and took appropriate disciplinary action. In many cases, a them-and-us mentality of management and the workforce resulted, with the workforce closing ranks in support of the poor performer. With the self-managing production teams, teams tend to manage poor performers, as this example shows. A production officer was repeatedly making mistakes that were having consequences for the operation of the plant. The worker's team initially tried to provide support by giving on-the-job coaching and training, but the production officer continued to make mistakes that threatened the plant's ability to operate within its license limits. Finally the team decided that the employee did not possess the competencies required to be a production officer and should be reassessed and, if found to be lacking the necessary competencies, be redeployed within the business. Team members spoke to management, and the production officer was subsequently reassessed and redeployed within the business.

Conclusions

This case serves to illustrate a successful major, strategic, human resource management initiative within an established, mature organization. Although a number of implementation problems have arisen or are continuing as a result of the change program, the broad spectrum of outcomes achieved paints an impressive picture of a successful change strategy. In doing so, this case study demonstrates that a partnering approach to reform driven by a consultative process can be successful in eliminating many of the potential hurdles to effective and timely implementation of workplace change. In terms of Storey's (1992) conceptualization of change management approaches, the change process may be best characterized as one of systemic jointism, where the complete reform strategy is the result of consultation and negotiation at a senior level between management and unions. Although Osterman's (1994) survey of U.S. industry found that the presence of unions did not appear to affect the extent of workplace transformation, it does appear that the likelihood of successful workplace reform in unionized settings is increased when it has been the subject of such strategic consultation between senior management and union leaders (Kochan, Katz, and McKersie, 1986).

Although research suggests that there may be many paths to reform (Osterman, 1994), the costs associated with transformation may be enhanced where change is negotiated piecemeal or where there is strong employee resistance to management's change attempts. Furthermore, the effective utilization of new transformed work structures will depend on organizational members' willingness to do so (Trist, Susman, and Brown, 1977). This is more likely to occur, and the potential costs associated with delays in implementation and industrial disputation minimized, when stakeholders in the new work system have been appropriately involved in the process of transition. Sydney Water's consultative process and transition arrangements provide a useful example of this.

Questions for Discussion

1. The design process for introducing self-managing teams began with the production process. What aspects of this design process were instrumental in developing a design that achieved the reported outcomes?
2. What were the key features of the organizational change strategy that facilitated the successful introduction of the new self-managing team job design? Why did these features have such a significant effect?
3. How central to the outcomes achieved in this case was the empowerment of the self-managing teams?
4. In light of the difficulties encountered in implementation, what aspects of the job design or organizational support systems could have been addressed in the initial design phase? How would you address these difficulties now?
5. Despite significant downsizing in the introduction of the new self-managing team job design, the outcomes are positive across a cross section of measures. How do you account for this when significant downsizing programs have been associated with falls in workforce commitment?
6. The responsibilities of the production teams illustrated in this case are extremely broad. Does such a broad range of responsibilities contribute positively to team performance, or could a greater focus on the central production function of the teams lead to greater performance outcomes? What is the appropriate balance between breadth of responsibilities and competence and depth of competence?

The Authors

Brett M. Wright is the group general manager human resources in Australian Water Technologies Pty Ltd., where he develops, implements, and reviews the effectiveness of organizational change programs. He has a Ph.D. in organizational behavior from the University of Western Australia, and his research interests include the effectiveness of self-managing teams and group process variables in work groups. Wright can be reached at Australian Water Technologies Pty Ltd., Level 1, 115-123 Bathurst Street, Sydney, NSW, 2000, Australia; phone: 612.9350-6946; fax: 612.9261.3130; e-mail: brett.wright@awt-pl.com.au.

John L. Cordery is professor of management in the Department of Organizational and Labor Studies at the University of Western Australia, where he teaches organizational behavior and human resource management. He has a long-standing research interest in work redesign, more recently involving the development of models of self-managing team effectiveness.

References

Barker, J.R. (1993). "Tightening the Iron Cage: Concertive Control in Self-Managing Teams." *Administrative Science Quarterly, 38,* 408–437.

Campion, M., G.J. Medsker, and A.C. Higgs. (1993). "Relations Between Work Group Characteristics and Effectiveness: Implications for Designing Effective Work Groups." *Personnel Psychology, 46,* 823–847.

Cherns, A. (1976). "The Principles of Sociotechnical Design." *Human Relations, 29,* 783–792.

Cohen, S.G., and G.E. Ledford. (1994). "The Effectiveness of Self-Managing Teams: A Quasi-Experiment." *Human Relations, 47,* 13–43.

Cordery, J. (1996). "Autonomous Work Groups and Quality Circles." In M. A. West, editor, *Handbook of Work Group Psychology* (pp. 225–246). Chichester, England: John Wiley.

Cordery, J.L., W.S. Mueller, and L.M. Smith. (1991). "Attitudinal and Behavioral Effects of Autonomous Group Working: AA Longitudinal Field Study." *Academy of Management Journal, 34,* 464–476.

Cordery, J.L., and T.D. Wall. (1985). "Work Design and Supervisory Practice: A Model." *Human Relations, 38,* 425–441.

Cummings, T.G. (1978). "Self-Regulating Work Groups: A Socio-Technical Synthesis." *Academy of Management Review, 3,* 625–634.

Emery, F.E. (1959). *Characteristics of Socio-Technical Systems.* London: Tavistock Institute of Human Relations, Document No. 527.

Goodman, P.S., R. Devadas, and T.G. Hughson. (1988). "Groups and Productivity: Analyzing the Effectiveness of Self-Managing Teams." In J.P. Campbell and Associates, editors, *Productivity in Organizations* (pp. 295–325). San Francisco: Jossey-Bass.

Hackman, J.R. (1977). "Work Redesign." In J.R. Hackman and J.L. Suttle, editors, *Improving Life at Work: Behavioral Science Approaches to Organizational Change* (pp. 96–162). Santa Monica, CA: Goodyear Publishing.

Hackman, J.R. (1987). "The Design of Work Teams." In J. Lorsch, editor, *Handbook of Organisational Behaviour* (pp. 315–342). New York: Prentice Hall.

Herbst, P.G. (1974). *Socio-Technical Design: Strategies in Multidisciplinary Research*. London: Tavistock.

Jacob, R. (1992, May 18). "The Search for the Organization of Tomorrow." *Fortune*, 52–58.

Kelly, J. (1992). "Does Job Re-design Theory Explain Job Re-design Outcomes?" *Human Relations, 45*, 753–774.

Kelly, J.E. (1978). "A Reappraisal of Sociotechnical Systems Theory." *Human Relations, 31*(12), 1069–1099.

Kochan, T.A., H. Katz, and R.B. McKersie. (1986). *The Transformation of American Industrial Relations*. New York: Basic Books.

Lawler, E.E. (1990). "The New Plant Revolution Revisited." *Organization Dynamics, 19*(2), 5–14.

Lawler, E.E., S.A. Mohrman, and G.E. Ledford. (1992). *Employee Involvement and Total Quality Management: Practices and Results in Fortune 1000 Companies*. San Francisco: Jossey-Bass.

Macduffie, J.P. (1995). "Human Resource Bundles and Manufacturing Performance: Organizational Logic and Flexible Manufacturing Systems in the World Auto Industry." *Industrial and Labour Relations Review, 48*, 197–221.

Majchrzak, A. (1988a). *The Human Side of Factory Automation*. San Francisco: Jossey-Bass.

Majchrzak, A. (1988b). "Towards a Framework for Identifying Organizationally-Compatible Amt." In W. Karwowski, H.R. Parsaei, and M.R. Wilhelm, editors, *Ergonomics of Hybrid Automated Systems I* (pp. 93–99). Amsterdam: Elsevier Science.

Manz, C.C., D.E. Keating, and A. Donnellon. (1990). "Preparing for an Organizational Change to Self Management: The Managerial Transition. *Organizational Dynamics, 19*(2), 15–26.

Manz, C.C., and H.P. Sims. (1987). "Leading Workers to Lead Themselves: The External Leadership of Self-Managing Teams. *Administrative Science Quarterly, 32*, 106–128.

Oldham, G.R., and J.R. Hackman. (1980). "Work Design in the Organizational Context. *Research in Organizational Behavior, 2*, 247–278.

Osterman, P. (1994). "How Common Is Workplace Transformation and Who Adopts It?" *Industrial and Labour Relations Review, 47*, 173–188.

Pasmore, W.A. (1988). *Designing Effective Organizations: The Sociotechnical Systems Perspective.* New York: Wiley.

Pearce, J.A., and E.C. Ravlin. (1987). "The Design and Activation of Self-Regulating Work Groups." *Human Relations, 40,* 751–782.

Pearson, C.A.L. (1992). "Autonomous Workgroups: An Evaluation at an Industrial Site." *Human Relations, 45,* 905–936.

Porter, M.E. (1985). *Competitive Advantage: Creating and Sustaining Superior Performance.* New York: The Free Press.

Roberts, K.H., and W. Glick. (1981). "The Job Characteristics Approach to Job Design: A Critical Review." *Journal of Applied Psychology, 66,* 193–217.

Storey, J. (1992). *Developments in the Management of Human Resources.* Oxford: Blackwell Press.

Susman, G.I., and R.B. Chase. (1986). "A Sociotechnical Analysis of the Integrated Factory." *Journal of Applied Behavioral Science, 22,* 257–270.

Trist, E.L., G.L. Susman, and G.R. Brown. (1977). "An Experiment in Autonomous Working in an American Underground Coal Mine." *Human Relations, 30,* 201–236.

Wall, T.D., J.M. Corbett, R. Martin, C.W. Clegg, and P.R. Jackson. (1990). "Advanced Manufacturing Technology, Work Design, and Performance: A Change Study." *Journal of Applied Psychology, 75,* 691–697.

Wall, T.D., N.J. Kemp, P.R. Jackson, and C.W. Clegg. (1986). "Outcomes of Autonomous Work Groups: A Long-Term Field Experiment." *Academy of Management Journal, 29,* 280–304.

Wall, C.D., and P.R. Jackson. (1995). "New Manufacturing Initiatives and Shopfloor Job Design." In A. Howard, editor, *The Changing Nature of Work* (pp. 164–211). San Francisco: Jossey Bass.

Walton, R.E. (1985, March). "From Control to Commitment." *Harvard Business Review,* 77–84.

Wellins, R.S., W.C. Byham, and J.M. Wilson. (1991). *Empowered Teams: Creating Self-Directed Work Groups That Improve Quality, Productivity and Participation.* San Francisco: Jossey-Bass.

Suggested Readings

Cordery, J.L., B.M. Wright, and T.D. Wall. (1997, April). "Towards a More Comprehensive and Integrated Approach to Work Design: Production Uncertainty and Self-Managing Team Performance." In P.E. Tesluk and J.E. Mathieu, co-chairs, *Work Teams and Their Environments: Exploring the Dynamic Team-Context Relationship.* Symposium conducted at the Society for Industrial and Organizational Psychology Annual Conference, St. Louis, Missouri.

Denison, D.R. (1992). "Sociotechnical Design and Self-Managing Work Groups: The Impact on Control." *Journal of Occupational Behaviour, 3,* 297–314.

Hilmer, F.G., M.R. Rayner, and G.Q. Taperell. (1993). *National Competition Policy: Report by the Independent Committee of Inquiry.* Canberra: Australian Government Publishing Service.

Johnson, M., and M. Paddon. (1995). *Keeping Our Heads Above Water: Is Privatisation of the NSW Water Industry Inevitable?* Sydney, Australia: Public Sector Research Centre, The University of New South Wales.

Kemp, N.J., T.D. Wall, C.W. Clegg, and J.L. Cordery. (1983). "Autonomous Work Groups in a Greenfield Site: A Comparative Study." *Journal of Occupational Psychology, 56,* 271–288.

Maddock, R., and N. Gonzalez. (1995). *Urban Water Markets and the Hilmer Reform Process: Research Report no. 89.* Melbourne: Urban Water Research Association.

Manz, C.C. (1992). "Self Leading Work Teams: Moving Beyond Self-Management Myths." *Human Relations, 45,* 1119–1140.

Wright, B.M. (1994). *Framework for Workplace Reform in the Waste Water Business.* Unpublished manuscript: Sydney Water Corporation.

Theory, Implementation, and the Measurement of Critical Success Factors

Malden Mills Industries

Mordecai Porath, Mindy L. Gewirtz, and Peter Gumpert

This case study reviews the creation, implementation, and initial in-process evaluation of a team-based management system that has been created in a well-known textile manufacturing organization, Malden Mills Industries, Inc., headquartered in Massachusetts. The project is ongoing at this writing, so it is possible to describe only part of the planning, implementation, and evaluation efforts. However, the authors describe the effort and its associated organizational dynamics in detail, and some outcome indicators provide evidence of early-stage successes.

Malden Mills Industries and GLS Consulting, Inc., a Boston-based organizational consulting firm, collaborated closely on the broad effort that this chapter describes. GLS had earned considerable credibility at Malden Mills through the completion of several projects in the organization over a five-year period. Referred to as TEAM, the effort had several initial champions in the organization: the owner and CEO of Malden Mills, the director of U.S. manufacturing, and the corporate quality director. These champions have been critical to the effort at every stage. As will be described, additional champions were added as the project proceeded.

Background and Overview
Malden Mills Industries has, since 1983, moved from being a manufacturer of superior commodity products in the textile market to

This case was prepared to serve as a basis for discussion rather than to illustrate either effective or ineffective administrative and management practices.

becoming what may be the world's first major creator and maker of branded high-technology textile products. Malden Mills has positioned itself as an innovative market leader both in product performance and product aesthetics. Its key markets include high-technology outerwear, leisure and lifestyle apparel, and home textiles. Its corporate headquarters are in Lawrence, Massachusetts, and it has facilities elsewhere in New England, in the Southeast, and in Germany. Malden Mills is an intergenerational business that is wholly owned by a single family. The principal owner also functions as its chief executive officer. The production workforce at Malden Mills is unionized; UNITE serves as the bargaining agent for most employees. A large number of members of the production workforce are not native speakers of English, and many enjoy only partial literacy.

In 1995, Malden Mills Industries' largest division, apparel (now called Circular Knit), was producing knit fleece apparel fabrics designed primarily for the high-end outdoor cold-weather sports market. The smaller division, upholstery (now called Woven), was producing upholstery fabrics of various types, and was using dyeing, weaving, flocking, screen printing, and face-finishing processes in manufacturing. This division was under a great deal of price pressure from the market, and it was struggling to find ways to achieve durable profitability despite environmental pressures. It had been forced repeatedly to cut costs, and was operating with a traditional management philosophy combined with an extraordinarily lean management group.

The Upholstery Division's management decided in 1995 that its supervisory workforce lacked important managerial and supervisory skills, and it asked the outside consulting firm, GLS Consulting, Inc., to conduct a thorough assessment of its training and other management needs. GLS interviewed almost all members of the managerial and technical staff of the division as well as a number of union workers. The assessment confirmed that there was much need for skill building among managers and supervisors. The study also pointed clearly to various systemic problems. For example, valuable information was frequently lost due to lack of communication and competitive relationships among divisions and departments. Employees saw the work as poorly planned and coordinated, resulting in considerable confusion and inefficiency. It seemed highly desirable to move from a traditional manufacturing system to a much more participative, cooperative, team-based system. The reasoning was that market requirements are very challenging, with rapid changes, and this requires both rapid product development and sustained high quality, despite quick changes. In this context, GLS and the Upholstery Division's management felt that simply improving skills and traditional processes would not be enough.

Accordingly, the Upholstery Division's management and GLS took a proposal for training and a pilot team project to top management. It was approved under the condition that the Upholstery Division accept accountability for dramatic improvements in its product quality.

The First Pilot Program

The division formed a steering committee to initiate the pilot program, specifically in the flock operation. In the beginning, the committee included managers at each level as well as technical specialists in flock and screen printing processes. After this group felt it had achieved some clarity about the usefulness of teams, the group invited the president of the local union and the union's regional business manager to attend a meeting, which the director of human resources also attended. This meeting led to the appointment of representatives of the union to the original steering committee, which was now designated as a union-management committee. The committee considered and contributed to the content of the proposed training program. It also created a team design for one area of the flock manufacturing section, and a management-technical support team that was to be the primary resource for this pilot production team. It is significant that this initial production team combined members of two separate departments that had historically blamed one another for manufacturing problems.

The training program created for managers, supervisors, technical personnel, and maintenance workers contained useful communication, supervisory, and participative management skills. It also contained an explicit and critically important subtext: trust building among participants and the formation of new cooperative relationships both within departments and across departmental and functional lines. The shorter training program created for production operators had a similar manifest content, and it also was designed to strengthen relationships and to empower workers.

A Tragic Fire

A tragic fire and an all-out rebuilding process slowed—and then fueled—implementation of the program. Midway through the initial round of the training program, a tragic midwinter fire destroyed the flock operation in particular, and all the face-finishing facilities that distinguished Malden from the commodity market. The owner immediately resolved to rebuild, and agreed to continue to pay employees for several months, even though Malden Mills was not in operation. A major rebuilding effort was undertaken that consumed the energies of virtually every active Mill employee.

The fire stimulated the purchase of new, state-of-the-art equipment and also led eventually to the decision to declare the flocking operation dormant for some time to come. Funds from the state and federal government were made available to retrain displaced employees and also to retrain retained employees in the operation of modern, computer-based manufacturing machines and systems. The arrival of state-of-the-art machinery also stimulated a reexamination of the company's production system and strategies, and strengthened corporate interest in teamwork and functional integration.

Thus in the spring of 1996, Aaron Feuerstein, the CEO, decided to restart training for the TEAM project, and to create a number of pilot teams in the smaller of the two manufacturing divisions (Woven). The tentative plan called for creating production teams organized by shift and function, and management-technical support teams to assist and support production floor teams in each manufacturing facility. Before the training of production operators began in the Woven Division, the steering committee took responsibility for creating and implementing a joint union-management committee to coordinate and monitor the training and the transition to teams.

Months later, the Circular Knit Division instituted the company's second steering committee. The impetus for its creation was that the manufacturing director was acutely conscious of the need for change in the division and was aware of the success of the Woven Steering Committee. Thus its initial charter was similar to that of the Woven's committee. This group oversaw the beginning of TEAM training for managers and technical personnel, but delayed the creation of operator teams on the production floor until they themselves had acquired direct experience working as a team.

During this latter period, GLS and management investigated the potential for synergy and integration between the TEAM program and additional change initiatives that were in progress at the company. These initiatives included a union-management safety program, a major technical training effort for new equipment in the various production facilities, and a major, computer-based production and customer service system.

Central Purposes of the TEAM Effort

The overall purposes of the effort the authors initiated can be summarized briefly:

1. to facilitate the transmission of information about performance, problems, and opportunities for improvement from person to person and department to department; to encourage innovation and creative problem solving in every aspect of the organization's functioning

2. to create an exceptionally agile, resilient organization that is closely integrated across departments at various organizational levels, with people working in close cooperation toward common goals

3. to cultivate in the entire workforce intrinsic motivation for constant improvement in manufacturing processes, quality, waste reduction, and other corporate and divisional goals

4. to function well with as little management presence as is possible, pushing decisions downward in the organization, and transforming the function of managers from drivers of performance to resources for planning and implementation

5. to improve the morale and corporate pride of members of the organization at all levels.

Obstacles and Critical Success Factors: The Management Process

Team management, like any so-called soft management practice, is susceptible to constant management scrutiny and can fall victim to budgetary cuts at the slightest hint of an economic downturn. If they have not taken root, these processes are difficult to sustain through times of economic upheaval or operational difficulties. We understood this fact throughout the creation and design of the change process and, therefore, implemented a strategy that was designed to minimize the adverse impact of typical environmental pressures. From the inception of the TEAM process, we created a strong linkage between:

- Teams and the company's strategic intent and vision.
- Teams and measurable, tangible business results and successes.
- Teams and the sustainability of what de Geus (1997) refers to as a living organization. It should be noted that the CEO's strong interest in communitarian principles—that is, community and social responsibility as well as his commitment to human values—made this linkage easier to build.

We felt it was imperative to convince major company stakeholders that sustaining market leadership through innovation requires an organization that is creative and agile through both the product development and the manufacturing processes and that this creativity requires some form of team management. It was important also to make clear that the successful commercialization and launching of new products are also highly dependent upon integration of functions and participative management. Commercialization requires that research, engineering, marketing, and manufacturing resources share a vision, a mission, and clear, specific objectives, and that their joint performance as a team can be measured and recognized.

As we anticipated, the process of forming teams at this level of management faced serious obstacles. The obstacles were not associated, however, with the abstract notion of team management; they were based on the uneasiness of certain key stakeholders about participating in a jointly controlled process. The fear of giving up unilateral control over the process of launching new products, for example, stems from concerns about the possible consequences of losing control of key resources, such as engineering expertise and manufacturing machinery, and from concerns about losing control of the final determination of which products will be launched. We were concerned, for example, that the resistance to blurring the boundary between research-and-development and marketing in team-based decisions about launching new products was likely to be an obstacle to successful implementation of teams for this process. Thus we had to consider how and where to start. We asked ourselves:

- What should be the initial organizational scope of the team process?
- What are the necessary preconditions to moving forward with team implementation?
- What kind of measurement system is required to monitor progress?

We were convinced that the readiness of major stakeholders is required at the earliest stages of implementation. For example, a decision to focus on manufacturing operations requires that the director of manufacturing operations be ready to embrace and carry through team management in terms of his or her management style, management philosophy, and overall management objectives. We selected manufacturing as the initial target precisely because its top management group believed that much would be gained from the process; these players had the long-term vision to realize that the team process had the potential to guarantee the success of manufacturing while also meeting the company's overall strategic intent.

Building on a core process first and then extending and expanding it to other areas was a key decision. By focusing on a core business function such as manufacturing, we would maximize our opportunity to succeed and simultaneously promote the company's core strategic intent with measurable results. Additional teams could be implemented later.

The second critical operational decision revolved around the following fundamental questions: Can we implement team management without concurrently building essential basic, technical, and interpersonal skills at the individual level? What are these fundamental skills? How does the process of building skills interact with the process of building team management?

The answer to these questions, we thought, was fairly simple: The individual must possess the basic skills required to perform his or her individual job before he or she can become an integral part of any participative management process. We identified required skills along four dimensions:

- technical and operational skills in a particular area (for example, dyeing, fabric finishing, or shipping)
- basic language skills that allow the individual to communicate clearly with peers, supervisors, and technical staff
- basic computer and math skills that facilitate a contextual focus rather than a simple, linear procedural focus among employees
- basic interpersonal and group skills that support a team management effort.

The basic technical and language skills were, we thought, preconditions for a fully successful implementation of team management. We sensed that ideally they should be developed prior to or in parallel with interpersonal and teamwork skills. Thus the team preparation process we designed was coupled with the process of developing these knowledge and skill preconditions.

According to de Geus (1997), the human element of a "living company" has four fundamental features:

- It values people as a critical asset.
- It loosens steering and control.
- It organizes its members for learning.
- It shapes a human community within which work is carried out.

Each of these elements has been a cornerstone of our TEAM program.

The TEAM program supports focusing on people as assets by encouraging a human infrastructure that promotes innovation (and thus presents human observation and thought as the prime corporate asset). By creating an organization in which all people participate in innovation and in which innovation becomes integral to the normal operating model, we shift the culture to one that recognizes and invests in participative innovation as a central operating paradigm. One of the difficult challenges in creating a "participative innovation" mindset in the TEAM program was preserving a trusting relationship with union employees when the need emerged because of technological changes to modify employee assignments, or to reduce the workforce in a particular area.

Loosening steering and control is another essential element that our TEAM process develops and monitors. Being a closely controlled company, Malden Mills must shift toward an organization in which ideas can develop at all levels of the organization and in which tolerance for encouraging moderate risk is culturally accepted at all levels of the organization. This shift secures the transition in leadership style and encourages a search for innovation in places never before explored. The TEAM program assumed that vertically—as well as horizontally—integrated teams whose members share common values and objectives maximize the achievement both of innovation and the company's broad objectives.

Organizing for learning is another element that we wished to achieve through the TEAM project. TEAM is geared to support organizational learning in four ways:

- to provide an environment in which the teams are able to modify the organization when market, business, or technological concerns require a shift or a transformation
- to provide an information-rich environment in which people at all levels are active in respect to the knowledge and information available to them
- to provide an environment in which skills can be transferred easily and efficiently, in time to sustain the company's competitive edge under changing conditions
- to provide the communication and cultural infrastructure for transmitting knowledge between individuals and between organizational units.

We hoped to achieve these learning objectives by taking a community-driven approach to teams. Rather than making the initial commitment to the inner circle of Malden's top management or to the broadest circle that includes of all of Malden's employees, we made a commitment to the community in which the vast majority of Malden's employees are employed—the manufacturing group—and we strove to shape teams within that community and to shape the community around teams. In so doing, we accepted as an asset the realities of the community in which we began the work. The realities included were that the manufacturing community was under tremendous pressure to increase production and reduce operating costs. Time was one of the most precious commodities that managers owned. We too had to be very productive in terms of how we used the managers' and operators' time. For example, we learned how to condense 90-minute meetings into an hour with no loss of effectiveness.

Assumptions and Components of the Implementation Model

Creating champions at different levels in the organization helped teams establish roots in the organization that strengthened the process. We thought of the process as entwining three strands of rope to create both a container for resistance and a strong force for the change process in the organization.

Change Champions at Several Levels

The CEO's role in championing the change project evolved over time. He knew it was the right thing to do and advocated for the program at critical points when other senior-level managers were uncertain of its value because of financial, production, and time pressures. As the CEO more clearly understood that the effort had to go beyond training and empowerment to a fundamental cultural transformation, he was determined to keep the process in motion.

The second set of champions was the corporate-wide manufacturing and quality directors who helped create the context for the change to occur. The manufacturing director, despite great production pressures, supported the change effort in the face of numerous attempts to delay implementation. With the quality director and a quality-training manager assigned to the project, we created a vision for the change process that could be sustained over a three-year time period.

The third level of change champions was the members of the steering committees who monitored the interpersonal skills training and helped design and implement the team structures. These managers and union representatives championed the effort in their own departments, and worked hard with their production and maintenance workers, managers, and supervisors to make the change process successful. These members also were willing to confront managers who put production pressures above the change process and who could otherwise have confirmed the cynicism of workers who expected the process to fail as soon as there was pressure. Union members of the committee were able to reassure coworkers who were uneasy about the implications of the change for their collective bargaining agreement.

What seems important as well as interesting in this context is that our change model defies conventional wisdom about the necessity of implementing the change from the top downward. We were deliberate in starting the change effort in the middle of the organization. In several cases, teams strongly influenced their managers or influenced teams above them in the reporting structure to change their normal modus operandi.

In Unity There Is Power: How Change Began and Grew

The development of the human systems infrastructure for an integrated organization can be divided into eight phases. We created momentum for change at the top level and linked it with a reconceptualization of the organizational structure and with the development of education for managers and operators that would help them become productive members of teams. Although the concept of phases suggests a linear process, the development of the change initiative was sometimes sequential, sometimes simultaneous, and always iterative. Each division customized its own learning and development sequence and methods.

Phase One: Launching and Sustaining Steering Committee Leadership

The Woven Division TEAM Steering Committee's mission was to coordinate and monitor team-related training, to design the team-based structure in its division, and to communicate, monitor, and evaluate the change process over time. Before operator training began in the Woven Division, the steering committee took responsibility for creating and implementing a joint union-management committee to coordinate and monitor the training and the transition to teams. Indeed the union members of the steering committee turned out to be a strong positive force in the process.

Significant concerns arose on the part of the union that management's implementation of teams could lead to a violation of the current contract. The steering committee collaborated with union officials to maintain the integrity of the contract, and it made sure that union members and officials would experience themselves as full members of the steering committee. The process of union and management's working together was slow and tenuous as business-as-usual activities fostered suspicion that nothing could ever change at

Malden Mills. Some union members on the committee worried that they might be viewed as betraying their members by collaborating with management. All these problems were, in time, overcome.

Phase Two: Training for Managers and Production Operators

Management training consisted of 16 four-hour sessions, given once a week over a four-month period. The topics included leadership, problem solving, communication, intergroup relations, managing diversity, coaching, planning, and conflict resolution. The training focused on knowledge and skill, and the methodology consisted of a balanced lecture and discussion format, linking conceptual input with experiential exercises and discussion. Each group of about 24 participants was further subdivided into small learning groups, where people experienced a safe place to try out new behaviors, particularly regarding presenting one's ideas to a group of people so that other people could hear them, and inviting feedback on behaviors and ideas.

The subtext, which people reported to be particularly significant throughout the training, was the way the small, stable learning groups naturally created new pathways that encouraged people to work together. Each of the training sessions contained people from a variety of departments and levels within the division; people in direct reporting relationships were in different classes. It was the first opportunity some members had to meet people in other departments with which they are interdependent. At the outset, many people had no idea of what others did, what their problems were, or how interdependent they were with the others to get a job done well. In some instances, people had spoken to one another over the phone for years and did not realize they worked nearby. People created lasting working relationships during the training sessions—sessions of working, laughing, risking, and daring to hope together that significant changes could be made.

The training for production operators consisted of nine sessions of four hours each. In most cases, operators attended the training sessions in intact teams. During the tenth session, each of the production facility managers took their people on a Malden-wide tour. There were many operators who had no idea of the internal or external customer-supplier relationship. For operators this was a significant indication that a new way of thinking could be created. Language difference was a significant hurdle that needed to be overcome. To facilitate implemen-tation, we translated handouts and overhead materials into Spanish and identified bilingual translators who could help monolingual Spanish speakers. Consultant-trainers learned to use principles based in teaching English as a second language (ESL) to guide delivery. They partnered with ESL-experienced trainers in the pilot groups to sharpen their curriculum development and delivery skills.

The first six sessions of the training mirrored some of the topics delivered in the management training. The last three sessions, however, were devoted to actual team development. Each training class consisted of at least one or two more or less intact teams. Each team worked on creating a mission and beginning performance goals for their team. They also worked on role and procedural clarity within their teams. Supervisors joined their operators for these last three sessions.

It is important to note at this point that resistance to as well as hope for change was evident in both training programs. Both defensiveness as described by Mazen (1997) and classic resistance to change emerged and will be discussed in some detail below.

Phase Three: Management Team Development

In the Woven Division, GLS provided team development for the Policy and Planning Team, the Division Operations Team, the Industrial Engineering Team, and for each of the four management-technical support teams in the Woven facilities. The purpose of team development was to help jump-start each of the teams by providing a structure within which they could develop a mission and a set of measurable performance goals, and attain clarity about roles and procedures for working together. The team development phase consisted of approximately 16 to 20 hours in either two- or four-hour blocks of time. One of the consultants who delivered the interpersonal skills training facilitated this series of meetings. Each team worked at its own pace and style, and set different goals. Members of different teams updated each other at the steering committee meetings, and shared systems and or materials they had created to facilitate the process. At the end of the eight to 10 sessions, the team worked on its own for about six weeks. Then the facilitator met with them for a "check-up" and to determine what further support the team needed. When the Circular Knit Division began to move to teams, team development was provided for their teams as well.

Production facility managers realized that supervisors were a critical but weak link in the implementation of teams. We took several steps to integrate supervisors. The first was to prepare them for working with their operators in the last three sessions of the training. There was great fear on the part of supervisors and operators that putting the two together could stifle creativity within the group. Some supervisors feared that operators would take the opportunity to complain and blame supervisors, and not be productive. Some operators feared that supervisors would quash the spirit of change in the team and not support the team effort. The production managers responded by forming supervisory support groups and integrating at least one or two supervisors into their management support teams. Consultants facilitated some of these support teams in the early stages, and others preferred to be self-managed once their team development sequence was complete.

Phase Four: Production Team Facilitation

Production floor teams that had completed training and team development received team facilitation for their first eight meetings. The facilitators knew their teams from the training and already had established relationships with them. The transition from the safe classroom environment to the day-to-day rough-and-tumble of the production floor was a significant hurdle for both operators and management personnel. Managers agreed to give up one hour weekly of precious production time so that operators could meet as a team.

We discovered that production floor teams were up and running more quickly, and were more effective, when the management support team presented its business goals to the teams and invited them to choose to work on those goals that were consistent both with their own priorities and with the goals of the department. Thus the progress of the production floor teams was related to the developmental level of the management support teams. Those production facilities that had clearly worked out their own goals and their communication processes with the production floor teams found they had well-functioning production floor teams. The ability to provide meaningful performance feedback consistently to the production floor teams was also very helpful in this respect. The production floor teams that could distinguish between issues related to the union contract and team issues had an easier time getting together than those that continued to argue about injustices regarding contractual issues. What eventually helped some teams become unstuck was the development of a separate union-management group in the department that worked to resolve union issues.

Finally, it is worth making explicit that the production facilities that were under great pressure (because they were starting up new processes or had become constraints in the manufacturing chain) had far greater difficulty with teams in the initial stages than did the facilities that were under less pressure and less scrutiny. It became clear that organizational pressure makes learning and change particularly difficult, at all levels.

The initial contract for team facilitation included helping the team to clarify its mission, operating philosophy, and potentially measurable performance goals—along with explicitly negotiated roles that team members would take on to achieve team goals. Facilitators also helped the team members rotate the meeting tasks of facilitator, recorder, timekeeper, and minute taker among them.

The steering committee helped shape the role of an internal TEAMS coordinator, whose task was to track and monitor the teams' success.

Phase Five: Performance Coaching

As training and team development progressed, it became clear that there were supervisors and managers who would welcome or needed coaching to help them through the difficult change process. Some managers met face to face with consultants on a weekly basis, whereas others utilized a phone coach system in which they connected with a consultant on an intermittent, as needed basis.

Phase Six: Senior Management Teams

Several cross-functional mid- and senior-level management teams emerged from the work of the steering committees, as table 1 shows. In the Woven Division, a Woven Operations Team and a Woven Policy and Planning Team were created at the recommendation of the Woven Steering Committee. The Circular Knit Operations Team and the Circular Knit Policy and Planning Teams were created after successes became visible in the Woven Division. All these teams were facilitated for several months as they created their own mission, clarified performance goals, decided upon roles and responsibilities of team members, and began their week-to-week work. The Woven Policy and Planning Team, for example, at the request of their subordinate Woven Operations Team, worked long and hard to create a realistic three-year plan that would bring the division back to profitability.

In the case of the Woven Division Policy and Planning group, this was the first time that managers could remember that the managers of sales and marketing, research and development, quality, manufacturing, finance, and planning sat down to talk together about creating a new future for the beleaguered division. Managers had to learn to have a dialogue rather than to posture or shift blame. They had to

Table 1. Team types at Malden Mills.[1]

Organizational Level	Name	Membership	Functions	Meeting Frequency
Executive and Corporate	Executive Team	CEO; chief operating officer (COO); chief financial officer (CFO); vice president (VP) manufacturing; VP marketing; director, human resources (HR); director, research and development (R&D); board rep; owner-family rep.	Long-range vision and leadership; major policy and long-term financial decisions; HR policy; career development; review of personnel actions	Twice per month
	Corporate Planning and Operations Team	Finance, HR, R&D, marketing, sales, merchandising quality, customer service, MIS, inventory/distribution, strategic planning, division manufacturing managers, commercialization, purchasing	Participates in creating the broad vision; advises executive team; ensures coordination of all functions; accountable as group for execution of plans; annual goal setting; medium-range implementation planning; career development and succession	Twice per month
Manufacturing Management	Woven Policy and Planning Team	Woven production manager, representative facilities managers, finance, marketing, sales, customer service, R&D, quality assurance	Provides long-range vision and broad leadership for the division; sets major policies and makes long-term plans and decisions; ensures the coordination of resources that affect the division; ensures the representation of requirements of corporate stakeholders	Twice per month

[1]Note that there is some cross-level membership overlap in each time. This is done to strengthen vertical communication throughout the organization.

continued on page 144

Theory, Implementation, and the Measurement of Critical Success Factors **143**

Table 1. Team types at Malden Mills (continued).

Organizational Level	Name	Membership	Functions	Meeting Frequency
Manufacturing Management (continued)	Woven Operations Team	Woven production manager, manufacturing facilities managers, quality assurance, safety, customer service, production control, HR, industrial engineering, inventory, logistics, distribution	Reports progress to Policy and Planning Team; accountable as a group for successful execution of plans; sets clear annual goals; medium-range planning to reach goals; execution of the broad vision; ensures coordination of essential functions; frequent information exchange and problem solving	Once per week
	Circular Knit Policy and Planning Team	Circular Knit production manager, representative facilities managers, finance, marketing, sales, customer service, R&D, quality assurance	Provides long-range vision and broad leadership for the division; sets major policies and makes long-term plans and decisions; ensures the coordination of resources that affect the division; ensures the representation of requirements of corporate stakeholders	Twice per month
	Circular Knit Operations Team	Circular Knit production manager, manufacturing facilities managers, quality assurance, safety, customer service, production control, HR, industrial engineering, inventory, logistics, distribution	Reports progress to Policy and Planning Team; accountable as a group for successful execution of plans; sets clear annual goals; medium-range planning to reach goals; execution of the broad vision; ensures coordination of essential functions; frequent information exchange and problem solving	Once per week

Manufacturing Management (continued)	Industrial Engineering (IE) Team	All industrial engineers	Provides IE services to Malden Mills; acts as consultant to all departments on planning and implementation issues	Once per week
	Distribution Division Policy and Operations Team	Warehouse managers, transportation team, warehouse team, domestic, export, HR	Sets direction for warehousing, export, and domestic shipping	Once per week
	BKM Knitting Leadership Team	Plant manager, directors of HR, production, quality control, maintenance, traffic, technical engineering	Sets operating philosophy and goals for overall results of facility; functions as a model team for other teams in the organization; provides support to production floor team; provides communication processes for adequate information flow; shares information from larger organization to all levels within the plant	Once per week
Facility-Level Management Teams	Distribution Transportation Team	Entire logistics staff, import, export, third-party shipping providers	Provides transportation services to internal and external customers	Once per week
	Manufacturing Facility Management/ Technical Support Team (one in each facility)	Facility manager, representative supervisors, quality, engineering, maintenance, representative team communicators	Sets goals; accountable for overall results of facility; provides support for production floor teams; provides results feedback to teams; ensures the coordination of resources	Once per week

continued on page 146

Table 1. Team types at Malden Mills (continued).

Organizational Level	Name	Membership	Functions	Meeting Frequency
Production Floor Teams	Production Teams (number varies)	Team communicator, team members, supervisor (by invitation)	Accountable to achieve goals that team sets; makes decisions consistent with its responsibility; requests assistance as needed; coordinates with internal customers and suppliers	Once per week
	Intershift Coordination Team	Supervisors, across shifts	Communicates problems; shares solutions; ensures that teams don't blame one another; provides information to other teams	Once every two weeks
	Supervisor Support Group	Team communicators, supervisors (by invitation)	Communicates problems; shares solutions; provides information, support, assistance to members	Once per week

learn to trust each other, and believe that by working collaboratively they had a much better chance to accomplish their daunting task than they did by continuing to work in isolation. The members of the team made significant strides in understanding other members' assumptions and constraints. They learned how to help each other and how to accept help from each other. They worked so well together, in fact, that they did not recognize the importance of bringing the chief operating officer (COO) into their process. When this error became clear, the COO was explicitly invited to attend team meetings at his discretion.

In a similar way, the Woven Operations Team worked together on developing business plans for each manufacturing facility to support the goals of the division. They collaborated on their most important goals in respect to quality, production volume, safety, waste reduction, communication, training, and productivity. The Circular Knit Operations Team, more recently established, is moving in the same direction.

The Circular Knit Policy and Planning Team had a very different dilemma from that of the Woven Division. In the Woven Division, the central problem was ensuring profitability. The Circular Knit Division was oversold, however, and had to deal constantly with shifting manufacturing constraints as it handled existing and expanding customer demand. The team's challenge was to create an implementation and monitoring plan that took into account the turbulent and unpredictable nature of the marketplace. One of its important goals, for example, was to create a product development process that was realistic and that minimized manufacturing problems. Its tasks were no less daunting then the challenges of the Woven Division.

Members of all these cross-functional groups have recognized the extent and importance of their interdependence. Thus the various functional areas and manufacturing facilities are working together in a very different way than ever before.

The news of the effectiveness of teams as a vehicle for creating meaningful change has spread through the organization at the middle-management and grassroots levels. The Distribution Division, charged with warehousing, export and domestic shipping, and receiving, established a top leadership team, a transportation team, and a warehouse team. The Malden Mills knitting facility in Bridgton, Maine, internally created the momentum to develop its own top leadership team. As a company plant located in another state, it has additional issues of integrating into the broader system because it has the experience of being perennial outsiders.

There has been agreement to create a Corporate Policy and Operations Team to bring together all corporate functions at a high level (including the plant in Europe). This group had not yet begun to meet at the time this was written.

Phase Seven: The Executive Team

The three top-level leaders in the company, the CEO, the COO, and the chief financial officer (CFO), have met once a month for the past six months to discuss where they wanted the company to go in the future, where it is at present, and what gaps between the present and desired future need to be addressed. As part of this facilitated process, members of the Executive Team worked on changing the way they themselves worked together, in growing recognition that their own interpersonal and group process would be reflected in the remainder of the organization, and that it had to be improved in order to make executives' vision of Malden Mills in the year 2001 a reality. Thus they achieved basic consensus on central values, came to understand more about each others' assumptions and motivation, and began to conceptualize the transition from a traditional to a team-based structure at the top of the organization.

The Executive Team decided that it would add to itself new members, including vice presidents of marketing, manufacturing, and human resources, the director of research and development, and representatives of the board and of the owning family. An executive committee would remain in place to work on major succession and capitalization issues and to respond to special requests of the broader Executive Team.

Phase Eight: Performance Measurement and Feedback

Performance measurement and feedback at the team level is an important cornerstone of a successful transformation to a team-based system. It is relatively easy for management teams to find indicators of the goals and successes of their performance because they are generally responsible for broad results and products that are straightforwardly measurable or visible.

Performance feedback for production floor teams is a more difficult matter. It requires much finer control and feedback of data as well as in-process and team-relevant measures of quality and internal customer satisfaction. It also requires the creation of measures of waste and other controllable costs at the team level. Despite the difficulties, such measurement is critical to teams' ability to recognize that their efforts have useful consequences. The steering committee recognized the importance of this issue early in its deliberations. In some cases, organizing performance data for teams was relatively easy. In other cases, it was quite difficult, and required continued focus and effort on the part of the Division Operations Team and other resources. At this writing, the task is only partially accomplished.

Dynamics of the Change Process

This section describes in some detail the group and individual dynamics of the change process, with particular attention to resistance to change. Our perspective on resistance—that it is normal, inevitable, and valuable—informs our strategy for approaching and dealing with it.

The implementation design was simultaneously structured and emergent. It is important to dispel the idea that a linear implementation model was followed, with orderly, sequential steps that can be deconstructed into a linear process. In fact, the implementation process grew like a three-dimensional chess game in which every move had unintended consequences for other parts of the playing field. The basic engines of the change process were the TEAM steering committees in each of the two manufacturing divisions. We began the process of change in the Woven Division because that is where the desire for change was most apparent. The stakes were particularly high in this group, and its steering committee worked hard to move the organization and its people from the survival mode it had been in for years to a process that could lead to a secure, profitable future.

Initial Defensiveness and Resistance

In the beginning, the Woven Steering Committee accepted its assignment with reluctance. Members wanted to believe in the future of teams and a new way of working together. They worried, however, that the organization's commitment would be temporary, and as soon as production pressures mounted, the program would be discontinued (like the fate suffered by the quality initiatives created with W. Edwards Deming and Philip Crosby Associates during the prior decade). It took several facilitated meetings and some discussions between the group and the division's manager for members to commit to the risk of initiating the process. The group read a widely popular book on teams (Katzenbach and Smith, 1993) and discussed a chapter a week at their meetings. These discussions provided a safe forum in which to discuss resistance to moving toward a team structure, and what the group could expect as the process unfolded.

The great skepticism in the early stages of the steering committee's development foreshadowed the resistance we would see enacted throughout the process. The first question committee members asked would be continuously asked in later stages: When will senior management go through the training program and the transformation process? People in the organization had learned to be oriented to personal power and were clear that those in power always determine what happens next. Most people seemed to look "upward," and experienced themselves as more or less helpless. They questioned whether their own supervisors, managers, and senior manager could ever change even if they did participate in the TEAM training. In their view, developed over decades, the hierarchical culture of Malden Mills was so deeply embedded that no amount of effort could change it. Indeed, the top executive team only began to meet to improve their own process about eight months into the project.

Over time, the Woven TEAM Steering Committee became a team, and a strong force for change in the division. As members realized that the division manager accepted their recommendations and proposals for the creation of actual teams, they began to feel more autonomous and empowered, and they were able to take on the next phase of the change process. There was also a great sense of accomplishment at the end of each of the first waves of manager and operator training. Managers and operators took group photos, received a signed certificate by the CEO and the manufacturing and quality directors, and asked when refresher sessions would be given.

Communication about the process of change required continuing attention. The Woven Steering Committee implemented a variety of creative ideas for keeping the program alive as other people waited to be assigned to teams or to go through the training. Team news was communicated monthly through a manufacturing newsletter produced by a member of the steering committee. Team news, photos of members on the plant tour, evaluation of the training, and articles on teams appeared prominently in the newsletter. People received updates on TEAM progress through bulletin boards throughout the Mill. Thus the steering committee took on the leadership tasks of containing resistance to change, and solidifying a vision of the future.

Using Teams as a Parallel Organizational Structure

The implementation of the TEAM project depended on the creation of a team structure that could exist in parallel with the traditional reporting structure of the organization. The traditional reporting structure maintained a sense of safety and control for some members of management, and the cross-functional teams created solid, measurable results that gave credit both to the change program and to the managers who were traditionally accountable for them. A schematic representation of the Woven Division's team structure appears in table 1. We assume that the production facilities of the Circular Knit Division will be similarly designed; its top two teams are in place at this writing, and an interfacility team of supervisors is being formed.

Riding the Resistance, and Containing Feelings About the Change Process

The context for the resistance to change was grounded both in the reality of the present and in the organization's painful memories of years past. Employees could easily rattle off the number of well-known consultants who had come to Malden Mills and applied their programs without lasting effect. Employees cited the history of beginning and not completing initiatives as proof positive that even the training would not be completed. When the training was completed, they were positive that production floor teams would never develop. When the production floor teams began to work and did well, people were sure the plug would be pulled at any time. Before managers were trained, operators were convinced that managers would not change. After the training, people gave some credit to managers and supervisors who did exhibit clear change, but continued to worry about those who had not yet shown signs of behaving differently.

Managers were as skeptical as production operators and believed that their senior managers would never give up the use of arbitrary power. Managers who attended training had to listen to their own bosses discount the team training and demand that the same level of work be accomplished on a day in which four hours were taken up by training. Some managers who attended classes and spoke politically correctly about teams and empowerment in class, quietly predicted that these team concepts would never change the way they themselves operated.

Parallel Process and Resistance

A broad parallel process permeated the organization. Each level both hoped and feared that change would actually occur. Each level gave evidence of a pervasive sense of helplessness in which it looked to the level above to give orders and take responsibility for results. When people were indeed told what to do, there was a general feeling that those giving instructions had no clear idea about the consequences of following the instructions, and that any direction that was set would soon change anyway. Risking empowerment meant taking responsibility (blame) for unambiguous results, and being unable to hide. Risking the empowerment of others meant losing control over tasks and results.

Time and financial resources were the two preeminent reality bases for resistance. Resistance was enacted either through passive, noncommittal compliance or through contemptuous, defiant challenges about whether this program was meaningful or could have an impact on people's lives or on the organization. People complained of being tired of going to training and team meetings while many other activities in the organization also demanded their time and energy. People who were willing to try to change their methods found it difficult to do so when there was no critical mass of others who shared the new language and attitudes.

There were also compelling reality factors underlying resistance to change. New buildings were being built and occupied, new machines were being installed and tested, much technical training had to be done, and there was enormous production pressure generated by unfilled customer orders. The production pressure on areas that had difficulty mastering their new equipment and processes quickly enough led to premature agreements to get up to speed, and to inevitable disappointment. Those who were geographically proximal to the problem were blamed, outside help was brought in to solve the problem, and the ensuing pressure and disempowerment made it even more difficult to stabilize the processes involved. In this way, the organization fed and perpetuated its own ineffectiveness, and slowed its progress.

Those of us who were leading the change effort, at times, also were captured by the resistance. Various employees periodically asked us to revise the training process or other activities we were pursuing, in the hope that a different intervention might fare better than the one we were engaged in. The focus on changing the training curriculum rather than on systemic and structural issues began to be highly predictable. The implication was that we should be able to create a training program so compelling that it would melt the resistance, and make all the difference; if the program wasn't able to do it, the blame was ours. Again the attribution of blame fell on the process or persons who were seen as proximal.

We provided containment for the change process by openly recognizing the resistance as real and valid—and something we needed to find room for and even partner with rather than push away. The hardest part of this was to avoid interpreting resistance as a personal attack on our own competence. Once we could be clear about that misattribution, we were in a better position to hear and respond to the real meaning of the resistance, rather than to the surface noise it made. We, therefore, could focus on interventions that would make a difference, usually at the structural level. This point about the relationship between our defensiveness and our ability to learn has recently been made by Mazen (1997) in a very useful paper about team defensiveness; it had, for us, clear implications for what inhibited learning in the organization.

Responding to Resistance: An Example

One example of this process occurred during the first wave of training for Circular Knit managers and technical personnel when managers told us that the training was seen as not useful and that we should consider replacing part of the curriculum with two sessions with each group to explore the problem. The training, we were told, must be so exciting that everyone would clearly see the benefits of going, and be delighted to take four hours out of their hectic schedule only to return to find their work waiting for them.

We decided to speak with the divisional manager and assistant manager to enlist their efforts in understanding and working with the resistance. The divisional manager came to the next steering committee to give the group a pep talk. In response, the group looked him squarely in the eye and said, "How can we design production floor teams, when we do not work like a team ourselves and with you?" The manager immediately heard and agreed. Within two weeks, the manager asked the group to broaden its role from a steering committee to a divisional operations team charged not only to work together as change agents but also to shape and direct the daily operations of the division. He also created a strong cross-functional policy and strategy team to plan the future of the division and to set broad policies for the future. Thus we moved beyond the surface manifestations of resistance and intervened in a very different way. Very soon afterward, sentiment in the TEAM training classes changed considerably. In the meantime, the people actually doing the training maintained a safe holding environment that recognized and understood the variety of feelings that the prospect of change generated.

In summary, resistance to change was our steady companion throughout the change process. We learned to respect the natural pull of the resistance, though we were often frustrated by the tenacious hold it had (and has) on individuals and the organization and by the surprising ways it is sometimes manifested. There is no simple, foolproof formula for managing resistance. What we can offer is our generally respectful and containing approach, and the critical importance of anticipating, talking about, and riding the waves of the process. Our broad strategy, then, was to respect the feelings that arose, to help people contain and manage the feelings, and to stay the course. In some cases, we built structures such as supervisor support groups to help people deal with a very rough ride.

The paradox here is that at various times many individuals experience hope and excitement, but at other times the same people might experience intense feelings of disruption, uncertainty, and fear about their future. Malden Mills employees at all levels expressed a strong wish to change the way people worked together, but they also shared a fear about the improbability of accomplishing this task. We expected resistance to surface, and we were not disappointed. But we also experienced the spontaneous initiation of teams in part of the corporate structure outside manufacturing and a variety of requests from people outside manufacturing to be involved in the training and for assistance in establishing teams of their own.

Our theoretical context for approaching resistance is broadly constructivist rather than rationalist (Kagan, 1995). Rationalists work from the premise that to overcome resistance to change, affect must be controlled. In a constructivist approach, affect cannot be controlled—it is respected, and its expression and exploration are encouraged. The belief among rationalists is that resistance is an obstacle to be overcome; constructivists view it as normal, self-protective, and adaptive. Indeed, we take the position that the recognition of affect is related to the ability to use intuition, and to the so-called emotional intelligence of the organization and its members.

From a rationalist perspective, reality is singular and stable, and knowledge is validated by logic or reason; learning and change are discrete, with events unfolding in a linear fashion. From a constructivist view, reality can have many perspectives, and the validity of knowledge is not as important as its value in helping individuals adapt. In the rationalist view, people passively receive information and try to adapt to reality. In the constructivist view, people actively shape and construct their social reality. Our constructivist approach allowed for greater flexibility in creating structures to allow for transformation while expecting and allowing for the oscillatory nature of resistance. The people in the organization are able to shift from a passive to an active, dynamic stance, and the organization follows.

Measurement of Progress and Success

We used a triangulation approach to measurement to capture the change over time. Both quantitative and qualitative methods were used to supplement the anecdotal data provided by teams at the various levels. This section outlines a score card of measures that include indicators of attitude, behavior, performance, and bottom-line results.

We were convinced from the beginning of our planning that team management must be linked to tangible business results. The long-range sustainability of any management process depends on hard-core contributions that can be clearly recognized as having a positive impact on the company's bottom line and overall financial health. Thus tying the progress of team-based management to bottom-line results is likely to secure sustainability and clearly identify areas that need improvement.

We had to develop a measurement system that was closely related to standard performance measurement systems (that is, acceptable by accountants and financial analysts). But we needed a system that also measured the less tangible aspects of the process—those aspects that demonstrate cultural transformation and presumably lead to improved business results. Thus a measurement system must be closely tied to our theory of how team management brings about results and also must be thought of as a score card mechanism to help us navigate through the process and help participants and stakeholders constantly evaluate progress and opportunities.

The score card included process measures and key elements of the company's business on which team management would have an impact. The measures of change we used to assess employees' attitudes and perceived behavior were:

1. Using members as observers of the change process. It was necessary, first of all, to obtain indicators of the consequences of the interpersonal skills training program and the new organizational structure in the smaller manufacturing division in which the program began. About midway through the training program, we asked managers and technical personnel who had gone through the training program to serve as informants about what changes they were observing in themselves and others. They completed a brief paper-and-pencil survey that asked them to comment on whether and how they themselves were different; on changes they had seen in others; and on what, if any, changes they had seen in performance that they could attribute to the program. They were asked to try to provide specific examples to illustrate their comments. Sixty percent of respondents reported they had themselves made some changes in the way they work with

others; 70 percent said that they were seeing differences in the attitudes and actions of managers; and about 40 percent reported that they were seeing changes in the way that hourly operators work. About a quarter reported that there was evidence of bottom-line effects on worker motivation, product quality, and overall participation.

2. *A periodic survey of members.* The Woven Division Operations Team also decided to administer a periodic questionnaire survey (at two- or three-month intervals) of members of the division at all levels. The 15-item questionnaire, administered both in Spanish and in English, contained the following:

- items assessing general work satisfaction and fair treatment
- items assessing the degree to which respondents felt informed about divisional and departmental goals, roles, progress, and events
- items assessing the quality of relationships with peers, with supervisors, and between respondents' own and other teams
- items indicating the degree to which respondents experienced themselves as autonomous and free to make decisions about their work.

An open-minded item asking respondents to inform the Operations Team about issues or problems that should be attended to soon.

A stratified random sample of division members at all levels and in all departments received the periodic survey. Its purpose is to provide regular, accurate information about divisional progress toward its human-process goals and to serve as an early warning device about emerging problems so they can be addressed before they reach crisis proportions. The survey also is intended to provide division management with regular information about employee sentiment in order to reduce the power of rumors and ad hoc assertions based on small samples. Other divisions will examine this survey measure, and we trust that manufacturing, at least, will adopt it.

We also decided to keep a record of the number of initiatives that teams generate and to create a ratio of initiatives implemented to initiatives proposed. We felt that this would be a useful measure for tracking the actual progress of teams in the organization.

Table 2 presents a summary of our scorecard approach to measurement. Key criteria include financial, customer relations, internal processes, and individual development and organizational learning. The table lists the business impact of each criterion as well as examples of measures and methods for each. At this writing, we are in the process of creating the necessary controls for the measurement of the individual components; we can comment on progress in only a few examples.

Table 2. Key criteria and measurement methods.

Key Criteria	Business Impact	Examples of Measures	Method
Financial	Productivity	Labor variances	Standard financial accounting
	Quality improvement	Off-quality variances	Percent off-quality
Customer Relations	On-time delivery	Product elapsed time index	End-to-end product time flow
	Customer satisfaction		Survey
Internal Processes	Waste reduction	Percent of waste to total input	Standard financial accounting
	Unscheduled downtime	Machine up-time variance	
	Safety	Lost hours due to accidents	Direct measurement with causal attribution
	Reduced number of nonattributable defects	Number of defects without clear root cause	Direct measurement
			Direct in-process and final inspection
Individual Development and Organizational Learning	Absenteeism	Variance	Direct measurement
	Tardiness	Variance	Direct measurement
	Sick leaves	Variance	Direct measurement
	Improved communication, relationships, experienced autonomy, work satisfaction	Index	Survey
	Process knowledge	Test results	Individual assessment
	Skills improvement	Test results	Individual assessment
	Cooperation between business units	Variance	Survey

Progress on Business Goals Linked to the Team Structure

Substantial progress is already evident, particularly in the Woven Division. At the production level, teams in three of the four departments have been established on two to three of the four shifts. They are making useful suggestions and taking increased responsibility for work output and quality. They systematically exchange information with the Management/Technical Support Team in their facility and they feel supported by it. Progress in the fourth department is slower because new machinery and new processes are complicating members' learning curve. Employees do not yet fully understand the new products, and the equipment and methodology are not fully documented, but production pressure is great. Overall in the division, quality has improved visibly, the number and type of undocumented defects have decreased, and progress has been made on the control of waste and other controllable costs.

Members of the Woven Division Operations Team now assist one another, instead of trying to avoid and shift blame. They have already met a number of the goals they set for the year, and experience themselves as being on or ahead of schedule. They share information and ideas freely and are learning as much as they can about one another's problems, methods, and solutions.

The Woven Policy and Planning Team responded to the strong request of the Woven Operations Team that they design a sensible, achievable, coordinated three-year business plan for the division. After some initial resistance, this cross-functional group began to work to develop a plan that was realistic as well as fully acceptable to research and development, marketing, sales, finance, customer service, manufacturing, and production control. The discipline of going through an iterative, complex, well-informed planning process to a solid draft has been exhilarating to the team members. They have submitted their plan to the Operations Team for input and to senior management for ratification.

On-time delivery is a central, high-priority management goal. It is achieved through integrating streams of complex market, scheduling, production, distribution, and customer information. The use of solid, well-integrated management information systems is only part of the solution to this enormously complex problem. Interpersonal communication channels must also be broadband and wide open, and stakeholders who recognize their interdependence and agree on their goals must plan and decide together. Teams have not yet taken on this task; it is anticipated that they will do so in the near future.

As quality and production data are generated at the production team level rather than the broader levels currently available, we hope to be able to specify and test a causal model relating the progress and success of teams to business results (see, for example, Van Aken and Kleiner, 1997). If this is not possible due to the nature and quantity of data available to us, we will use techniques such as pooled time series analysis or hierarchical linear models to test our model. Qualitative measures will enhance and enrich the picture. In the meantime, the successes of existing management teams have already been substantial and easy to document. As we progress in our ability to measure individual development and organizational learning, we will also progress in strengthening the data-based link between team management and sustaining a living and learning organization.

Summary

Much has been accomplished in the transition of Malden Mills to a team-based organization. We have used a broad combination of approaches to the change, including individual skill building, group training processes, the establishment of a parallel team structure, careful attention to resistance, and the creation of progress metrics that can be fed back to the organization and its teams. Teams are beginning to make their presence felt and are creating visible results.

Both the broader change process and the program to measure the success of teams are, however, far from complete. Much remains to be done. For example, teams must be established and broadly appreciated at the level of senior corporate management. Compensation and other human resources programs must be reexamined so that team performance can be fully incorporated into and maintained in the culture of Malden Mills. Additional support for first-line supervisors must be created in manufacturing, and teams must take root in the remainder of the manufacturing organization and, at a minimum, in the various groups that are interdependent with manufacturing. We believe, however, that something close to a critical mass is near and that the change to teams has a solid chance of becoming stable, and ensuring the future of Malden Mills.

Questions for Discussion

1. Most people assume that in order for change from a traditional to a team-based organization to be successful, teams must be installed from the top of the organization downward. Why did the method used in this case succeed?

2. Can you think of potentially useful process and outcome measures that were not mentioned in this case? How, for example, would you measure the return-on-investment for teams in this organization?

3. In thinking about the sustainability of the change effort described in this case, what additional barriers or obstacles would you anticipate (for example, financial, cultural, interpersonal)? What strategies might be used to manage them?

4. The initial effort described in this case began in manufacturing and did not involve human resources (HR) in a central way. Nevertheless, HR will become important at a later stage. What infrastructure should HR develop in order to maintain and extend the gains that have been achieved?

5. In the organization described in this case, do you see an important function for teams in the sales organization? What shape might such teams take, and how might marketing and product development figure in?

6. In the case described here, the segments of the organization under greatest pressure also had the greatest difficulty establishing effective teams. How would you explain this? What implications do you see for implementation strategy?

The Authors

Mordecai Porath has been involved for over 15 years in business transformation and organization development through the use of high technology. His academic and professional focus has been on utilizing modern networking technology to facilitate teamwork and organization development. He joined Malden Mills in 1994 as director of quality assurance, where he focused on leveraging individuals' technical skills and the utilization of modern manufacturing technology to enhance organizational effectiveness, and championed the change process. Currently, he is senior vice president, with responsibility for part of the company's electronic commerce, at the FundTech Corporation, a software company that specializes in electronic fund transfer and trade. He received his B.Sc. in industrial engineering and operations research from Tel-Aviv University in 1976 and his M.S. in operations research from the Massachusetts Institute of Technology in 1982. Porath may be contacted at the FundTech Corporation; phone: 781.674.0300; e-mail: motip@fundtech.com.

Mindy L. Gewirtz is a partner in GLS Consulting, Inc., a Boston based management consulting company that specializes in creating, sustaining, and measuring large systems change. She received her doctorate in organizational sociology and social work from Boston University, and has 20 years combined experience as an organizational consultant, psychotherapist, and educator. Some specific areas of expertise include leadership development, executive coaching, and helping organizations design, develop, and implement collaborative, high-performance work systems.

Peter Gumpert is a clinical and organizational psychologist practicing in Boston. He was educated at both Stanford and Columbia Universities (Ph.D. 1967). He is a partner in the organizational consulting firm GLS Consulting, Inc., and a member of a group clinical practice known as PsycHealth. He is a faculty member and senior clinical supervisor at Boston Institute for Psychotherapy, working with advanced trainees in both psychotherapy and organization development. Gumpert taught social and organizational psychology at the doctoral level for 17 years, and has done consulting in both private and public sector organizations since 1966.

References

de Geus, A. (1997, March-April). "The Living Company." *Harvard Business Review*, 51–59.

Kagan, D. (1995). "Why Entrepreneurs Ignore Good Advice: A Study in Non-Linearity & Ego." *Human Systems Management*, 327–333.

Katzenbach, J.R., and D.J. Smith. (1993). *The Wisdom of Teams*. Cambridge: Harvard Business School Press.

Mazen, A. (1997). "Team Defensiveness: A Neglected Root Cause." *Quality Management Journal, 4* (2), 24–50.

Van Aken, E., and B. Kleiner. (1997). "Determinants of Effectiveness for Cross-functional Organizational Design Teams." *Quality Management Journal, 4*(2), 51–79.

Pay for Knowledge
and Skill System

Chemainus Sawmill Division
of MacMillan Bloedel Limited

Ann Armstrong

The case presents a detailed description of the pay-for-knowledge and skill system at an innovative sawmill in Canada's largest forestry company. In addition to the pay system, it presents detailed information on the organization, its environment, its technology, its processes, and its outcomes. The teaching note provides current information on the sawmill and on the company.

Introduction

The case study describes the pay-for-knowledge and skill system (PKS) at the Chemainus Sawmill Division (the Sawmill) of MacMillan Bloedel Limited (MB). MB is Canada's largest forestry company with sales of about $5 billion Canadian a year. (All financial data are in Canadian dollars.) The Sawmill produces high-grade lumber for use in exposed areas, both interior and exterior, of buildings. Local 1-80 of the International Woodworkers of America (IWA) holds the certification for the Sawmill. MB's senior management considers the Sawmill a model for how to operate effectively in the 1990s and beyond.

The author collected data for the case in late 1989 and early 1990. She updated that information through informal interviews with employees in January 1998 and from articles in such newspapers as *The Globe and Mail's Report on Business*, January 21-22, 1998, and its monthly magazine in February 1998. The views of various employees, as told to the author in interviews on-site and by telephone, appear in quotation marks throughout the study.

This case was prepared to serve as a basis for discussion rather than to illustrate either effective or ineffective administrative and management practices.

History

The Sawmill opened on January 2, 1985, and is the fifth in the 123-year history of sawmilling at Chemainus, a small town on Vancouver Island, British Columbia. The previous sawmill, constructed of wood in 1920, was shut down permanently in June 1983 because it had lost $16.5 million between 1980 and 1983: Its equipment was outdated, its productivity low, and both the number of housing starts and the market price for lumber had plummeted in the 1981 recession. Its 700 employees were fully severed according to the terms of the then collective agreement, and they lost any recall and seniority rights.

By 1979, it was already evident that the old sawmill would have to be replaced, and the previous mill manager had been involved in a project to assess the feasibility of establishing a new sawmill at Chemainus. Because the old sawmill was constructed of wood, it required considerable and costly maintenance to operate at all. The sawmill that the manager proposed was considered too costly a capital investment, and the project was sent back to the drawing board. It was then put on hold when the old sawmill was shut down. However, a joint management labor committee was created in 1982 to determine if the old sawmill could be run profitably through such plans as reduced personnel and drastic cost cutting. The committee failed to satisfy both union and management needs, and, in August 1983, the old mill was permanently shut down and severance was paid out. The new mill and its team system were designed by management alone.

A further impetus to reviving the sawmill was that the provincial government, through its forestry minister, declared that "if MB won't use the logs, then it will lose the logs." (Most woodlands for logging are owned by the crown—the government—and sublet to different firms.) MB then decided to build a sawmill, made of steel, for a relatively modest capital investment of $25 million.

The town of Chemainus is trying to break its one-industry past; in 1985, it won first place in the international Downtown Revitalization Awards for a project started in 1981. At the heart of the project is the painting of large murals on the exterior walls of many of Chemainus's buildings. By the end of 1982, the outdoor art gallery had five murals and now there are a total of 25. Once nearly a ghost town, Chemainus is now a tourist area with many craft and other retail shops and 250,000 visitors each year. A documentary about the town is entitled "The Little Town That Did." Even so, there remain considerable anger and bitterness about MB's 1983 shutdown of the old sawmill because only a few of the 700 employees have been rehired.

Competitive Environment

The Sawmill's competition is international. Its primary competition abroad is with sawmills in Sweden, and, nationally, with several sawmills owned by Noranda Inc. (Noranda). In light of the plummeting market price for lumber coupled with the increasing demands from its customers for particular grades and sizes of lumber, the key success factor for the Sawmill has become getting quality or value out of logs.

A log produces sawdust, chips, and lumber. The Sawmill must pay to dispose of sawdust, but chips can be sold and lumber is the principal and major source of value. (The Sawmill does not produce plywood veneer.) In MB's woodlands, employees harvest two species of logs (Douglas Fir and Pacific Coast Hemlock) for the Sawmill. The challenge is to try to recover the highest-grade fiber of lumber from each cut log. The value of a log increases if it is cut so that the lumber is clear (that is, free of knots) and thick. (There are numerous grades of lumber, ranging from Ô2 and better clear, the best, to shop, merch, and utility, the worst. Use of the lumber varies according to the grades. Both Ô2 and better clear can be used as exterior trim in rooms, whereas utility can be used as interior framing for houses.) The Sawmill is trying to cut its logs so that lumber to be sold at the lower merch grade does not include any clear grade. In the old sawmill, most logs were cut as merch and thus the value for clear, approximately four times greater than that for merch, was not recovered.

There is also an increasing demand, particularly from the Sawmill's Japanese customers, for consistency of lumber in each pallet. As a result, packaging, like quality, has become very important for showing off the best features of the lumber. Customers inspect the lumber on-site and "appearance has become two-thirds acceptance." (To increase quality control awareness and skill, the Sawmill offers and pays for an after-hours course that the quality control supervisor teaches. It enables the operators to learn "the [difficult] art" of lumber grading and to earn their grading tickets. The supervisor evaluates operators by written and practical tests. Operators that pass the tests receive a premium on their hourly rate. Several employees from the office have taken the course.)

Labor Market

The 1988 unemployment rate on Vancouver Island was approximately 13 percent. Sources of employment on the island include craft and other retail shops, three pulp mills, nine sawmills, and several logging camps. Most of the jobs in the forestry industry are unionized and well paid.

The rates of compensation (and any changes to the rates) for sawmilling jobs are set by a rate determination committee, an industry joint-management labor committee, as part of the negotiation process for the industry's master collective agreement. The Sawmill does not deviate, by choice, from the principal terms of the master collective agreement by paying any additional benefits, for example.

In early 1984, the Sawmill hired its foremen. Shortly thereafter, the management team selected from the 2,400 applicants "a hand-picked, committed crew" of 73 because of their sawmilling skills, experience, and their attitude toward working in teams. A few were hired at the top rate of compensation. Those hired initially received training in effective problem-solving and decision-making techniques, but those hired later have not. New employees, however, do have a one-day orientation session with the personnel supervisor, who explains the nature of the Sawmill's PKS.

There are, in total, 137 operators, shippers, and maintenance staff of whom approximately half had worked at the old sawmill. The staff are covered by the same collective agreement. Their average age is 37 years, of whom most are men and have 12 years of schooling. There is one woman and a member of the First Nations. There are 25 management staff. (Eight of the 137 are temporary or part-time employees, or both, "casuals or floaters on a call list" to serve as buffers for the Sawmill's vacation, sickness, and banked overtime system. Call list employees cannot answer temporary postings or switch shifts. They can accumulate qualifying hours only at the entry-level workstations. Should they become permanent employees, the hours they have already accumulated would be applied to the hours for qualification.)

Recruitment is conducted by a panel made up of the personnel supervisor and the foremen of the department for which there is a vacancy. On occasion, production operators have sat in as observers, but, by choice, they have had no involvement in any hiring decisions. To fill vacancies in the maintenance department, however, the entire maintenance team sits in on the panel along with the personnel and maintenance supervisors. The team participated in the hiring of a warehouse supervisor who works in the maintenance department, for example.

Any prospective employees must have, as well as sawmilling experience, their grading ticket, which shows they know how to grade different qualities of lumber, and first aid tickets, which demonstrate first-aid training. (The company requires first aid tickets because there is no designated first aid position.) On average, one of 10 prospective employees is hired.

Manufacturing Process

The manufacturing process, although similar to traditional sawmilling in that it employs hydraulic and pneumatic technology, also uses computerized precision scanning technology to facilitate "getting value out of logs." It involves 10 steps.

1. *Barker:* All logs entering the Sawmill must first have the bark removed by the 72-inch mechanical barker. The finished logs are put back into the water, and the bark is pulverized in a grinding machine for use as fuel for the power boilers at MB's pulp mills.

2. *Log cut off saw:* As logs are brought into the Sawmill, a computerized scanning system determines the exact length of each log and gives the operators three cutting solutions for the best utilization of the logs. The logs are then cut by a 9-foot chain saw.

3. *Head Rig:* The head rig is a 9-foot double-cut band mill with a 60-inch carriage. It is the job of the head rig to break down the logs for further processing by the edger or cant quad.

4. *Edger:* The edger is a 10-by-72-inch six-saw splined arbor machine that is used to cut side cants from the head rig into high-value finished lumber.

5. *Cant quad:* The cant quad consists of four 6-foot band saws. It breaks down partially sawn logs from the head rig into finished products. The accurate cutting helps to enable maximum lumber recovery from the logs.

6. *Trim line:* The trim line consists of an edger drop sorter, a mountain trimmer, and a resaw drop sorter. All lumber is end trimmed to remove waste and is cut to length. Finished lumber is sent either to the automatic sorter or to the timber deck if it is over 4 inches thick.

7. *Remanufacturing:* The *reman* process consists of two machines: a 6-foot vertical band saw that remans width and thickness of all off-size or off-grade lumber; and a three-saw hula trimmer that retrims incorrect lengths or end defects and also remans for grade improvement.

8. *Timber deck:* The timber deck consists of the timber grader who grades and tallies all timbers in the sawmill and can retrim to higher values; and the timber crane and chaser who work together to sort and package all timbers from the Sawmill.

9. *Lumber sorters/stackers:* Two lumber sorters make up the automated green chain, which has 90 bins in total. Lumber is graded and sorted by lumber graders, and a bin patrolman monitors the transfer system and assists two stackers with building packages.

10. *Chipper area:* The chipper area consists of two chippers: a 76-inch horizontal feed disc chipper used for chipping side edgings; and a drop-in 59-inch drum chipper used for chipping trim ends. All chips are screened for size and are stockpiled for shipment to MB's pulp mills where they are used for making pulp and paper.

Although the Sawmill itself is compact, the geography of the Sawmill is not. It is set back from the water to increase space for lumber loading. "[It] is more isolating for the operators" than a traditional sawmill. The core of the manufacturing process consists of the head rig, edger, and cant quad. The entire process is operator paced, and any operator can shut down the conveyor system for safety or quality considerations, or both, and any operator can refuse to perform unsafe work. The batch sizes are large, and only one species of log is processed at one time, usually in production runs of two weeks. The Sawmill ships lumber by MB's deep-sea vessels or by truck, from the yard.

Organization

Each division (for example, a pulp mill or a sawmill) of MB operates as a profit center, but interdivisional competition does not occur because each of MB's sawmills has its own supply of logs from MB's woodlands. MB is owned by Noranda but remains a publicly traded corporation.

Goals

The goals of the Sawmill, according to its documentation, are two-fold: "to be first choice with customers and with the community." The Sawmill thus strives for the following:

- to provide a high value product in terms of its size, grade, and presentation
- to provide dependable delivery
- to respond proactively to market [demands] by being organizationally flexible and to be cost effective
- to respond to feedback [from customers]
- to provide personally rewarding work
- to provide a safe and healthy workplace
- to develop and maintain trust [within the Sawmill and the community].

Structure

The Sawmill consists of several teams, and internally its structure is described as the team concept. There are six production teams with varying numbers of workstations:

- log prep, six workstations
- log breakdown, three
- trim, eight
- grading, five
- merchandising, four
- yard, seven.

Although members of the yard team (that is, shippers) work only on the day and afternoon shifts, the members of the other teams (that is, operators) work on one of three shifts. Those with the highest seniority originally were able to select if they wanted to work on the graveyard shift. The day and evening shifts swing every two weeks, but those on the graveyard shift do not. New operators work on any of the three shifts, depending on the opening they are filling. (The day shift consisting of one log prep, log breakdown, trim, grading, and merchandising team is called the A crew; the evening shift, the B crew; and the graveyard shift, the C crew. Each crew comes in a little prior to the start of its shift.) The Sawmill has no time clocks, no whistles, and no status parking spaces.

The operators and the shippers are expected to rotate through all the workstations in their teams to become multiskilled and to train others in the skills they have mastered. They also are expected to make safety their first concern in the workplace. The Sawmill has instituted a safety program called Take Two, which involves a monthly meeting of one hour. The Sawmill pays for half the time, and the lunch break falls during the other half. At the meetings, the operators and the foremen watch videos and then discuss ways to improve safety procedures in the Sawmill. The Sawmill provides most of the necessary safety equipment, such as ear protectors, hard hats, gloves, and coveralls for all the team members. In addition to the Sawmill's own safety committee, the Sawmill participates in an industry joint-management labor safety committee with approximately five other firms. The group holds seminars on a rotating basis at each of the firms. An equal number of representatives of management and labor from each firm attends, tours the Sawmill, and makes recommendations for improving safety procedures and practices.

The shippers report to the yard foreman, and the operators report to a shift foreman who, in turn, reports to a department foreman. The department foremen swing (to use the company's terminology) every three months, whereas the shift foremen swing with their crews. They are responsible for daily operations, that is, to ensure that the flow of logs into the Sawmill meets customers' orders and that the logs are cut for value extraction.

The maintenance team consists of several millwrights, filers (that is, benchmen, fitters, and round sawmen), electricians, oilers, and mechanics. They report to charge hands who, in turn, report to the maintenance supervisor. Although members of the maintenance team work on the day shift, they are on call at all times.

The management team, headed by the mill manager, consists of the operations superintendent, the personnel supervisor, the accountant, the sales superintendent, quality control (QC) supervisors, and other managerial staff. The Sawmill has its own importer (another of MB's divisions) with offices in Osaka and Tokyo because its number of Japanese customers continues to increase. (The Sawmill had no QC function until 1986, its second year of operation, when it was established at the behest of the sales superintendent. The QC supervisors check grades, measure widths, and manage any exceptions to the lumber. They work flexible hours but essentially work on the day shift, although every two months, the assistant QC supervisor will work on the graveyard shift for one week.)

Much of the design vision and impetus for the team concept (and the PKS) came from the previous mill manager. He was convinced that there must be a better way to operate a sawmill and was particularly impressed by his visits to sawmills in Sweden and to MB's wafer board plant in Thunder Bay, Ontario (since sold to a Japanese firm). As a result, along with the previous operations superintendent, the previous personnel supervisor, and the three department foremen, he developed the team concept for the Sawmill. The Sawmill has considerable operating autonomy as long as "it stays within the terms of MB's policies and those of the collective agreement."

Central to nurturing the team concept is the Sawmill's communications network. The network consists of a series of meetings of production team, crew, and others to facilitate the process of employee input. Any member of the production team may call a meeting to discuss any problem. No agenda is set, and no minutes are taken.

Each production team on each shift and the yard and maintenance teams have a team representative. On some teams, the representative is elected, whereas on others the role rotates among the members. Team representatives participate in meetings designed to deal with issues that affect the Sawmill as a whole. Recently, the monthly general team representatives' meeting looked at several issues, including the following:

- How work orders could be more expeditiously communicated and implemented. The Sawmill has a work order system designed to encourage improvements to the manufacturing process. Employees can initiate work orders—and they do—and the maintenance staff clarifies and verifies the work orders and, subject to safety considerations, implements them.

- Where, on-site, hard hats had to be worn. A committee, comprised of representatives from the three crews and chaired by the personnel supervisor, was created to address this contentious issue.
- What changes, if any, are necessary to the local addendum to the master collective agreement.
- How to improve the sawmill's ventilation.
- The desirability of moving the parking lot closer to the sawmill. Both the current and previous mill managers had turned down the request to move the lot.

The subject of an earlier meeting had been team participation in the recruitment process. The teams rejected participation out of concern that they would become involved in both firing and hiring decisions. In addition to the meetings, data on the sawmill's performance are posted daily in the lunchroom, and the accountant presents monthly results to each crew.

The team concept seems to receive ambivalent reviews. Although many team members are supportive (one employee said, for example, "It's fantastic as everyone is not so bored"), some express concern that, as one said, "It could be manipulated by the management or by the union." Some felt that the communication process was "time-consuming and frustrating, although it's easy to find out what's going on." The long-term goal continues to be to built on the process of involvement so that safety, productivity, and job satisfaction can continue to increase.

The Union

The International Woodworkers of America (IWA) represented the employees at the old sawmill. When the Sawmill was opened, MB made a commitment to remain unionized and negotiated an addendum to the industry's master collective agreement with the local IWA officials. The local addendum specifies the design characteristics particular to the Sawmill. Its preamble and background sections read as follows:

Since January 1985, Chemainus Sawmill Division has embarked upon a program to effect change in traditional employee relation practices. The objective is to develop a co-operative working environment that will encourage employee participation in managing and operating a sawmill, and to encourage individual multi-skill development. This agreement reinforces the commitment of the union, the employees and management to work together to ensure the viability of a productive, efficient and safe operation within a participative work environment for the mutual benefit of all parties.

Since the start up of the new mill, management and employees of [the Sawmill] have been working together in developing a nontraditional work environment and manning concept. Through countless team discussions, a great many proposals have been evaluated. The result has been the development of work practices referred to as "Team Policies" [which include only the following:] the organization of work stations into teams; the progression sequences for training and advancement; team posting systems and requirements; qualification requirements; and personal pay rates.

The addendum goes on to note that certain policies do not (yet) apply to the maintenance staff. For example, there is official union opposition to developing some sort of multiskilling system for the maintenance staff for fear that jobs will be lost or safety be compromised.

In June 1986, the sawmill's employees voted on the local addendum and accepted it. The Sawmill has a plant committee, comprising elected representatives from the yard, the sawmill, and the maintenance staff. There are six (and alternates), none of whom is a union official. The committee meets regularly and is "a good solid plant committee." Both managers and unionists regard the Sawmill as having "harmonious industrial relations" because "everyone understands that there's a need for a bargaining agent and for rules to be followed." The committee keeps local union officials updated regularly about any proposed changes to the local addendum or any decisions about it, or both. As a result, union officials seldom visit the Sawmill except to manage local elections.

The Pay-for-Knowledge and Skill System

The current department foremen designed the PKS in 1984 with some assistance from a consulting firm. There was no union involvement in the design process. As part of the development of the team concept, production teams had been created using the following grouping criteria: the proximity of the workstations, compensation rate compatibility, and logical skill progression. On the basis of the groupings and the knowledge and skill requirements for each workstation, the consulting firm developed training manuals for all the workstations. The PKS was in place for the opening of the Sawmill, but the process of rotation did not begin until July 1985, because the employees, at the outset, had been hired to do a particular job for six months. The PKS covers only the operators and the shippers, not the office staff or the maintenance staff.

A working committee that comprises five elected representatives from the maintenance staff and several managers has been examining how to reward the development of multiskilling in the maintenance staff. By virtue of the sawmill's computerized technology, the different trades are working together more closely than they would in a traditional sawmill. They are learning one another's trades without substantively crossing trade lines. The maintenance staff wanted some financial recognition for doing extra. Management offered a premium of 65 cents an hour, but the maintenance staff categorically rejected the offer as too low.

The issue of rewarding the development of multiskilling remains contentious and complicated, particularly as trade lines are very tight in the pulp mills and sawmills on Vancouver Island. If an electrician is needed to perform a task but is unavailable, for example, the other trades cannot and do not do any of that work. There is also a rotation system already in place for the filers. Historically, filers have been able to rotate among the three filing workstations of fitter, round sawman, and benchman, and thereby earn the filer's top rate (that is, the top rate of compensation in the maintenance team). There has always been a certain mystique about filing—filers used to work behind black curtains—and thus the filers, unlike the other trades, earn a premium. The issue is "demoralizing" and unresolved.

The principle underlying the PKS is that "as and when an employee qualifies at a work station," that employee is paid for having acquired the knowledge and skill for the particular workstation (or job). When an employee starts at a workstation, that employee works with someone who is already qualified at the workstation (the trainer) and a foreman to learn all the tasks of the workstation. The new employee is expected to study, at home, the training manual for the workstation and to learn, on the job, how to perform the tasks safely. The trainer demonstrates the tasks, and then the employee performs them under the trainer's supervision. Each training manual has five sections: The first outlines the role of the workstation in the manufacturing process, its safety requirements, and its major machine components; the second, its operational procedures; the third, its quality and quantity requirements; the fourth, its maintenance and troubleshooting procedures; and the fifth, a checklist for the workstation's tasks and procedures.

After a week or so, an employee becomes validated (that is, the trainer and the foreman determine that he or she has "a basic understanding" and is capable of doing the job safely without assistance). Then the employee performs the job in two-hour increments (daily, if possible) until such time that he or she has met the specified total number of hours required to master the workstation. To master the edger workstation on the log breakdown team, an employee must work on the edger for a minimum of 350 hours, most of which is done in 175 increments of two hours each, to a maximum of 400 hours. (The foremen and the operators established the minimum and maximum hours jointly as reasonable time frames in which all employees could be expected to master the workstation. The hours spent to become validated are not included in the minimum and maximum hours to become qualified.) An employee who has put in the minimum number of hours must demonstrate, using the training manual's checklist, that he or she is qualified at the workstation. There is no other formal performance appraisal process. Figure 1 shows an example of a checklist. If the trainer or supervisor, or both, are not satisfied that the employee has achieved visible competence, the employee must re-do the workstation, up to a maximum of an additional 200 hours. In the event of a disagreement between the trainer and the foreman, the foreman's view prevails. To date, most employees have been able readily to become qualified at the workstations, so there are no specific provisions for handling any extreme difficulty in learning.

During the two-hour increments at which the employee is learning the job (that is, after becoming validated but prior to becoming qualified), he or she receives the pay for the particular workstation being mastered. For the other six hours of the day, the employee is paid at the highest rate for the workstations mastered already (that is, at the personal rate). Once the employee becomes qualified, the higher rate for the particular workstation becomes his or her personal rate. Then the employee can learn the next workstation and rotate through the workstations mastered already while maintaining his or her personal rate. At that point, the employee is expected to train another employee on the workstation that he or she has mastered. Although the employees are not required formally to give training, most do so.

Rotation through the workstations occurs in a specified sequence. For example, on the trim team, an operator enters at the edger drop

Figure 1. Sample training manual checklist.

	Demo ✓	Check ✓✓
Re-entry transfer deck	_____	_____
Quad outfeed transfer deck 1	_____	_____
Quad outfeed transfer deck 2	_____	_____
Dead skids on quad outfeed transfer deck 2	_____	_____
Air cylinder operating	_____	_____
Dead skids	_____	_____
Edger outfeed deck	_____	_____
Storage transfer to trimmer	_____	_____
Storage transfer to trimmer stop pins	_____	_____
Dropgate to waste conveyor	_____	_____

✓   Denotes that the trainer has shown the employee how to perform a particular task.

✓✓   Denotes that the employee has demonstrated visible competence in a particular task.

workstation and then goes on to master the chipper, the hula trimmer, the mountain trimmer 1 and 2, the resaw drop, the quad drop, and, lastly, the vertical resaw workstation. The yard team members, for example, rotate in their own subteams of shipping or processing. Those in the processing subteam will fill in for the shipping subteam members when they are sick or away on holidays.

Some teams set their rotation schedules informally, whereas others develop a monthly rotation schedule. For example, if Person 1 is in the process of mastering the resaw drop workstation, then in addition to the time spent learning the resaw drop, he works only on those workstations at which he was already qualified (that is, edger drop, chipper, hula trimmer, mountain trimmers 1 and 2). If Person 2 were hired at the penultimate rate and then qualified at the vertical resaw workstation (the highest rate), however, she may be required to train down to learn every workstation (with a lower rate) in the team. It takes about three years to master all the trim team's workstations. Although there is no formal, mandated requirement to rotate in order to receive additional pay, an employee must do so. (There are eight workstations but 10 employees on the team because the extra two are used as rovers for the Sawmill. When an operator is about to train on a new workstation, there is a need to double up for the first few days. The rovers fill in, as required, so that the training can take place. For example, there are two rovers on the trim team; they cover any training needs and absenteeism.)

Should a permanent vacancy occur on a team, an opening is posted as a team position. It is open first to permanent qualified team members of the same team on the other shifts and to other qualified employees. (Permanent team members can switch shifts within their own teams. Posting is then awarded on seniority; however, the members of both teams and the foremen must agree to the switch.) In the event that several employees are equally qualified, the most senior will receive the team position. All vacancies now are at the entry level and, therefore, the employee enters the sequence behind the team's incumbent members. An employee who posts to another team keeps his or her personal rate unless it is higher than that of the highest paid workstation for the new team. If it is, the employee's personal rate will be lowered to that of the highest paid workstation for the team. Should an employee leave temporarily, his or her qualification time stops until the person returns. Short temporary team vacancies are filled from within the team.

Although there is no requirement per se to rotate through all the workstations of a team, all the employees must master two workstations. On average, the employees have mastered five. Those employees hired originally at the top rate for their specialized expertise for the sawmill's start-up are training down to learn all the workstations and are becoming multiskilled without receiving any additional compensation.

The employees keep logs of their hours at each workstation, on a daily or weekly basis. The foremen sign off that an employee has qualified at a particular workstation and inform the personnel supervisor that the employee should receive the corresponding rate of compensation. The employee receives the additional compensation and a memo outlining all the workstations at which he or she has already qualified. The personnel supervisor manages "the minimal amount of administration for the PKS." Record keeping is computerized on a "mill-wide net" so any rate changes can be easily noted and made.

Advantages and Disadvantages of the PKS

The employees the author interviewed identified a variety of advantages of the PKS. They include the following individual and organizational advantages:
• The PKS increases job variety.

- The increased job variety decreases boredom and, therefore, increases safety.
- It enables operators to acquire a broad understanding of the manufacturing process, thereby facilitating improved decision making.
- It decreases job dissatisfaction in that "[the operators] are not just bodies being bought or used."
- It makes operators more marketable in the event of a downturn in the sawmill's fortunes.
- "It holds the team concept together" as it recognizes multiskilling financially.

The employees identified very few disadvantages because "the PKS isn't a problem at all" for the union or for management. The few include:
- "The PKS is taken for granted."
- It provides no incentive for those earning the top rate to rotate.
- It creates the topping out problem—it is anticipated that most operators will reach the top compensation rate in two years.

Outcomes of the PKS

The variety of outcomes of the PKS included the following:
- Operators are "happier"—they display "a better attitude as [they don't] mind coming to work now."
- Operators are enjoying the opportunities to receive and to give training.
- Operators are better able to receive and to give performance feedback.
- Operators are paying greater attention to "getting value out of logs."
- There has been an increase in flexibility as more operators are becoming multiskilled (two other divisions of MB are in the process of implementing some form of PKS because "it is a competitive advantage").
- Because rotation is not required, some "dogging of work" and "hogging of jobs" still occur (for example, the lamb crane workstation is considered to be the most prestigious in the merchandising team and, therefore, is one from which the operators do not want to rotate).

Issues

Several issues are under active discussion or consideration, or both, at the Sawmill. They include the following:
- How should the team concept be strengthened so that the communications network works consistently and so that more participation is encouraged?

- What kind of training is required so that consensus in decision making can be achieved?
- What should participation entail—having input or exercising substantive decision-making power?
- How should commitment to the process of rotation be fostered?
- What kind of gainsharing system (if any) can be implemented within the terms of the master collective agreement?
- How can knowledge about selling and marketing lumber be diffused throughout the Sawmill?
- How can the development of multiskilling in the maintenance staff be effectively implemented and rewarded?

Performance Data

In 1988, the Sawmill had the best performance record in MacMillan Bloedel. The amount of lumber recovered from every cubic foot of log cut has increased steadily, and the percentage of shop, or better grades of lumber, has increased likewise. Each day, 137 employees produce half a million board feet.

There has been one grievance since start-up because one of the foremen made a mistake about seniority rights. Absenteeism is so low that it is not monitored. The Sawmill received several awards for its 1987 safety record, because there had been no lost-time accidents, but the next year, there were two. Management and union alike considered the increase to be a serious one because the expectation then was that there would be none. Although sawmilling is recognized as less hazardous than logging, almost everyone at the Sawmill has vivid memories of a fatality that occurred in 1988. Even so, the employees and the community regard the Sawmill as a good employer.

Current Situation
Compensation Systems

In 1991-1992, a modified Scanlon (gainsharing) plan was implemented for the Sawmill. In its first year, the payout was about $11,000. A committee comprising management and employees redesigned the plan in 1993 to eliminate any uncontrollable costs or artificial gains (for example, fluctuations in the exchange rate). Now the gainsharing plan incorporates only those costs that are controllable onsite. The gain is calculated from data on log recovery, the value of lumber that is shop or better, the volume produced, log cost, manufacturing and processing costs, and claims for off-grades or off-orders. All full-time employees of the Sawmill (including the mill manager) participate in the plan. A training module on the gain-sharing system is now being prepared so that everyone has an enhanced understanding of the plan and its mechanics. Last year was the second-best year for the gainsharing plan, and the payout was approximately $6,000 per employee. The gainsharing plan added approximately $3.5 million to the sawmill's revenues in 1997; approximately $1.2 million were shared, and the remainder contributed to the sawmill's profitability.

Teams

The teams continue to evolve. The only turnover has been from retirements. Teams have worked on major capital projects, such as the rebuilding of the packaging unit, and on major systems projects, such as the design of what the Sawmill calls setworks computer programs, which are programs unique in the industry that the company is copyrighting.

Outcomes

The Sawmill is the only one on Vancouver Island that has always run three shifts and has been able to adjust to market curtailment. In 1997, the Sawmill had its best safety record.

The Company

Tom Stephens, who took over as CEO in September 1997, is implementing a major restructuring of MB because the company has reported losses for four consecutive quarters and another was expected in the 1997 year-end results. Its shares have traded between $15 and $25 for the past 10 years. MB is laying off one-fifth of its workers and selling or closing down some of its operations, including its research and technology center. It is focusing on its value-added businesses, employing flexible work practices, such as those at the Chemainus Sawmill. MB also plans to reduce its "exposure to lumber markets in Japan," according to the February 1998 *Globe and Mail's Report on Business* magazine. After the announcement of the restructuring plans, MB's share price went up $1.20, closing at $16.80.

Questions for Discussion

1. How well does the PKS support the organizational structure and communication network? How and why (not)?
2. How flexible is the organization and how multiskilled are its operators?

3. What is your assessment of the strengths and weaknesses of the PKS design?

4. What are the challenges and the opportunities of implementing teams supported by PKS in unionized organizations?

The Author

Ann Armstrong got her Ph.D. in organizational behavior at the University of Toronto. For her dissertation, she studied nine North American manufacturing organizations using PKS, and in one part of her research, she did not find support for the topping-out phenomenon in PKS. Armstrong founded the firm, Learning+Earning Systems, through which she consults on PKS and provides training and development in managerial skills. She teaches at the Universities of Toronto and Guelph. Armstrong can be contacted at Box 6507 STN A, Toronto, Ontario M5W 1X4; phone: 905.939.7381; e-mail: lrn-ern@aol.com.

Suggested Readings

Cohen-Rosenthal, E., and C.E. Burton. (1987). *Mutual Gains: A Guide to Union-Management Cooperation*. New York: Praeger.

Kochan, T.A., and T.A. Barrocci, editors. (1985). *Human Resource Management and Industrial Relations*. Boston: Little, Brown.

Lawler, E.E., III. (1990). *Strategic Pay: Aligning Organizational Strategies and Pay Systems*. San Francisco: Jossey-Bass.

Ledford, G., Jr. (1995). "Designing Nimble Reward Systems." *Compensation and Benefits Review*, 27(4), 46–54.

Sustaining Teams

Fernco, Inc.

Stewart L. Tubbs, Joseph H. Kryska,
and Darrell H. Cooper

Moving an organization to a team environment is certainly a difficult challenge, but it is even more difficult to sustain a team over a long period of time (Stoltz, 1997; Tubbs, Ebrom, and Widgery, 1995). We have attempted to conceptualize a model for both creating and sustaining teams over the long run.

The model presented in this study has guided us for several years in creating a team environment in many organizations. We have utilized this model in organizations ranging from 100 to 6,500 employees; in both union and nonunion organizations; and in both for-profit and not-for-profit organizations. Data are now available to demonstrate the results over a seven-year period in one company, Fernco, Inc., an injection-molding manufacturer of flexible plastic couplings located in Davison, Michigan, and Manchester, England.

Conceptual Foundations

In 1978, Fernco had approximately 12 employees and slightly more than $1 million in annual sales. By 1988, the company had grown to almost 100 employees and sales of nearly $15 million annually.

The company's annual sales actually dropped in 1989, as did profits due to competitive pricing. However, the total units shipped continued to increase. Through effective team building and training the company's annual sales and profits slowly began to increase until 1995, when profits and sales increased dramatically.

In late 1988, the authors began a systematic organizational-development process that was designed to improve an already successful

This case was prepared to serve as a basis for discussion rather than to illustrate either effective or ineffective administrative and management practices.

company. Figure 1 shows the process model. The conceptual under-pinnings of the study were based on the writings of the late Rensis Likert (1967; Likert and Likert, 1976) and developed by one of the authors (Tubbs, 1998). The basic premise is that the company's leadership behaviors are the driving force that is manifested in several intervening variables and eventually in bottom-line outcomes.

In late 1988 and through 1989, it was becoming apparent to the authors that changes had to be made in the way the business was run. Competitive pressures and declining profitability created a sense of urgency. Because Fernco had invented its line of connector products, the company had had the market pretty much to itself for many years. Because high profits breed competition, the market field grew from only Fernco to a field of 17 competitors by 1988.

Many companies attempt to follow current management fads and fail to accomplish any lasting changes. After studying other companies that went through changes, we concluded that a long period of time for effective change was required and that we had to target key areas of the business for change (see Miles, 1997). We felt we needed an updated vision, leadership behavior training for all of our employees, and extensive team training to help us establish team-based managing entities and an empowered workforce.

Fortunately, we had what was needed most, a senior management that recognized that in order to transform this company we had to accept that maintaining the status quo requires "management," but making and creating change and coping with its results requires leadership.

Fernco had what was needed to make this leap of faith by creating what we call a change culture and a continuing organizational development program. In our judgment, this is the single overriding principle that has made this sustained change possible.

Methodology

In 1989, 1990, and again in 1996, the authors measured employees' attitudes through use of a modified form of the survey of organizations, which the Institute for Social Research at the University of Michigan had developed. The findings created an internal benchmark to track the organizational development program's progress.

The surveys in all three years indicated that most work was needed in relationships within the various work groups (that is, satisfaction with work group rather than satisfaction with company, job, pay, or supervisor). As a result of these conclusions, we continued the extensive team leadership training with all of our employees. All employees

Figure 1. Process model for organizational development.

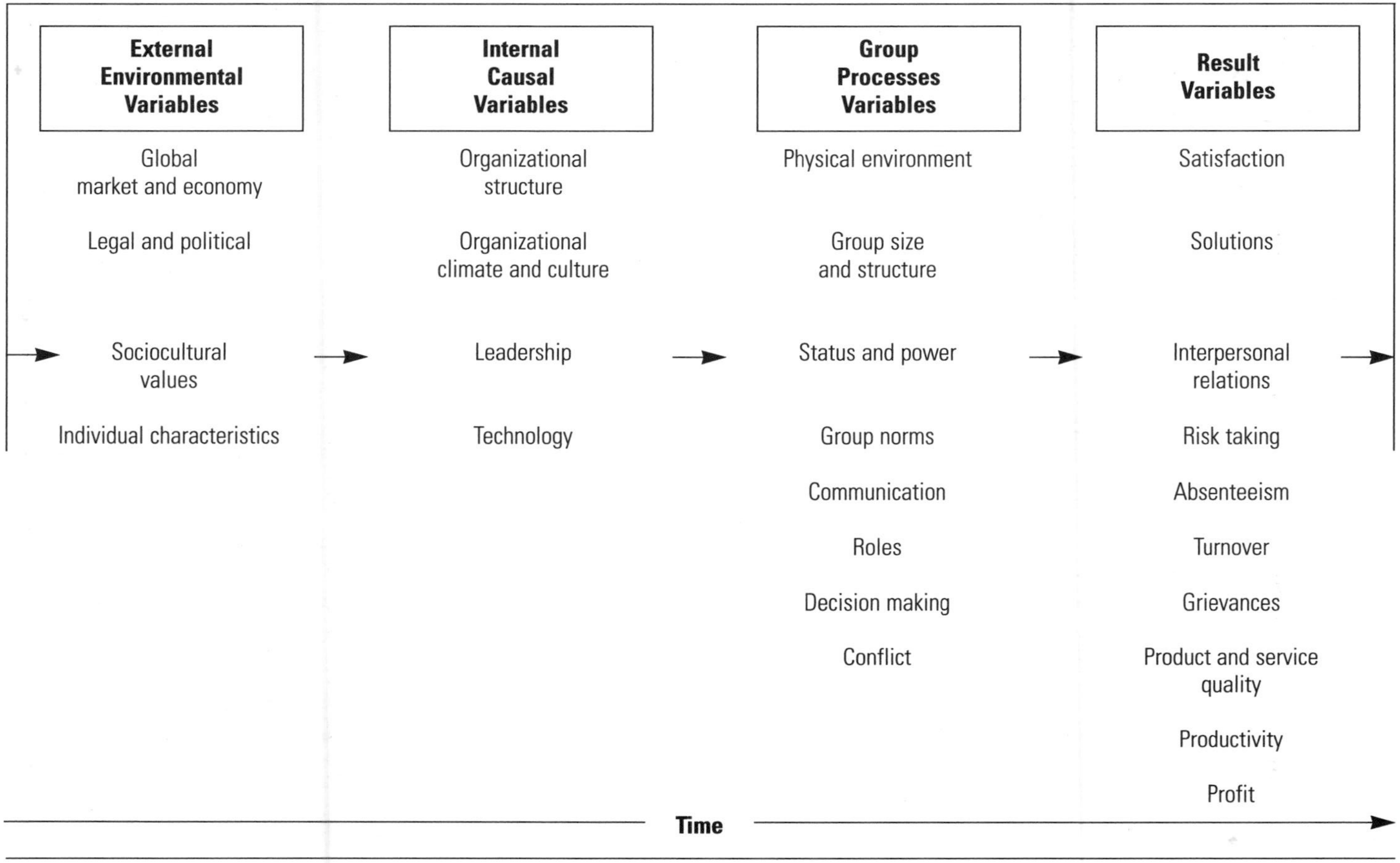

External Environmental Variables	Internal Causal Variables	Group Processes Variables	Result Variables
Global market and economy	Organizational structure	Physical environment	Satisfaction
Legal and political	Organizational climate and culture	Group size and structure	Solutions
Sociocultural values	Leadership	Status and power	Interpersonal relations
Individual characteristics	Technology	Group norms	Risk taking
		Communication	Absenteeism
		Roles	Turnover
		Decision making	Grievances
		Conflict	Product and service quality
			Productivity
			Profit

Time

received team leadership training because we intended to have as much empowerment as possible of everyone in the company. It was our hope that all employees would exercise leadership skills when needed on micro and macro levels. Quinn (1996) emphasizes that organizational changes rely on the change beginning with each individual. Top management, supervisors, and employees all went through the training together. We set a goal of 30 hours of formal training per employee per year. This training goal has been achieved and exceeded in four of the last six years.

We have conducted the following training programs during this period of time:
- high-performance leadership
- team leadership
- problem solving
- communication
- total quality management
- teamwork training
- synchronous manufacturing.

Most of the training had its basis in material found in earlier editions of Tubbs (1998) and Tubbs and Moss (1994).

We utilized all of these training programs to continually reinforce our vision of growth for Fernco, and for all of its employees. We told all of our employees that we did not intend to copy other companies' strategies but that our change culture and operating style would have to fit our company personality.

Our journey started in 1989 with team leadership training for all employees. It was near the end of that year that we laid out for all of our employees the path we intended to take, and the goals we hoped to achieve and the work groups and departments that would be affected first.

We started by eliminating the company plane and company cars for the executive group. We made sure that everyone understood that the organizational changes were starting at the top. This was communicated to employees by their supervisor in the daily briefings. It was done to show that the company needed to reduce costs and that everyone needed to sacrifice. The employees seemed to like seeing the executive perks reduced. It showed that top leaders were willing to walk the talk in cutting costs. The training programs continued through 1990 and 1991.

One of the initial transition moves toward building the team approach in the company was to form a steering committee made up of employees and a few members of management. The steering committee consisted of representatives from each department, and it met weekly for an hour. This group was responsible for establishing program policies, procedures, objectives, and resources. It provided guidance, direction, and support for the teams program. The steering committee stayed in place for one year and then was disbanded because the members felt that its goals had been accomplished.

From 1989 to 1991, the company established several cross-functional pilot teams from its production area to address specific problems. Over several years of experience we have found that it is more effective to begin organizational changes on a small scale with pilot projects than to implement a change program organization-wide. Pilot projects enable companies to make their inevitable mistakes on a small scale so they can improve the process before they implement a program throughout the organization. The pilot teams identified specific company improvements and were empowered to carry them out. For more on this, see Katzenbach and Smith (1993). The pilot teams were disbanded once they had accomplished their specific tasks.

Starting in 1991, the company underwent some other major changes. A new president was named, and the team deployment was expanded. Teams were formed among the office employees and among the sales staff. Then all the office and sales staff members were cross trained so that they became one cross-functional team. Physical changes were made in the office locations; walls were replaced with a U-shaped module so that more cross-office communication could occur.

In 1992, the production employees were informed that more team changes would be forthcoming. By 1993, all pay grades and job classifications were eliminated for production employees. Instead of bringing everyone down to a common denominator, everyone was brought up to the highest pay grade to ensure a more positive employee response to the changes. Employees thought that this was extremely generous.

By December 1993, the announcement was made to begin self-directed work teams throughout the company, and a new pay for knowledge plan. Another change was the introduction of an at-will policy for all employees. All employees sign an agreement to the effect that they serve at the pleasure of the company. All hourly employees were upgraded to salaried management status. At-will status is the opposite of just-cause status, which requires that managers give employees just cause before terminating them. The just-cause policy tends to instill in employees the feeling that their employment is a right regardless of their performance or market changes. Employers who have a problem worker whom they want to terminate must have a significant amount of documentation and face legal complications. Many companies are moving to an at-will relationship with employees. The overall plan for Fernco was to increase the teamwork and accountability of every employee.

In 1992, we started to streamline our organization, beginning with the office employees. Two office clerk positions were eliminated. We set up self-directed work teams and started to empower these work groups. Changes and training continued through this year as well as continual communications to all employees on the status of our change journey, good and bad news, right and wrong decisions.

Throughout 1992 and into 1993, we started to let our production employees know that they would be the next to move to self-directed work teams. The training continued.

From the end of 1993 through today, we have made changes in the production employees. As we implemented the self-directed work teams with the production employees, the following activities occurred:
1. We eliminated all different pay and job classifications and upgraded all employees to the highest pay grade.
2. We began cross training for all jobs in their department for maximum job flexibility.
3. We eliminated seniority as a basis of any consideration.
4. We eliminated shift preferences that were based on seniority.
5. We replaced shift preference with flextime at the suggestion of the production employees.
6. We started a pay-for-knowledge and a gainsharing program. (See also Gross, 1995.)

Although we began this organizational development effort focusing primarily on the formation of self-directed work teams, it has grown to include total quality management (TQM), participative management, and open book management, all of which utilize teams in one way or another to improve productivity and bottom-line performance. (See also Case, 1995; and Stack, 1992.)

Results

It is gratifying to see the results after seven years. First, the overall employee attitudes show significant improvements from 1990 to 1996 on nine different dimensions. These dimensions are as follows: decision making, coordination, supervisory team building, peer team building, peer team goal emphasis, peer goal emphasis, intragroup coordination, peer group problem solving, and satisfaction with work groups. These results are reflected similarly in all three shifts and to some extent among office employees.

As one might expect, the full-time employees and the contract employees have different attitudes. Contract employees are paid less and are not eligible for the profit-sharing program. Consequently, contract employees are less satisfied with pay than full-time employees. This is certainly to be expected.

Second, the financial measures of success also show significant improvements.

Discussion

Anyone who has tried to change an organization knows how difficult that task is. Similarly, if you have ever tried to sustain a high level of team performance, you know that it is even harder than achieving it in the first place. It is similar to losing weight. Although it is hard to lose weight, it is even harder to keep the weight off. Some research shows that fully 95 percent of attempts to lose weight fail within one year. Similarly, with organizational changes, teams have several predictable difficulties that seem to arise and create challenges for the teams' long-term success. Rayner (1996) in his book *Team Traps* identifies 12 predictable types of problems that teams face: manager abdication, successionless planning, downsizing, political suicide, team arrogance, undefined accountability, short-term focus, disruptive team member, poor teamwork habits, decision by default, uneven team-member contributions, and participation gimmickry.

In addition, many organizations create improvements in financial results at the expense of employee morale. Because the definition of productivity is output over input, if you decrease the input, you easily can improve productivity. This is sometimes referred to as "denominator management" (Hamel and Prahalad, 1994). However, this is often a short-run strategy. Numerator management, which tries to build the organization through growth, is an entirely different way of thinking. This study used both methods. The predominant method was to build the organization by improving leadership through employee teams. This method leads to increased employee satisfaction, which in turn increases the human elements in the organization and improves financial performance. It is exciting to see that this method works, and we hypothesize that other organizations can use it as well.

Questions for Discussion

1. Using the conceptual model in this chapter, explain the influence on Fernco of the external environmental factors, as shown in the first column in the process model (see figure 1).
2. Using the conceptual model in this chapter, explain how the processes described in this case fit or don't fit the model.
3. Given all the changes described in this study, which ones do you think were the most important in bringing about these changes?
4. Give examples from your own work experience that illustrate the conceptual model from this chapter.
5. If you were the CEO of Fernco, what things would you do to continue to improve the company?

The Authors

Stewart L. Tubbs is dean of the College of Business at Eastern Michigan University. He is also a contributing editor for *The Journal of Leadership Studies*. He has been named an outstanding teacher three times and an outstanding scholar twice. In addition, he has consulted extensively for *Fortune* 500 companies and is past chairman of the organiztional communication division of the Academy of Management. He recently received the outstanding leadership award in London, England, from the Academy of Business Administration. He can be contacted at The College of Business, Eastern Michigan University, Ypsilanti, MI 48197; phone: 734.487.5875; e-mail: Stu.Tubbs@emich.edu.

Joseph H. Kryska attended Northern Michigan University and Wayne State University, and he served three years in the Army Security Agency, a branch of the U. S. intelligence network. He is now president of Fernco, Inc., a manufacturer of plumbing products located in Davison, Michigan, where he previously served as a plant manager and vice president of manufacturing. His work experience includes four years as an hourly employee and foreman at GM Fisher Body and 11 years as a general foreman, superintendent, personnel manager, and West Coast operations manager for Allen Industries, an automotive supplier.

Darrell H. Cooper graduated from Arkansas State University with a B.S.E. degree in 1964. He has also completed postgraduate study at the University of Michigan and Harvard University Business School and has received an honorary doctor of business degree from Eastern Michigan University in 1994. He has served as chairman of the College of Business Development Board from 1989 to 1992. He also served as a member of the Eastern Michigan University Foundation Board of Trustees and as its treasurer, 1992; chairman of the Investment Committee, 1992; and board chairman, 1993–1995. His business affiliations include having been chairman and CEO of Fernco, Inc., and majority shareholder and director of Gunnell, Inc., and of Leaseline Financial, Inc. Cooper is also the author of two books.

References

Case, J. (1995). *Open Book Management*. New York: Harper Business.

Gross, S. (1995). *Compensation for Teams*. New York: Amacom.

Hamel, G., and C.K. Prahalad. (1994). *Competing for the Future*. Cambridge: Harvard Business School Press.

Katzenbach, J., and D. Smith. (1993). *The Wisdom of Teams*. Cambridge: Harvard Business School Press.

Likert, R. (1967). *The Human Organization*. New York: McGraw-Hill.

Likert, R., and J.G. Likert. (1976). *New Ways of Managing Conflict*. New York: McGraw-Hill.

Miles, R. (1997). *Leading Corporate Transformation*. San Francisco: Jossey-Bass.

Quinn, R. (1996). *Deep Change*. San Francisco: Jossey-Bass.

Rayner, S. (1996). *Team Traps*. New York: Wiley.

Stack, J. (1992). *The Great Game of Business*. New York: Currency/Doubleday.

Stoltz, P. (1997). *Adversity Quotient*. New York: Wiley.

Tubbs, S.L. (1998). *A Systems Approach to Small Group Interaction* (6th edition). New York: McGraw-Hill.

Tubbs, S.L., R.P. Ebrom, and R.N. Widgery. (1995). "Implementing Team Leadership." *The Journal of Leadership Studies, 2*, 36–49.

Tubbs, S.L., and S. Moss. (1994). *Human Communication* (7th edition). New York: McGraw-Hill.

A New Paradigm:
Industrial Teamwork Dynamics

Automobile Parts Manufacturer

Masahiro Nowatari

This case study introduces a new paradigm: industrial teamwork dynamics (ITD), which is rooted in the concept of group dynamics. The ITD measurement system is capable of testing and evaluating multiple work teams with quantitative results, as this case study of its use with a Japanese manufacturer's industrial work teams demonstrates. It also explores efficiency and productivity management from the fields of social psychology and industrial engineering. This unique quantitative approach investigates the teamwork level and productivity of industrial work teams, and the relationship between the two. Appraisal factors of teamwork (AFTs), teamwork levels, and productivity were measured by designated questionnaires to determine how those values were related. Because of its quantitative measurement, ITD can be easily modified for various industries or adapted for different cultures and countries. The ITD measurement system enables human resources development practitioners in various industries to maximize productivity, efficiency, and team member welfare.

It has been several decades since the Japanese industrial society first received international attention for its high productivity and quality products. Now, managers in related industries and researchers in the field of industrial engineering (IE) strive to find the secret of Japan's rapid economic success. During the 1980s, human resources development (HRD) practitioners and researchers began to pay special attention to Japanese management strategies. These strategies were

This case was prepared to serve as a basis for discussion rather than to illustrate either effective or ineffective administrative and management practices. All names, dates, places, and organizations have been disguised at the request of the author or organization.

grounded in sophisticated management systems such as quality control (QC) and just-in-time (JIT). Since their creation and implementation in Japanese industrial society, QC and JIT have become international benchmarks of the IE field.

Because the objectives of the QC and JIT systems were heavily focused on technology and productivity improvement, critics began to argue that those systems left employee welfare and compensation behind. To improve both productivity and employee welfare, IE needed to move in a new direction. The new paradigm, industrial teamwork dynamics, opens the door to a concept that incorporates social psychology with productivity.

Implication of Social Science

Since the end of WWII, improvements in productivity and efficiency and innovations in technology have been major objectives in the IE field in Japan. To achieve highly efficient production, it was necessary for various industries to develop new hardware, such as robotics and control mechanisms. Software that operates the hardware systems was studied and developed to maximize manufacturing productivity and efficiency. IE researchers have deemphasized areas of humanity, such as employee interaction and the working environment culture. The study of humanity, or humanware, in the industrial society could prove to be a significant factor to facilitate efficiency and productivity.

Industrial teamwork dynamics (ITD) includes objectives in industrial hardware, software, and humanware fields. ITD was developed to incorporate concepts of social science into traditional IE concepts. It focuses on teamwork levels and productivity among work teams in manufacturing plants. ITD shows HRD practitioners how employees appraise their work teams and how the appraisal values affect productivity. With the quantitative results, HRD practitioners are able to evaluate work teams precisely.

Methodology: Its Quantitative Approach

Begun after WWII, ITD is a quantitative measurement system that incorporates concepts of IE and social psychology. Most publications suggest that strong leadership is critical to teamwork development and productivity, but there have been only a few quantitative studies about industrial teamwork.

To evaluate productivity, the ITD measurement system makes use of Steiner's Group Dynamics Model, which says group productivity is produced through group process by an interrelationship of task demand and resource. That is, good team productivity is produced through good teamwork, and good teamwork is produced by union of team task and cumulative team resources, including humanpower, machine power, and so on. Individual work team members complete designated questionnaires with responses that enable collection of appraisal factors of teamwork (AFT) values. Each questionnaire specifies five appraisal levels (-2, -1, 0, 1, 2) for 12 AFTs consisting of a total of 79 items. The AFTs are divided into two categories: workability and cohesiveability. To evaluate AFTs' statistical significance, the K-J method, a multivariate analysis method, and principal component analysis (PCA) are used. Regression analysis also is used to evaluate the correlation between AFT and productivity. Productivity is defined in the following formula:

$$\text{Productivity} = \text{estimated working hours} / \text{actual working hours}$$

ITD also investigates how teamwork levels affect productivity. From the application of PCA, teamwork levels can be defined as closeness (that is, the range between positives and negatives in the factor loading values on the principal component axis of AFTs).

Automobile Parts Manufacturer

A study of the ITD measurement system was conducted in 1994 in an automobile parts manufacturer listed on the Tokyo Stock Exchange. AFTs, teamwork levels, and productivity were measured through questionnaires to determine how those values were related. The study was to test the following two hypotheses:

- Team work levels are positively related to productivity.
- Factors of workability (competency levels) and cohesiveability (cultural levels) are equally related to productivity.

The manufacturer, with approximately 2,000 employees, recorded capital of 5 billion yen and sales of 100 billion yen. ITD-designated questionnaires were given to 506 individuals including team leaders and their subordinates. There were 199 study subjects, and they were categorized into two team clusters. Cluster H, for high, consisted of 99 responses from individuals who belonged to teams that performed in the top 20 percent of productivity. Cluster L, for low, was made up of 100 responses from individuals who belonged to teams that performed in the bottom 20 percent of productivity.

The questions cover a broad range of subjects that focus on such topics as allocation of work, clarity of instructions, knowledge of colleagues' duties, atmosphere at work, and employees' enjoyment of their work. Following are a few of the questions:

- In your group, are there sharp divisions among the kinds of the work or jobs employees can do?
- Is everyone in your group willing to grapple with his or her assignments?
- Does your supervisor give instructions about the work or jobs in a systematic manner?
- Is your supervisor willing to pay attention to employees' opinions or suggestions?
- Do you think that you are well suited to your present work or job?
- Do you always want to work with the members of your current group?
- Do you think that you are lucky to be employed by your company?
- Are you happy in the atmosphere in your group at work?
- Do you think your group is well suited to do its job as a team?

To test the first hypothesis, the values of teamwork levels were compared. As a whole, cluster H's teamwork level values, 0.259, were lower than cluster L's, which were 0.384. According to the definition, cluster H has better teamwork levels than cluster L. Better teamwork levels show a narrower range of factor loading values on the principal component axis of AFTs. Moreover, cluster H rated higher teamwork levels than cluster L on both AFTs (workability and cohesiveability). These findings show that the teamwork levels were positively related to productivity and that the first hypothesis was accepted.

The study also found that the correlation between productivity and teamwork levels was stronger with higher AFT values of cohesiveability than with high workability values. AFT values of cohesiveability needed to become greater in order to increase productivity through improvement of the teamwork levels. The second hypothesis, as a result, was rejected. This means that factors of workability and cohesiveability are not equally related to productivity.

Challenges of the ITD Measurement System

ITD is rooted in the fields of industrial engineering and social psychology. Its unique quantitative approach investigates teamwork levels, productivity, and the relationship between the two. The ITD measurement system can be used to test multiple work teams and to precisely evaluate the work teams with quantitative results. However, ITD methodology is not easy for some to understand. Technology transfer is required before HRD practitioners implement the ITD measurement system in a real working environment. This means that the ITD measurement system could be transferred to computer software so that HRD practitioners can access and implement the system more readily. In addition, the data-entry process could be minimized by the use of Internet technology (such as developing a questionnaire Web site). Through Internet access, large corporations are able to investigate work teams consistently and instantly at any location. It is possible that such a technological transfer facilitates cross-cultural or international evaluation, or both, to improve overall productivity.

Conclusion

ITD was developed to form a new concept of IE that synthesizes the concept of social psychology with the traditional concept of IE (improvement of technology and productivity). Because of its quantitative measurement, ITD could be easily modified for work teams in various industries or adapted to different cultures and countries. With such modification and adaptation, ITD facilitates cross-cultural studies among HRD practitioners and researchers in the field of social science and industrial engineering. In summary, this new concept will help to maximize productivity, efficiency, and team member welfare.

Questions for Discussion

1. Do you have a quantitative measurement for teamwork?
2. Do you have a quantitative measurement for group productivity?
3. Is your team more affected by workability or cohesiveability?
4. Are the members of your group able to establish enough solidarity so that they can perform their work or jobs as they should?
5. In your group, are all the members able to cooperate sufficiently enough with one another so they can establish a good relationship?

The Author

Masahiro Nowatari is professor in the Graduate School of Engineering, specializing in industrial sociology, at Tamagawa University in Tokyo. As a distinguished international scholar, he was a visiting professor at the Institute for Social Research at the University of Michigan from 1989 to 1990. He also has been a member of the American Psychological Association and the American Psychological Society. In his home country, Nowatari serves as an editorial board member for *IE Review,* a journal issued by the Japan Institute of Industrial Engineering (JIIE). He is an active member of the Japan Industrial Management Association (JIMA), the Japanese Association of Industrial/Organizational Psychology (JAIOP), the Japanese Group Dynamics Association, and many other professional organizations. Nowatari can be reached 6-1-1 Tamagawa Gakuen, Machida, Tokyo 194-8610 Japan; e-mail: nowatari@eng.tamagawa.ac.jp.

Note

Many thanks to my special friend Mr. Masateru Uema for his assistance developing the contextual part of this paper and Miss Souko Suzuki for translating my original text in English. To my wife, Keiko, for all of her support.

Suggested Readings

Nowatari, M. (1989). "Relationship Among Group Integrative Determinants for Group Work: Based on Rate of Leader's Direct Work in his Total Work." *Journal of Japanese Association of Industrial & Organizational Psychology, 3*, 7–17.

Nowatari, M. (1990). "Relationship Among Group Integrative Determinants for Group Work: Relationship by Every Group Size Model and Extraction of Teamwork Determinants From Group Integrative Determinants Through Principal Component Regression." *Journal of Japan Industrial Management Association, 41*, 153–164.

Nowatari, M. (1991). *The Third Technology: Extraction of Teamwork Determinants in Japanese Manufacturing Industries*. Paper presented at the meeting of the 1991 International Industrial Engineering Conference: Institute of Industrial Engineers, Detroit.

Nowatari, M. (1992). "Group Dynamics in Japanese Manufacturing Industries: Confirmation and Verification of the Teamwork Determinants Conclusion of Succeeding Researches for Group Work." *Journal of Japan Industrial Management, 43*(4), 241–252.

Nowatari, M., and A. Aswad. (1993). "Extraction of Teamwork Determinants in Japanese Manufacturing Industries." *The Japanese Journal of Experimental Social Psychology, 32*(3), 269–283.

Nowatari, M. (1994). "Relationship Among the Teamwork Determinants of Work Groups in the Japanese Manufacturing Industries." *The Japanese Journal of Experimental Social Psychology, 34*(1), 1–9.

Nowatari, M. (1994). "Relationship Between Teamwork Level and the Team Productivity of Work Teams in the Automobile Related Parts Manufacture: Industrial Teamwork Dynamics. Part 1. *Journal of Japan Industrial Management Association, 45*(5), 479–487.

Nowatari, M. (1995). *Industrial Teamwork Dynamics (ITD): Relationship Between the Teamwork Level and Their Group Productivity of Work Groups in Japanese Industries*. Paper presented at the meeting of the 4th Industrial Engineering Research Conference, Nashville, Tennessee.

Nowatari, M. (1997). *Verification of Japanese Teamwork: Teamwork on Member Within Work Teams in the Japanese Manufacturing Industry.* Paper presented at the meeting of the 14th International Conference on Production Research, Osaka, Japan.

Nowatari, M. (1997). *Teamwork in the Japanese Work Teams: Introduction of Appraisal Factors of the Teamwork by Case Studies.* Paper presented at the meeting of The 1997 Eighth Annual International Conference on Work Teams, Dallas, Texas.

Nowatari, M., and S. Nanboku. (1997). "Quantitative Estimation on Relationship Between Work Types and the Teamwork Level of Work Teams in the Ladies Innerwear Sewing Maker Plants: Industrial Teamwork Dynamics, Part 2. *Journal of Japan Industrial Management Association, 48*(4), 166–173.

Primary Health-Care Teams

United Kingdom National Health Service

Julie A. Slater and Michael A. West

The aim of this chapter is to discuss the failures of primary health-care teams in the United Kingdom. The chapter begins with a description of primary health care within its organizational and historical context. We describe how the history of primary health care has led to failure in effective teamworking. We suggest some solutions, and we draw on basic tenets of teamworking in the organizational sciences to propose a model for teamwork in health care.

What Is Primary Health Care?

Primary health care is the first level of contact that people have with their health system, the first element of a continuing health-care process that brings health care as close as possible to where people live and work (World Health Organization, 1978). It addresses the main health problems in the community by providing appropriate promotive, preventive, curative, and rehabilitative services. At the Alma Ata Conference in 1978, the World Health Organization (WHO) set a target that by the year 2000, all peoples of the world should attain "a level of health that will permit them to lead a socially and economically productive life." It saw primary health care as the key to attaining this target. The Alma Ata declaration specified that primary health care should provide the following: health education and promotion, maternal and child health care, immunization, prevention and control of locally endemic disease, appropriate treatment of common diseases, and essential drugs. This broad interpretation suggests

This case was prepared to serve as a basis for discussion rather than to illustrate either effective or ineffective administrative and management practices.

the necessity of involving a wide range of health-care professionals who need to collaborate over a wide range of issues. It follows that if primary health-care practitioners are to coordinate care for people and offer them a flexible mix of skills, then they must work together in coordinated ways that embody a wide range of skills within primary health-care teams (PHCTs).

Primary health care is the central component of the UK's National Health Service (NHS). From its inception in 1948 and throughout its development, the NHS has mirrored a national commitment to providing health care, free at the point of service, to those who are in need, according to principles of equity and equality.

The organization of primary health-care delivery in the community, in the UK, has recently increasingly emphasized team-based working, but teamwork in primary health care is not a new idea. Its development began in 1920 when local health authorities established health centers. They thought these could provide a focal point for provision of health services, and there was an assumption this would encourage family doctors to work in a team with other family doctors and with community nurses (district nurses, health visitors, and midwives). Prior to the NHS Act of 1948, however, these professions continued to work quite independently, and there was little evidence of collaboration. As Taylor explains, "Many of the tensions and problems of professional co-operation found in today's NHS can be traced back into the history of each groups' separate development" (1991, p. 8).

Following the creation of the NHS, and after a bitter struggle, family doctors were permitted to maintain their independent contractor status. Separate organizations administered services that family doctors and community nursing and allied services provided. Although family doctors and community nurses were expected to collaborate in providing primary health care to their communities, no physical structures or management policies were in place to ensure that this happened. Today, the extent of joint working varies considerably between practices. In some instances collaboration is facilitated by shared premises, although studies have indicated this is not a necessary requirement (Cant and Killoran, 1993; McClure, 1984). Since 1948, numerous governmental reports have urged teamworking in primary health care, though legislation has not been implemented to make this happen.

The composition of PHCTs across the UK now varies from small general medical practices comprising one family doctor, receptionist, and practice nurse to large primary care networks that include multiple family doctor partners, receptionists, managers, practice nurses, and attached community nursing, health visiting and midwifery staffs. Such networks may include nurse practitioners, pharmacists, chiropodists, clinical psychologists, and social workers.

Since the origin of the NHS, family doctors have been self-employed, under contract to the NHS to provide 24-hour care for patients registered on their list. Each family doctor cares for an average of 2,000 patients (Marsh, 1992). Family doctors accept responsibility as first-line diagnosticians, referring their patients to hospitals for further specialist treatment or to other members of the primary health-care team or to social welfare services. They also provide 24-hour care for their patients and offer home visits for those too infirm to visit their premises.

The Problems of Health-Care Teams

Problems currently facing primary health care are an outcome of its history of ad hoc development coupled with the common assumption that if groups of primary health-care professionals are given the title of *teams,* joint working will result.

Although many reports refer to the primary health-care team, none provides a usable or practically meaningful definition of what one is. It is generally assumed that a team is always the best arrangement, and that telling practitioners that they are members of one will in itself bring all the cooperation necessary (Øvretveit, 1986, p. 2).

A number of UK Department of Health reports have attempted to define the primary health-care team. One of the most quoted reports emphasizes interdependence of complementary skills and common purpose of primary health-care workers:

> A primary health care team is an interdependent group of general medical practitioners and secretaries and/or receptionists, health visitors, district nurses and midwives who share a common purpose and responsibility, each member clearly understanding their own function and those of the other members, so that they all pool skills and knowledge to provide an effective primary health care service. (Department of Health and Social Security [DHSS], 1981, p. 2)

Why is the rhetoric of teamwork in health care not applied in practice? Below we consider historical obstacles created by the organizational context, lack of clear objectives, team composition, team size, and team communication and decision-making processes—basic concepts in the organizational sciences that have not been utilized in the development of teamwork in health care.

Most primary health-care professionals would recognize the need for interdependence and shared purpose, although studies have shown little appreciation of the roles and responsibilities of other team members (Poulton, 1995) and some role ambiguity and conflict among team members (Slater, 1996). Indeed, difficulties associated with co-ordinated teamworking were recognized in national reports (DHSS, 1981) that reviewed community nursing services in England and concluded that many primary health-care teams exist in name only. As recently as 1992, the UK Audit Commission Report (Audit Commission, 1992) drew attention to a major gap between the rhetoric and reality of primary care:

> Separate lines of control, different payment systems leading to suspicion over motives, diverse objectives, professional barriers and perceived inequalities in status, all play a part in limiting the potential of multi-professional, multi-agency teamwork...for those working under such circumstances efficient teamwork remains elusive. (p. 20)

Thus, the piecemeal development of primary health care over its history has led to a number of structural, historical, and attitudinal barriers that stand in the way of efforts to promote teamwork in primary health care. More specifically they include:

- the independent contractor status of family doctors and their unique payment systems in the primary health-care team
- separate lines of management
- lack of an agreed model of leadership
- lack of professional mutual role understanding and respect
- dominance of family doctors and the medical model
- lack of understanding of organizational factors affecting teamwork
- lack of prequalification teamwork training for professionals in primary health care
- lack of clear team objectives and feedback on performance for primary health-care teams
- failure of many teams to establish even minimum opportunities for team meetings and team reviews of strategies, processes, and objectives

- the unmet need to base practice and teamwork on strategic identification of health needs of local populations
- deep historical professional divisions, exacerbated by gender differentiation, which characterize the primary health-care context (West and Slater, 1996, p. 29).

Organizational Context

Below we consider how the organizational context of these groups, their lack of clarity about objectives, and problems of composition, leadership, and team processes have historically created these difficulties.

In recent years, models of team effectiveness have tended to emphasize the organizational context within which teams perform (Hackman, 1990). This includes consistent reward systems for the whole team, including payment methods (such as team-based bonuses) and recognition. Education and training also influence team effectiveness, but the management and organizational structures may be critical above all.

Clear team tasks and objectives, guided by the wider organization, are vital if teams are to perform effectively. In particular, it is essential to ensure that management systems do not give teams conflicting objectives, and, in general, single lines of management are required to support and guide teamwork. Where there are multiple lines of management (as is the case in primary care with different managers for district nurses, midwives, practice managers, health visitors, receptionists, and family doctors), problems of teamwork are exacerbated to an extent that threatens people's ability to function as a team.

Øvretveit (1986) notes that it is essential that the service be properly coordinated and managed in order to ensure that there are no gaps or duplications of services. Many of those in primary care do not regard organization and management as central issues, and these are seen in health care as issues that will sort themselves out. Further, the organization of a high-quality and effective service for clients is considerable and complex. Because basic aspects of team organization are neglected, primary health-care teams spend valuable time struggling with major problems that could have been avoided if managed strategically from the outset. Øvretveit emphasizes that:

> Structures, boundaries and objectives are especially important in
> view of the emotionally-demanding work which most team members

undertake, the high workload, and new and challenging types of work in the community. The role of senior management is crucial in defining and agreeing on organization, and their commitment to teamwork and to resolving the problems presented by new types of service and professional practice is essential. (1986, p. 58)

Recent models of team performance (that Guzzo and Shea, 1992, described) consistently emphasize the powerful impact these organizational context factors have in directly and indirectly determining team performance.

The degree to which the organization encourages participation, of all team members, in objective setting and decision making are also important factors in developing collaboration. Organizations can also provide relevant information that enable teams to effectively achieve their objectives. Availability of resources, such as people (for example, sufficient nurses to administer immunizations), equipment, money, and constraints in the work technology (for example, repeated malfunctions in the primary-care team's computing system or too few workstations) are also dependent on the organization.

Unclear Team Objectives

Professionals working in primary care and particularly family doctors, practice nurses, health visitors, district nurses, midwives, receptionists, and practice managers have (theoretically at least) collective and interdependent responsibility, along with patients and carers, for promoting the health and well-being of the local population. However, the extent to which that collective and interdependent responsibility is overtly recognized and acted upon varies considerably. Similarly, the clarity of shared objectives varies from crisp annual primary health-care team objectives to nebulous mission statements about improving the health of the local population.

West and Poulton (1997) in an examination of primary health-care-team functioning in 68 practice teams in the United Kingdom compared team processes of primary health-care teams with those of NHS management teams, community psychiatric teams, social services teams, and oil company teams. They used a well-validated and widely used quantitative measure of team functioning: The Team Climate Inventory (Anderson and West, 1994). On four dimensions of team functioning—clear objectives, participation in decision making, task orientation, and support for innovation—primary health-care teams scored significantly lower than the other team types. Their research suggested that primary health-care teamwork is less well developed than these other groups and that the main predictor of primary health-care team effectiveness is the clarity of and commitment to team objectives of members of the primary health-care team (Poulton, 1995).

However, attempts to overcome these problems are often unsuccessful because of the deep historical divisions between the professional groups involved. In one study by Wiles and Robison (1994), interviews were conducted with practice nurses, district nurses, health visitors, and midwives in 20 general medical practices. Midwives and health visitors were generally the least integrated. Topics identified as issues were team identity, leadership, access to family doctors, philosophies of care, and misunderstanding and disagreements about team members' roles and responsibilities. They concluded that attempts to change attitudes within the primary health-care team in an effort to produce greater democratic teamwork appear to bring only limited change. It seems likely that significant change will only be achieved if the circumstances under which the professions work change in ways that elevate their status (p. 330).

Team Composition

The size of primary health-care teams varies from small general medical practices comprising one family doctor and three or four other people to large practices with more than 40 primary health-care workers. The concept of team, therefore, historically has been applied to a wide range of organizational entities in primary health care, and, in some circumstances, the term is an inappropriate description, especially where it applies to a group of professionals who make little or no attempt to collaborate in the delivery of primary health care. This seriously adds to the confusion and frustration of those attempting to promote teamwork in health care.

Stott (1994) has remarked upon the interpersonal implications of larger primary health-care teams. He explained that there are new and greater communication needs in the big primary care networks of the 1990s. Every additional team member takes more formal and informal time for interaction, and these complex contexts absorb more time than simple working arrangements.

Team composition refers not just to the size of the team, but also to its homogeneity or heterogeneity in terms of demographic factors such as age, sex, educational level, training, ability levels, status, attitudes, personality, and values. Research has indicated that different aspects of homogeneity and heterogeneity affect different team outcomes (Jackson et al., 1991). For example, teams composed of people from diverse professional backgrounds (such as primary health-care teams) have the potential to produce better and more creative decisions than professionally homogeneous teams, but only if they can effectively manage the conflict characteristic of such teams.

Such issues of professional division, status, and gender differences are highly salient in primary health-care teams. Further, different socialization processes for doctors and nurses and separate basic and postbasic training for primary health-care professionals are significant in shaping attitudes toward teamwork. Stokes (1994) suggests that attitudinal barriers to teamworking, which function at an un-conscious level, are a product of these different backgrounds and training, which shape values, attitudes, and priorities. Medical training involves institutionalized and prolonged dependency of junior doctors on their seniors, from which the junior doctors eventually emerge to defend their new independence. This can degenerate into a counterdependent state of mind, denying the mutual interdependency of teamwork and the actual dependency on the institutional setting of general medical practice.

Group Processes
Communication, Decision Making, Participation

Interaction between team members also depends greatly on local circumstances, with some teams holding regular meetings to review strategies, objectives, and team processes and others never holding team meetings. However, in general there is a relatively clear role definition and differentiation and particularly where primary health-care professionals share premises, they have an organizational identity as a work team.

Bond and others (1985) examined interprofessional collaboration in primary health care via a survey of health visitors, district nurses, and family doctors. They used interviews, questionnaires, and records of 309 pairs of professionals (comprising 161 family doctors and health visitors, and 148 family doctors and district nurses) that had patients in common to explore the extent of collaboration. The research results suggested that family doctors had a moderately good understanding of the district nursing role but a very poor understanding of the health visitor's role. Levels of collaboration between family doctors and community nursing staff were low. There is little evidence that this has changed in the last 12 years (Field and West, 1995). Mc-Clure (1984) conducted a survey of 48 health visitors and 45 district nurses attached to general practices, one-third of whom were working from premises with attached groups. Health visitors were not enthusiastic about progress in teamwork, and community nurses generally reported that communication with practice staff was usually only about specific immediate patient issues rather than team objectives, strategies, processes, and performance review.

Having described rather pessimistically the historical obstacles to teamworking in primary health care, we conclude by describing the more limited research on successes, and offer prescriptions for improving teamworking in this health-care setting.

Developing Effective Teamwork in Primary Health Care

The work of the primary health-care team is now subject to measures of performance effectiveness and increasing accountability for meeting objectives and attaining standards of care, especially given central government concerns with value for money in health care. There are clear relationships at the level of provider unit between inputs (material and human resources) and outputs (standards of patient care, health gain). Increasing accountability means that practices now need to undertake population health needs analysis, set objectives, decide on processes for achieving these, and perform practice audit and measurement of objectives. If these outcomes are to be achieved, team members must work together to most effectively maximize the use of their scarce resources. Previous research clearly demonstrates this.

For example, primary care teamworking has been reported to improve health delivery and staff motivation (Wood, Farrow, and Elliott, 1994) and to have led to better detection, treatment, follow-up, and outcome in hypertension (Adorian, Silverberg, Tomer, and Wamasher, 1990). Jones (1992) reports on one American study in a primary health-care setting showing that families receiving team care had fewer hospitalizations, fewer operations, more physician visits for health supervision, and less physician visits for illness than control families. Overall, research-based evidence of teamworking in primary health care in the UK is consistent with research in other sectors in suggesting the value of this way of working for effectiveness and efficiency. However, the context of primary health care is such that there are substantial historical barriers to cooperation and collaboration in its delivery. Researchers repeatedly have called for these to be removed or reduced if the efforts of those who seek to build more effective teamwork are not to be frustrated.

Developing Effective Teamwork in Health Care

How can the organizational sciences be used to improve the team-based delivery of primary health care? In an authoritative review of teamworking, Shea and Guzzo (1989) make a series of research-based recommendations for developing effective teamwork:

1. *First, individuals should feel that they are important to the success of the team.* When individuals feel that their work is not essential within a team, they are less likely to work effectively with others or make strong efforts toward achieving team effectiveness. Roles should be developed in ways that make them indispensable and essential.

2. *Moreover, individual roles should be meaningful and intrinsically rewarding.* Individuals tend to be more committed and creative if the tasks they are performing are engaging and challenging. If their work is monotonous or partial, people are less motivated (Hackman, 1990).

3. *Teams also should have intrinsically interesting tasks to perform.* Just as people work hard if the tasks they are asked to perform are intrinsically engaging and challenging, when teams have important and interesting tasks to perform, they are committed, motivated, and cooperative (Hackman, 1990).

4. *Individual contributions should be identifiable and subject to evaluation.* People have to feel not only that their work is indispensable, but also that their performance is visible to other team members.

5. *There should be, above all, clear team goals with built-in performance feedback.* Research evidence shows very consistently that where people are set clear targets at which to aim, their performance is generally improved. For the same reasons it is important for the team as a whole to have clear team goals with performance feedback.

To what extent are these conditions met in UK primary health-care teams? By and large, the first three conditions generally hold true for such teams. However, it is rare for individual contributions to be measured and for feedback on performance to be given. Moreover, primary health-care teams tend not to have clear, specific objectives and goals (West and Poulton, 1997). And feedback on their performance against those objectives is rarely available. This represents an area where there is great opportunity for improved team functioning. The UK government is directly addressing this in its white paper (National Health Service Executive, 1996a), *Choice and Oppor-*

tunity, which encourages pilot schemes to promote these ways of working. So the key challenge for any team is to develop clearer objectives to guide work activities and coordination among team members. How can this best be achieved in primary health care?

Weldon and Weingart (1994) describe the importance of planning in teams for achieving team goals, and propose five ways of supporting team work:

1. Goals should be set for all dimensions of performance that contribute to the overall effectiveness of the team.

2. Feedback should be provided on the team's progress toward their goals.

3. The physical environment of the team should remove barriers to effective interaction (consider the difficulties faced by cross-surgery nursing teams).

4. Team members should be encouraged to plan carefully how their contributions can be identified and coordinated to achieve the team goals.

5. Team members should be helped to manage failure, which can damage the subsequent effectiveness of the team.

The NHS, therefore, should give guidance on setting local objectives for primary health care. Primary health-care teams then must set and monitor progress toward objectives locally. If these are truly primary health-care objectives, rather than only general medical practice objectives, the whole team, including community nurses and other professional groups and patients, should be involved in determining them (in accordance with central government targets).

A further potential difficulty is that family doctors are rewarded in different ways from their professional counterparts in primary health care. The latter are salaried by their respective employing organizations. Family doctors' reward arrangements comprise bulk payments, salary, performance-related pay, and a piece-rate system. Research in organizational behavior suggests that the application of individual bonus or performance-related pay systems is often ineffective in promoting productivity (Markham, 1988; Marsden and Richardson, 1992) and may militate against team working. Incentives have proved rather more successful where they are used to reward groups for group performance. Such schemes lead to small but significant improvements in group performance.

Recent UK government initiatives (National Health Service Executive, 1996b) offer some important possible solutions in the form of the following: salaried options for family doctors employed within the NHS, thereby regularizing team payment systems; practice-based contracts enabling team-based objectives to be derived; and flexibility of appointments encouraging consideration of human resource needs beyond professional boundaries.

As long as the structure of health care militates against the development of clear, shared team objectives, then attempts to encourage effective teamwork require health-care practitioners to swim against a powerful tide. Nevertheless, it is clear from a wealth of previous research that teamwork is precisely the means by which to best achieve the effective delivery of primary care to local populations (West, 1994; 1996). In the organizational sciences, the challenge is to draw upon the knowledge we have gained from theory, research, and practice and to apply them to primary health care.

Questions for Discussion

1. How does organizational culture influence the effectiveness of teamwork?
2. What types of culture are most conducive to teamwork?
3. What effects do team members' status, power, and professional diversity have on team working?
4. Does gender influence team processes and outcomes?
5. How can organizational context influence team functioning?
6. Is the context of health care inappropriate for the introduction of team-based working and why?
7. How can teamworking be most effectively promoted in health-care settings?
8. Should the health-care team include the patient or clients?

The Authors

Julie A. Slater has a Ph.D. in occupational stress and teamworking from the University of Wales College of Medicine (UWCM) and is a lecturer in nursing research at the University of Wales, Swansea. She has had posts as research fellow at the Sheffield School of Health and Related research and the Institute of Work Psychology, Sheffield University. Prior to that she was a clinical fellow with the Teamcare Valleys' Project (UWCM), where she worked as part of a multidisciplinary team supporting primary health-care workers in the development of research projects and teamworking. Slater can be contacted at University of Wales, Swansea, School of Health Science, Meadow Building, Singleton Park, Swansea, Wales, SA2 8PP; phone: 01792.518577; fax: 01792.518581; e-mail: j.a.slater@swansea.ac.uk.

Michael A. West is professor of organizational psychology at the Aston Business School, University of Aston, Birmingham, England. He has authored, edited, or coedited eight books including *Women at Work* (with Jenny Firth-Cozens, Open University Press, 1990), *Innovation and Creativity at Work* (with J.L. Farr, 1990, Wiley), *Managerial Job Change* (with N. Nicholson, 1988, CUP), *Effective Teamwork* (1994, BPS), the *Handbook of Workgroup Psychology* (1996), and *Developing Creativity in Organizations* (1996). He also has written more than 100 articles for scientific and practitioner publications, and chapters in scholarly books. His research interests are in innovation and creativity at work, team and organizational effectiveness, and mental health at work.

References

Adorian, D., D.S. Silverberg, D. Tomer, and Z. Wamasher. (1990). "Group Discussions With the Health Care Team: A Method of Improving Care of Hypertension in General Practice." *Journal of Human Hypertension, 4*(3), 265–268.

Anderson, N., and M.A. West. (1994). *The Team Climate Inventory: Manual and User's Guide.* Windsor, England: NFER-Nelson.

Audit Commission. (1992). *Homeward Bound: A New Course for Community Health.* London: HMSO.

Bond, J., A.M. Cartilidge, B.A. Gregson, P.R. Philips, F. Bolam, and K.M. Gill. (1985). *A Study of Interprofessional Collaboration in Primary Health Care Organisations* (report no. 27, volume 2). Newcastle-upon-Tyne, England: Health Care Research Unit, University of Newcastle-upon-Tyne.

Cant, S., and A. Killoran. (1993). "Team Tactics: A Study of Nurse Collaboration in General Practice." *Health Education Journal, 52,* 203–208.

Department of Health and Social Security (DHSS). (1981). *The Primary Health Care Team. Report of a Joint Working Group of the Standing Medical Advisory Committee and the Standing Nursing and Midwifery Advisory Committee (The Harding Report).* London: DHSS.

Field, R., and M.A. West. (1995). "Teamwork in Primary Health Care 1. Perspectives From Practices." *Journal of Interprofessional Care, 9*(2), 123–130.

Guzzo, R.A., and G.P. Shea. (1992). "Group Performance and Intergroup Relations in Organizations." In *Handbook of Industrial and Organizational Psychology* (volume 3, pp. 269–313), M.D. Dunnette and L.M. Hough, editors. Palo Alto, CA: Consulting Psychologists Press.

Hackman, J.R., editor. (1990). *Groups That Work (and Those That Don't): Creating Conditions for Effective Teamwork.* San Francisco: Jossey Bass.

Jackson, S.E., J.F. Brett, V.I. Sessa, D.M. Cooper, J.A. Julia, and K. Peyronnin. (1991). "Some Differences Make a Difference: Individual Dissimilarity and Group Heterogeneity as Correlates of Recruitment, Promotions and Turnover." *Journal of Applied Psychology, 76,* 657–689.

Jones, R.V.H. (1992). "Teamwork in Primary Care: How Much Do We Know About It?" *Journal of Interprofessional Care, 6,* 25–29.

Markham, S.E. (1988). "Pay-for-Performance Dilemma Revisited. Empirical Example of the Importance of Group Effects." *Journal of Applied Psychology, 73,* 172–180.

Marsden, D.M., and R. Richardson. (1992). *Motivation and Performance Related Pay in the Public Sector: A Case Study of the Inland Revenue* (Discussion paper no 75). London: London School of Economics, Centre for Economic Performance.

Marsh, G.N. (1992). *Caring for Larger Lists in The Future of General Practice.* London: BMJ.

McClure, L.M. (1984). "Teamwork, Myth or Reality: Community Nurses' Experience With General Practice Attachment." *Journal of Epidemiology & Community Health, 31*(1), 68–74.

National Health Service Executive. (1996a). *Choice and Opportunity—Primary Care: The Future.* London: HMSO.

National Health Service Executive. (1996b). *Primary Care: The Future.* Leeds: Department of Health.

Øvretveit, J. (1986). *Organization of Multidisciplinary Community Teams: AA Health Services Centre Working Paper.* Brunel, England: Brunel University, Brunel Institute of Organizational and Social Studies.

Poulton, B.C. (1995). "Effective Multidisciplinary Teamwork in Primary Health Care." Ph.D. dissertation, University of Sheffield.

Shea, G.P., and R. Guzzo. (1989). "Groups as Human Resources." In *Research in Personnel and Human Resources Management* (volume 5, pp. 323–356), K.M. Rowland and G.R. Ferris, editors. Greenwich, CT: JAI Press.

Slater, J.A. (1996). "Occupational Stress in Primary Health Care." Ph.D. dissertation, University of Wales College of Medicine.

Stokes, J. (1994). "The Unconscious at Work in Groups and Teams." In *The Unconscious at Work: Individual and Organisational Stress in the Human Services,* A. Obholzer and V.Z. Roberts, editors. London: Routledge.

Stott, N. (1994). "The New General Practitioner." *British Journal of General Practice,* January, 2–3.

Taylor, D. (1991). *Development of Primary Care: Opportunities for the 1990s.* London: Kings Fund Institute and Nuffield Provincial Hospitals Trust.

Weldon, E., and L.R. Weingart. (1994). "Group Goals and Group Performance." *British Journal of Social Psychology, 32,* 307–334.

West, M.A., and B.C. Poulton. (1997). "A Failure of Function: Teamwork in Primary Health Care." *Journal of Interprofessional Care, 11*(2), 205–216.

West, M.A., and J. Slater. (1996). *The Effectiveness of Teamworking in Primary Health Care.* London: HEA.

West, M.A. (1994). *Effective Teamwork.* London: British Psychological Society.

West, M.A. (1996). "Introducing Work Group Psychology." In *The Handbook of Work Group Psychology,* M.A. West, editor. Chichester: Wiley.

Wiles, R., and J. Robison. (1994). "Teamwork in Primary Care: The Views and Experiences of Nurses, Midwives and Health Visitors." *Journal of Advanced Nursing, 20*(2), 324–330.

Wood, N., S. Farrow, and B. Elliott. (1994). "A Review of Primary Health Care Organization." *Journal of Clinical Nursing, 3*(4), 243–250.

World Health Organization. (1978). *Alma-Ata 1978. Primary Health Care: Report of the International Conference.* Geneva: World Health Organization.

Redefining the Team Implementation Strategy

Blue Cross Blue Shield of South Carolina, Myrtle Beach Operations

Myriam G. Alonso, Robin Tebben, and Frances Cahill

This case describes how Blue Cross Blue Shield of South Carolina, Myrtle Beach Operations, seized the opportunity to start a new facility as a team-based organization, its largest full-scale organization-wide implementation of teaming. This study explains the pitfalls of the endeavor, which required the organization to redefine the team-implementation strategy, and it describes the experiences of two teams to illustrate how its teams function.

Background

The Myrtle Beach Operations, a division within Blue Cross and Blue Shield of South Carolina (BCBSSC), does business as Palmetto Government Benefits Administrators (PGBA). It is a TRICARE (formerly known as CHAMPUS) health insurance claims-processing center for retired military members and their families and for the families of active-duty members.

The division opened its doors in February 1994 with 550 employees, and it almost doubled its size in 1996, after a sister division won another contract. Today it has more than 1,000 employees and processes approximately 9 million claims every year for 19 states.

Getting Started

When preparing to write this case study, Myriam Alonso asked Jeff Littlefield, vice president of operations, what prompted the organization to utilize teams. He responded, "I am afraid we always viewed

This case was prepared to serve as a basis for discussion rather than to illustrate either effective or ineffective administrative and management practices.

ourselves as more of a paper-processing organization, not as a customer-driven organization. The main reason for us to move to any form of teams is for all associates to know that the work they do ultimately affects the customer."

Customer service has become a decisive factor in maintaining and growing any kind of business. TRICARE Management Activity (TMA), the government office that administers TRICARE contracts, is increasing its focus on customer satisfaction. In anticipation of higher expectations from TMA and other customers, upper-level management continues to align business strategies with the team-based organization to exceed the customers' expectations. The teams implementation is an example of the business strategies to accomplish that. It allows work teams, or PODS (an abbreviation for Processing Operations with Dedicated Services), to perform most of the functions the different departments handled in traditional claims processing. As will be discussed further, teams were designed to improve responsiveness and customer satisfaction by having each team retain the ownership of the claim it handles until it has completed processing the claim. Another key element of the business strategy is known as the 1-1-1 Initiative, which focuses on achieving the following:

- A customer should only have to contact us 1 time to get a problem resolved.
- The PODS team will resolve the customer's problem within 1 week of identification.
- If requested, a manager will speak to a customer within 1 hour of request.

With the teams implementation, Littlefield created a new organization structure based on the PODS team to overcome the limitations of traditional health insurance claims-processing operations. Figure 1 illustrates the traditional process.

In the traditional system, employees in the Coding Department were responsible for applying the various codes to claim forms and circling and highlighting information to facilitate the keying process. The Keying Department was responsible for the data entry of the fields on the claim form. If the claim did not present any problems, it would result in a processed claim, paid or denied. Claims needed intervention about 40 percent of the time and would be sent to other departments, depending on the nature of the discrepant information. The Suspense Department was responsible for resolving on-line edits that appeared when a claim was keyed (for example, discrepancies such as different spellings of a patient's name on the claim form and in the file).

Figure 1. Traditional claims processing.

Wide arrows represent the direct processing of a claim. Fine arrows represent the processing of a claim, depending on the kind of intervention required.

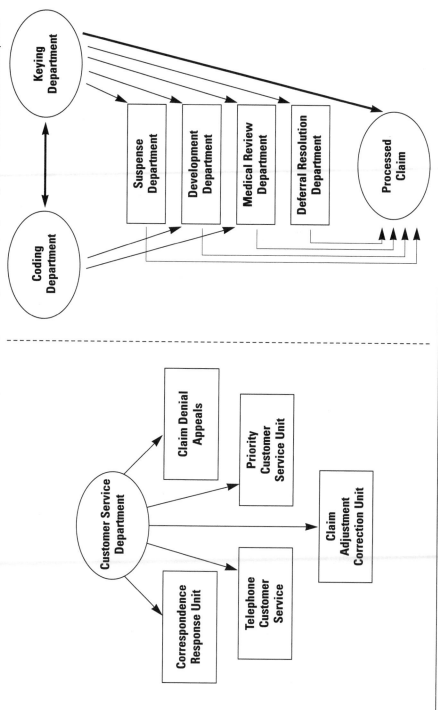

In the Development Department, employees researched, by telephone or correspondence, information that was incomplete or missing. If a claim required research for medical necessity, it would be sent to the Medical Review Department where claims were resolved based on TRI-CARE policy (for example, questionable procedures). To handle additional review of claims for the more complex set of edits that TRICARE prescribes, claims were sent to the Deferral Department (for example, duplicate claims or pricing inconsistencies). The Customer Service Department was a completely separate division that had very little interaction with the Claims Division. Separate units handled correspondence response, telephone customer service, claim adjustment correcting, priority customer service, and claim denial appeals. When corrective action was necessary because of contact with a customer, the claim could be routed to different units for resolution. No one associate had accountability to resolve a customer's problem.

With the new team-based organization, a different process was put in place, which had a direct impact on the type and composition of the work teams. The new work teams include three levels of claims associates—claims associates I, II, and III (CAI, CAII, and CAIII). Currently all three levels are in direct contact with customers. CAIs and CAIIs research claim information by communicating with customers via telephone or mail, and CAIIIs answer telephone inquiries from customers. The functions are currently organized as follows:

- CAI
  —coding
  —keying
  —suspense
  —development
  —customer service
- CAII
  —deferrals
  —adjustments
  —reprocesses
  —customer service
- CAIII
  —telephone inquiries
  —correspondence
  —adjustments
  —customer service.

The next step for the customer service strategy and the composition of the PODS teams is to phase out the three job levels to replace them with one position—the claims service associate—which will encompass all the functions described above.

Work teams were designed so that each team could perform most of the functions different departments handled in traditional claims processing. A PODS team contains between 20 and 25 members with the following typical composition:
- CAI, 10 employees
- CAII, 4
- CAIII, 6
- workflow clerk, 1
- medical review nurse, 1
- manager, 1.

The CAI codes and keys each claim's information into the computer system and researches and develops any required information missing from a claim. The CAII reviews deferred and suspended claims, researches and corrects any discrepancies, and updates files and third-party liability claims. The CAIII researches and responds to telephone inquiries and written correspondence from customers and reprocesses and adjusts claims as needed. Other required team members are the nurse, who investigates and researches medical necessity according to policy for services provided, and the workflow clerk, who sorts incoming claims and correspondence, distributes them for processing and performs preliminary research. Finally, the manager role is to ensure the accurate processing of claims, correspondence, and telephone inquiries, to motivate and direct team members, and to achieve and maintain optimum levels of performance. From the PODS, claims also may be routed to specialty teams as needed.

The most specialized functions were assigned to support teams outside the PODS. Figure 2 illustrates the system of team-based claims processing within the PODS and support teams. The new team structure was designed to allow the team to own each claim throughout the entire process, as opposed to the traditional structure where the claim goes from department to department until completion. Each associate in the team became accountable for the correct resolution of the customer's claim or service request.

Initial Implementation

A consulting firm assisted BCBSSC during the first year by delivering team training. Strengths of this initial implementation were upper management buy-in and excitement and that team training became part of the job requirements, just like technical training. The

Figure 2. System of PODS and support teams-based claims processing.

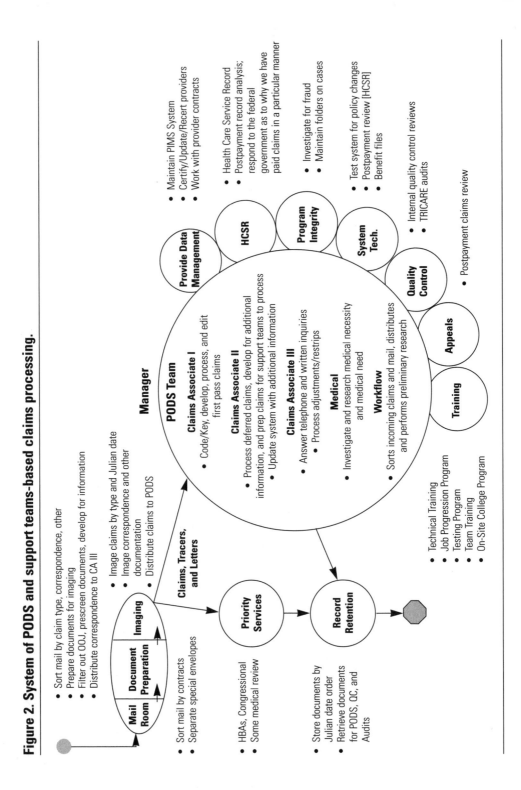

Mail Room
- Sort mail by claim type, correspondence, other
- Prepare documents for imaging
- Filter out OOJ, prescreen documents, develop for information
- Distribute correspondence to CA III

Document Preparation / Imaging
- Image claims by type and Julian date
- Image correspondence and other documentation
- Distribute claims to PODS

Manager

PODS Team

Claims Associate I
- Code/Key, develop, process, and edit first pass claims

Claims Associate II
- Process deferred claims, develop for additional information, and prep claims for support teams to process
- Update system with additional information

Claims Associate III
- Answer telephone and written inquiries
- Process adjustments/restrips

Medical
- Investigate and research medical necessity and medical need

Workflow
- Sorts incoming claims and mail, distributes and performs preliminary research

Provide Data Management
- Maintain PIMS System
- Certify/Update/Recert providers
- Work with provider contracts

HCSR
- Health Care Service Record
- Postpayment record analysis; respond to the federal government as to why we have paid claims in a particular manner

Program Integrity
- Investigate for fraud
- Maintain folders on cases

System Tech.
- Test system for policy changes
- Postpayment review [HCSR]
- Benefit files

Quality Control
- Internal quality control reviews
- TRICARE audits

Appeals
- Postpayment claims review

Training
- Technical Training
- Job Progression Program
- Testing Program
- Team Training
- On-Site College Program

Claims, Tracers, and Letters
- Sort mail by contracts
- Separate special envelopes

Priority Services
- HBAs, Congressional
- Some medical review

Record Retention
- Store documents by Julian date order
- Retrieve documents for PODS, QC, and Audits

opportunity to be part of a new strategy that could overcome the limitations of the old way of doing things was also a strength.

In 1995, after the first year of operations, several events interrupted the progress of the team implementation. First, continuation of the government contract was in question because of an obscure federal acquisition protest that had nothing to do with BCBSSC's performance. Second, it became apparent that it was too expensive to continue using the external consultants, and BCBSSC wasn't able to take over the team training without the use of external consultants. Finally, another subcontract award required the Myrtle Beach Division to rapidly expand and double its number of employees. These factors did not change the initial structure of the team-based organization, but it wasn't possible to continue with the teams approach for a period of time.

Redefining the Team-Implementation Strategy

In 1996, as the Myrtle Beach Operations almost doubled in size, Jeff Littlefield, the vice president of operations, decided to redefine the team strategy. At his impetus, the company added more teams and reconfigured most of the existing ones. He realized that it would be better to address employees' changes in behavior, expectations, skills, and attitudes through an internal training department.

As a consequence, he created the training department, and, in the summer of 1996, one of the authors, Myriam Alonso, joined the BSBSSC Myrtle Beach Division as the director of the Training and Career Development Department. Over time, Littlefield and Alonso and colleagues in her department identified the following weaknesses in the original teams implementation: The goals for implementation were vague, it lacked a needs analysis, it didn't have training reinforcement or support, and it used off-the-shelf curriculum. Kathy Norton, a director in the operations recalls, "There were no mechanisms for us to continue that path on our own and also integrate new team members into the team environment."

Alonso conducted research to find a new consulting firm to work with the Training and Career Development Department for the initial phase of training implementation with the expectation that her department would eventually assume full responsibility for maintaining and developing teams as internal consultants. The department consisted of two teams, technical training and team training, each of which has a training manager who was already on staff when Alonso was hired.

Currently, the department has 23 team members and 16 training specialists, of whom six were assigned to the Team Training Division.

Knowing that the Training and Career Development Department was responsible for team implementation, Alonso decided to begin implementation with her own team. She and the training managers began with a series of sessions called The Dream Team Workshop, which included team-building exercises to help the employees get to know one another, opportunities to bond, the development of goals and ground rules for each team, and development of the departmental mission statement. Once her department was functioning as a team, it led the company's journey to full team implementation with Wendy McKewen, the team training manager, and with the inspiration and direction of Littlefield.

The Training and Career Development Department also began to work with a second consulting firm. Together, they identified more missing pieces from the initial implementation and identified action plans. The following sections describe the key factors they identified as having impact on the success of team implementation and how they were addressed.

Creation of the Team Steering Committee

The department and the consulting firm created a steering committee to own the implementation process. Before redefining the team-implementation strategy and setting goals for the first and second years, the committee members developed a how far–how fast graph that depicts the level of responsibility each team owns. The committee also was responsible for moving the empowerment goals along on schedule and for taking the pulse of the team-implementation process. The committee is led by the training management. Originally, there were seven members, but the committee grew to 12 after representation issues arose. Figure 3 presents the how far–how fast graph for the entire operation.

Needs Analysis

Needs analysis questionnaires were administered to three levels of employees: workforce (a random sample of 10 percent), managers, and directors. The analysis for managers and directors made use of a multirater system that included peers, directors, direct reports, and self-assessments. There were needs analysis feedback sessions scheduled for all employees. The results of these sessions provided individual feedback for managers and above and provided information about the skills

Figure 3. How far–how fast level of team responsibility.

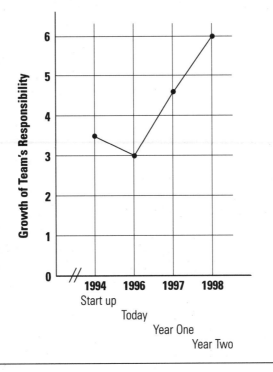

that were necessary to address in the team-training curriculum. The training management designed the curriculum. Some of the topics and workshops follow:

- Working in Teams
  —Clarifying Your Role in a Team-Based Organization
  —Participating in Meetings
  —Reaching Agreements in Teams
  —Making the Difference
- Communicating With Others
  —Personal Empowerment
  —Building Trust
  —Valuing Differences
  —Leading Effective Meetings
- Handling Conflict
  —Partnerships for Improvement
  —Taking Action
  —Rescuing Difficult Meetings.

Definition of Organizational Vision, Values, and Critical Success Factors

The team of directors and Littlefield held off-site vision and values sessions, which the consulting firm facilitated, in an effort to reach a consensus on the vision, values, and critical success factors for the changed organization. They reported the outcome of those sessions with the management team. During work in subgroups with facilitators they defined each value, its importance in the plan, and the observable behaviors that demonstrate them—behaviors to support those values that are expected from all of us. The outcome of the sessions was the following vision for BSBSSC:

> To be the premier integrator of health care delivery programs, customer service and technology by consistently exceeding our customer's expectations through highly involved employees committed to excellence.

We Value

Customer Focus
Accountability
Open/Effective Communication
Human Dignity
Integrity
Excellence
Teamwork
Innovation

BCBSSC published the vision, values, and critical success factors in a pamphlet that each employee received at one of a variety of get-togethers for employees at which Littlefield spoke. Employees said they appreciated the opportunity to speak with Littlefield about the company and its future. The training department also incorporated the vision, values, and critical success factors in its orientations for newly hired employees.

Determining the Business Case for Teams

Executive management reached a consensus on the most important reasons for a successful team implementation. The key reasons it identified were to have a significant impact on customer focus, timeliness, process improvement, and quality of life.

Determining Objectives and Scope of the Team Implementation

In the team responsibility continuum, the steering committee established a long-term goal that teams will handle work inputs and outputs, including dealing with external customers and vendors, selecting team members, and scheduling their own time. Managers share expertise in personnel functions while transferring other functions to the team. We also determined the need to develop organizational support and allocation of resources; to focus on overall process improvements in claims processing versus fragmented departmental functions; to clarify the emergence of new roles for employees in each organization level; and to design systems for continuous learning aligned with new systems such as team compensation.

Setting Specific Empowerment Goals

The steering committee prepared a team responsibility schedule in order to empower the teams with new responsibilities and decision-making authority. It explained the team's responsibility, job, and duties. Prior to its release, the management team was responsible for planning and making arrangements to provide all the resources the teams needed to assume the new responsibility (for example, training, availability of reports, equipment, and materials). The schedule was shared with team members during the presentations of the workshop *Clarifying Your Role in a Team-Based Organization*. Table 1 on page 227 shows a sample of a team responsibility schedule. Teams will get additional responsibilities in another phase that management will introduce later.

Creation of CORE Teams

To enable the PODS to carry out the new responsibilities and assume the new decision-making authority, new small teams, known as CORE teams, were created within each PODS team. CORE, for coaching, operations monitoring, resource coordination, and excellence assurance, became the most important vehicle, along with the new team structure, to make teams come to life.

In general, CORE teams have the following functions:
- C—coaching
  —peer coaching
  —team interviews for personnel selection
- O—operations monitoring
  —productivity reporting
  —help desk contact
  —team meetings
  —ordering of materials
  —coordination
- R—resource coordination
  —scheduled time off

—work schedule
- E—excellence assurance
  —problem identification
  —quality control (QC) reporting
  —continuous improvement
  —bright idea program.

Subgroups of the 45 managers determined the needs of each CORE team and prepared the documentation showing what each team needed. The needs included both optional and required tools and resources. The number of members in each CORE team (usually referred to as the C team, O team, and so forth) fluctuates between two and six in each PODS. Members rotate every six months with some members participating longer for transition purposes.

CORE teams are working extremely well for those managers who are supportive of the team-based organization. There are still other managers that are resistant to change, perhaps because they are threatened by the shift of managerial responsibility to the team. The difference between their teams is evident during team-training sessions. Off-site meetings are planned with managers to celebrate the CORE teams successes and to discuss barriers to implementing them. The meetings are part of the preparation to move forward with the other phases in the team responsibility schedule.

Clarifying Expected New Roles for Leaders

Executive management determined current and future levels of management responsibility for the following categories in an effort to define the managers' new roles:
- team performance and productivity
- quality
- business and finance
- customers
- managing performance
- training
- human resources
- coaching
- planning
- specialty projects
- personal development.

A successful transition to the new role is essential to the team strategy, but it proved to be one of the most difficult challenges to implementation. On the basis of our experience, we recommend that

Table 1. Sample team responsibility schedule, March–July 1997.

Category	Job	Duties and Description
C	Peer coach	Provide coaching and help to other team members; train new members; conduct training to improve team member technical skills.
C	Interview	Provide input to selection of new team members; serve on PODS interview team.
O	Productivity reporting	Compile PODS productivity report; coordinate reporting of team and division productivity with managers and directors.
O	Help desk contact	Maintain equipment and files and notify help desk when needed; keep log of equipment malfunction, downtime.
O	Team meetings	Determine when to call meetings (minimum of one per month required); establish agendas; schedule room; notify staff.
O	Ordering	Requisition supplies, equipment, and materials within budget, as needed.
O	Productivity reporting	Obtain and communicate data on performance of all teams to aid in meeting performance objectives.
O	Coordination	Contact other teams, departments, and shifts to obtain information, materials, services.
R	Scheduled time off	Determine leave schedules (cannot schedule time off you do not have).
R	Work schedule	Determine work hours within established core hours; determine phone schedule.
E	Problem ID	Identify claims and service quality problems and share results with team.
E	QC reporting	Monitor rebuttal process with Quality Control Department, enter internal QC results into system; share internal and QC Department statistics with PODS; coordinate internal claims QC efforts.

planning for the managers' new roles take place at the time of the needs assessment. Early planning would provide the opportunity to prepare and develop responses to those needs prior to releasing the team responsibility schedule that delegates new responsibilities and decision-making authority to team members. The results of the analysis and goals for future levels of responsibilities are summarized in figure 4.

During the team-training sessions and the team meetings that training specialists attend in order to provide feedback, it became evident that some managers were having difficulty transferring responsibilities and allowing team members to assume their new roles in the team-based organization. Therefore some of the differences in teams' levels of development were not a reflection of natural differences between teams but because of their managers' resistance to change.

To gather feedback and evaluate the progress in the team responsibility schedule, an off-site meeting took place with managers, directors, and vice presidents. As a result, a CORE teams survey was conducted to determine how far each team had progressed on the schedule. A needs assessment for managers also was conducted. The findings were used to design a curriculum and individualized development plans. Individualized plans are used to improve both management skills and relevant skills needed to develop their teams through the team responsibility schedule.

The Role of the Team Training Unit

The creation of the Team Training Unit within the training department was based on the premise that people who have close working relationships can be trained to work as a team. Team training improves employee performance both as team members and leaders. Participants learn to build effective working relationships, to engage in joint problem solving, and to reduce interpersonal friction, and the results are expected to be improved communication, creativity, decision making, and team performance. But getting participants to buy in and actually use the skills learned in training is not always easy.

At BCBSSC, team trainers do a good job at attending one team meeting (for each assigned team) per month. Trainers model the use of skills learned during the training sessions and reinforce practical process skills. They provide balanced feedback to the team on development areas and positive aspects of the team skills to ensure application of skills learned. Trainers also have proved to be valuable at facilitating interventions to guide teams through conflicts and problem solving, among other things.

Figure 4. Leader role clarity.

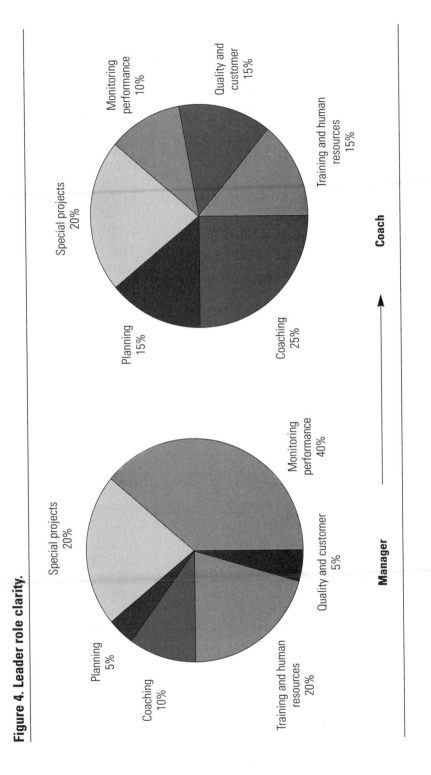

A Look at Two PODS

The process BCBSSC went through as it became a team-based organization is most evident through the experience of the teams. Following are the descriptions of the transition by the managers of two PODS, both of which exceed acceptable levels of team performance. Robin Tebben, manager, wrote the description of PODS 12, and Frances Cahill, manager, wrote the description of PODS 23.

Experience of Members of PODS 12

In a new team situation, I have learned, everyone is looking for his or her place on the team. "Will I be a leader or a follower?" "How will I get along with other team members?" "How will I fit into this new situation?" All the employees are concerned about how the situation will affect them individually. Everyone is apprehensive about leaving a comfortable, long-term situation. But change is good and can be used productively. At BCBSSC, fortunately (or unfortunately), upper management chose a group of associates with strong personality traits to be on my team. Most were up to the challenge.

As a manager, I discovered that the use of *we* and *our* in daily vocabulary helps form a bond—a sense of ownership among team members. I also have found that the team mirrors the manager's thoughts, feelings, and attitudes. Therefore, the success of the team begins with the manager, who must always be positive even in difficult situations. Things are always changing and the manager, or the first leader of the team, must be flexible to these changes.

START-UP OF PODS 12. I am proud to say that our PODS, then PODS 16, was the first to conduct a team launch in conjunction with the Team Training Division. Even before the team moved to its new area, I felt that we needed to get together in a nonthreatening but professional social setting. I had many years of experience as a manager for other companies, but I was a new manager with Blue Cross and Blue Shield of South Carolina and was excited to meet all the new team members. I threw a pizza party luncheon, and afterward the Team Training Division held a team-building session. It was a fun way to break the ice because no one really knew anyone else. It went very well, and using the activities during the team-building sessions, the Team Training Division helped to give some insight and understanding.

Part of this first team meeting was to set ground rules. The team members and the trainer discussed and agreed to the following rules:
- Establish agenda, set priorities.
- Conduct round robin at each meeting, option to pass always available.

- Be polite, respect others, listen, use the Golden Rule.
- Allow constructive criticism, don't put others down, leave out personal problems.
- Stay positive, be open minded.
- Maintain focus, arrive at a team consensus.

Two years later, and with the addition of new associates, we are still following these same ground rules. These rules help establish one's place on a team because expectations are clearly defined.

During the beginning of PODS 16, we went through many changes. We had to move from our assigned workstations, and we packed and moved no less than four times in about two months! Jeff Littlefield, the vice president of operations, indirectly helped during this bonding time. During a four-month transition, he allowed us to dress casually, which promoted a feeling of freedom to be ourselves. Team members were relaxed; they didn't form cliques or set up barriers around themselves. The situation created an atmosphere of acceptance.

Another icebreaker occurred in 1996, when PODS 16, calling ourselves the Robert Palmer Girls, won the Best Group Award for Halloween. In a parody of a rock video, the 22 women in our team dressed in black. With Robert "Bert" Palmer, our only male associate, singing in the front, our PODS performed a rendition of "Addicted to Love." It was a lot of fun and a great stress reliever. It also gave us time to be silly, which is a requirement if you want to enjoy your job.

Since that time, PODS 16 has worked through many changes and challenges. I continually request special projects for the team. Our team was originally selected to be one of two teams to handle the difficult and time-consuming task of processing durable medical equipment (DME) and intravenous (IV) drug therapy claims exclusively. Because of this job and the fact that a large number of associates were new in their positions, our production started to drop. The person who keyed the largest number of DME claims in one day received what I called the DME crown, which I made from a manila folder and painted with magic marker. This recognition was such a success that two years later, that same crown has been passed around our PODS and has moved into other PODS and other departments.

After the crown moved to another department, I tried a new tactic. The division goal for claims associates 1, is to key 85 claims a day. I offered anyone who could key over 100 claims in one day—a large number for even experienced associates—an award and a McDonald's Happy Meal. When I first made this offer, the team told me that it would be impossible to achieve that number of claims. Occasionally, one or two would make the goal and receive the award and a Happy

Meal. One day all team members ganged up on me—the eight claims associates 1, five claims associates II, and nine claims associates III. All but a few of the CAIIIs keyed over 100 claims. I had to buy 16 Happy Meals to congratulate the members of the 100 Claims Keyed Club! Now, we've done better and have a 150 Claims Keyed Club, a 200 Claims on History Club, and Most Claims Keyed in One Day for PODS 12, which currently is 380 claims.

As a team, we successfully lobbied to have all teams trained on DME and IV processing. Two of the associates on our team conducted the original DME training and assisted the Training and Career Development Department in writing desk procedures. This team is still the only one that processes contracted IV claims, and that work necessitates that associates get additional training and responsibilities. Because of these responsibilities, we were asked to move (again) to the PODS 12 area, which reflects the relevant contract numbers, and we became PODS 12.

STRENGTHENING THE BOND WITH TEAM-BUILDING EXERCISES AND TEAM MEETINGS. During a regular workday, we do not have time to interact with other team members so we must schedule for team-building exercises and team meetings. As a manager, sometimes I hear, "We have too much work to do. Can we reschedule?" My answer is always no. I feel that you must make time for your team members and their concerns. Everyone's questions and ideas are important. If you solve a problem in the beginning, it will not become a crisis. We consistently have regular team meetings and try to include team-building exercises at each meeting. These exercises are great ways to relieve stress, and my associates are better producers after these sessions.

One team-building exercise that our group enjoyed was also a real eye-opener. Associates wrote on a piece of paper an inanimate object they felt best described them, but didn't reveal it to anyone else. The pieces of paper were collected and randomly taped to associates' backs. Each associate then had to ask questions that the group would answer to help in identifying the word. Much laughter erupted during this part of the exercise. After everyone had correctly guessed the words taped on their backs, the group had to determine who originally wrote down that object.

The exercise was an eye-opener because associates discovered that they did not see one another the same way. Shy people, for example, did not see themselves as shy, but as outgoing. Someone wrote down an iron because she felt that she was always smoothing things out. The group incorrectly guessed that the word had been written by another associate whom they felt got upset easily and was, therefore, hot all the time. Everyone guessed that the object rock was the selection of one associate who argues every point, but that team member had written down a clock because she just "keeps on ticking." The rock was the choice of the quiet team member who felt she goes by the book. Another wrote down a diving board because it was necessary for her to dive right into the work to get all of it done. Still another wrote down a river because she flowed over the daily rocks, rolled through the twists and turns, or rolled with the flow. The exercise was great fun and a stress reliever, and it gave everyone insight into the other associates he or she is working with. The Team Training Division and upper management chose PODS 12 to demonstrate team-building exer-cises to reporters from Myrtle Beach's Sun News, which was featuring a story on it in a Sunday focus article.

There also need to be limits set. We always have an agenda and follow the team's ground rules. Training courses are provided when needed. The small amount of time that is required to learn the correct procedures is a time saver in the long run because it ensures that procedures are done correctly the first time.

I have heard other managers make statements like, "I have been a manager since _____, and we have never needed this team thing," "I am the manager, and they should do what I tell them to do," or "It's a waste of my time and my employees' time. We have to make our production numbers." Typically these statements come from managers who have had difficulty with teaming and have reverted to the old methods. The best method is to keep an open mind and incorporate the best of the old method into the new.

In every management position I have ever had, I have always felt strongly about two things that were told to me long ago:

- *I should be the best employee that I have.* What I mean by this is, How can you expect your associates to respect you and learn from you if you cannot do the job yourself? I have had management positions where I have done data entry, opened cases of merchandise, stocked shelves, or mopped floors—whatever was needed. If your people see that you are interested in doing a good job, whatever the job is, then they will respect you and model their behavior after your example. One-on-one training, as well as cross training, is vitally important. I treat people, whether it is an associate, peer, or upper management with respect and professionalism. These three elements—ability to do the job, one-on-one training, and treating people well—are basic requirements for excellent communication.

I am also the first to use the expertise of my associates if I am uncertain. This helps to build their confidence.

- *You are only as good as your employees.* The idea behind this statement is that your employees reflect your training and your ideas. As the manager, your job performance is judged on the performance of your staff. If you do not train your associates and support your associates, it reflects on your management style. I am always open to new things, especially knowledge, and I hope that I have given this idea to my people. My one goal is to inspire my team to be confident and enthusiastic about their position.

CORE TEAMS. PODS 12 was empowered with various CORE team responsibilities before the CORE guidelines were implemented. From day one of PODS 16, I gave ownership of certain responsibilities to different associates to help them bond. At the time, we did not call it CORE teams, but it did create an atmosphere where they had to work together.

Under coaching, we had always teamed experienced associates with new associates. We have three different coaching teams: New CAIs teamed with experienced CAIs; CAIIs teamed with CAIs to help with deferrals and keying errors; and CAIIs teamed with CAIIIs to work difficult adjustment and reprocessing deferrals. Some team interviews had been completed prior to CORE implementation.

Under operations monitoring, our workflow had organized many of the responsibilities along with the coteam captains. During one of our first meetings, we determined that we needed two team leaders, one to handle organization of office-related meetings and scheduling and one to be the social director. So the two team captains and the workflow clerk handled the team meeting schedule and agenda, called the help desk when needed, and ordered supplies. Productivity reporting was done on a marker board at the department level. For resource coordination, we had a calendar centrally located to log any requested leave. It was based on the honor system and was never abused. Guidelines were given to all and were followed. One of the team captains took care of correcting any operational productivity analysis system (OPAS) variances.

We established a QC team early on for the excellence assurance group. Selected members of the QC team would review all quality control errors, send rebuttals to the QC department, and then share any information, good or bad, with the whole team.

Thanks to the management skills and team training that the company offered, I feel that I have the skills to be a successful team manager. Training was extremely helpful in many ways but I have found it most helpful in resolving those negative situations that are difficult to handle but occur in every team. I have always had an open mind and have been confident enough in my ability, as well as my associates' abilities, to allow my team to succeed or fail in whatever they try. I was very open to the formal conversion to teams and, due to my associates' success, have become even more open to the changes and opinions they offer. I feel fortunate that I work for a company that continually looks to the future.

Experience of PODS 23

PODS 23 has been a team since April 1996. When the team was formed, it was made up of existing BCBSSC employees and associates new to the organization. We recognized that we were a mix of new and experienced talent with varying strengths and weaknesses. As a team, we were all eager to focus on getting our jobs done well while having a good time.

It was evident that there was a lot of energy in the new PODS 23. As the manager, I knew that I had to direct this energy in a positive way in order to make things work. I knew my job as the coach would be scrutinized by the team, and they would react accordingly. With this in mind, I knew I had to be positive, outgoing, and honest. After all, that is what I would want in a manager. I know that if I work hard and follow through, they will too! I can only expect from them what I would expect from myself.

PODS 23 had its introduction at a pizza luncheon, and those luncheons became very popular. In the beginning, the team tried to have one at least once every other month on a Friday. Those Fridays became special because we worked 7:30 a.m. to 4:00 p.m. with a half-hour lunch. I know this is not anything spectacular, but it was a nice reward for a job well done and a good way to start off the weekend. We have these luncheons occasionally now as well as occasional small breakfasts. All of us laugh about the fact that we like to eat together—and often. Around the holidays, we have a voluntary potluck team luncheon or breakfast. It gives us another chance to get together and get better acquainted. The team also has a community bowl that members fill with whatever goodies they choose—candy, vegetables, chocolate, fruit, and the like. It's nice to see different people filling the bowl.

In addition to our own activities, we attend the sessions that the Team Training Division offers us. It provides team members with an avenue that allows us to relax and get away from our everyday jobs while giving us an opportunity to bond with one another and voice ideas, opinions, and concerns. I feel the team training has helped to fine-tune our teamwork skills. And as associates join and leave the team, team-building exercises are a way for us to break the ice and get to know one another. As a manager, I have attended several manager-related training sessions, including The Changing Role of the Manager, Guiding Conflict Resolution, The Empowering Leader, and Interpersonal Skills. These sessions are geared to assist in effectively coaching teams. I particularly enjoyed The Empowering Leader workshop, where I learned concepts that motivated associates. After I attended the workshop, my PODS team attended a similar training session. Toward the end of the session, I joined the team. All of us evaluated our team empowerment on a scale of one to five (with five being the highest level of a self-directed and highly motivated team) on where we currently feel we stand and where we would like to be in the future. I am proud to say we all felt we were currently between level three and level four, which is a transition level working toward a partnership with the leader in the decision-making process. We agreed that we would like to progress to a level where we are a highly functioning partnership, level four, but not a complete level five, because we think the manager should maintain responsibility for disciplinary actions and work reviews.

PODS 23 has regular team meetings. The duration depends on the agenda. Every meeting has an agenda and involves almost all of the team. During one of our first team meetings that a Team Training Division representative attended, we came up with meeting ground rules. All of us discussed them and agreed to them, and we now attach them to the team meeting agenda. Our grounds are as follows:

- Respect.
- Speak one at a time.
- Share information.
- Keep things positive.
- Stick to the agenda, come to a consensus.
- Be on time for meetings.

I feel the team members of PODS 23 are at a comfortable work level with one another. If issues arise, a meeting is called to address the situation or problem immediately. It is nice to know that the people I work with are concerned about having an open environment and feel comfortable to address issues as needed.

CHANGES AND CHALLENGES. PODS 23, along with other PODS, successfully transitioned from an outgoing standard contract to a new managed-care contract. The work levels and information were all different. This really made us stronger. There were a lot of technical training courses that I made sure we all attended while still attending the scheduled team-training sessions. Everyone was helping others with their workloads and checking on their neighbors to make sure they were doing okay. We had more meetings at which strategies were planned to balance the workload. Projects were delegated not to just one person, but to several people. This sharing conveyed the message that I do not play favorites, but rely on everyone to do an outstanding job. And we had more meetings to go over our numbers and percentages. I felt it was important that team members knew where we stood in regard to productivity and efficiency. We made time for meetings and training, to help one another, and to learn, relax, and have team luncheons. We did not put things off by saying there was no time because policies like that may cause situations to snowball and hurt everyone later. We made time. As a team, we realized that, yes, work is important, but it is just as important to have a smile while working. It makes the atmosphere much more pleasant.

Along with the changes and challenges of work, individuals and the team have goals to meet. Team members get status reports on our performance at team meetings, through e-mail, through feedback sessions, through status reports that an associate or I put on the marker board, and through rewards for a job well done. The PODS had a toy called the flinger, which was a rubber ball of all fingers. Each day we gave the flinger to the associate who was most productive that day. We also gave candy bars for a job well done; no level of associate was left out because everyone has to work hard to do a solid job. I rewarded associates who met their goals by taking them to lunch in the cafeteria or at a local restaurant. These occasions also helped me to learn more about the individual and vice versa.

CORE TEAMS. The PODS were empowered with various CORE team responsibilities, even before the CORE guidelines were implemented, and I know that these responsibilities made us a success.

Currently the coaching team trains new associates as they enter the PODS through a formal desk procedure process. They attend production and change order meetings and participate in team interviews. PODS 23 had new associates sit and work with the associate level that they were currently in training for and, of course, we always made them feel welcome.

The operations monitoring team handles the daily CHOS (claim productivity report) and sends this info via e-mail to the team. That team also obtains the daily ending unkeyed claims report and sends this information to the appropriate person via e-mail. The associates involved in this group also help me run reports and input the numbers into the computer so team reports can be analyzed and distributed. I feel team members have a better understanding of what is going on with our workload through this activity because they are not just hearing it from me, but actually seeing the results firsthand. The operations group also prepares the team agenda and facilitates the meeting. PODS 23 had associates involved in preparing the team agenda and meeting, CHOS, and unkeyed reports prior to the CORE team implementation. We also had a team leader, and CAI, CAII, and CAIII captains to help in organizing meetings and workload information and reports.

The resource coordination team currently handles the time sheets and OPAS completion. In addition, the team assists in monitoring the leave calendar. These new CORE groups are a delightful addition to the team. They fully understand the necessity of completing the time sheets in an accurate and timely manner.

The excellence assurance team is responsible for handling the team's QC rebuttal of claims. Upon completion of the QC audit and rebuttal process, the E team associates share the information with each associate that was audited. In addition, they also share the overall general results with the PODS during our team meetings. Any important information that needs to be shared for educational purposes through findings in the QC is done by these associates through a PODS minitraining session or e-mail, or both. (PODS 23 performed these QC duties from the beginning to ensure that associates were performing quality work and that everyone was sharing and learning information on proper procedures.)

CORE teams are a great mechanism in welcoming new associates and getting them on the right track. Recently we had a new associate with a high QC error rate due to payment errors. The associate made errors when selecting the rendering provider and when calculating dollar amounts when the other health insurance paid prior to TRICARE. One hundred percent of her claims were audited for quality control. The peer coach from the C team and a member of the E team assisted her with her questions, reviewing her claims audit, showing the errors and how to resolve them. QC audits showed a reduction in payment errors from more than 3 percent to less than 1 percent (the standard is 2 percent or less payment error rate). Expertise within the PODS together with the new CORE teams responsibilities and decision-making authority allow the team to meet and exceed its standards without the manager's intervention. PODS 23 is also known for maintaining its employee morale index above the acceptable level. In the yearly morale survey, PODS 23 is consistently found among the top six teams.

I am proud to say that I am very happy with my job. I love to feel challenged and produce quality results with associates whom I know are working just as hard as I am. I know these facts make PODS 23 what it is today. I have attended management skills and team training sessions in addition to our team-building sessions. I feel the information and skills learned and shaped in these sessions along with my own strong work ethics will only help my team and me become stronger. I am lucky to work for a company that strives to succeed in technological areas while focusing on the people too!

Lessons Learned and Challenges Ahead

According to Myriam Alonso, these two teams are not the only ones who have seen results, learned, and grown.

Team training curriculum has been delivered for all levels on schedule. For the most part, it has been maintained even when the claims volume dramatically increased unexpectedly and the pressure to meet the standards also increased.

Among the results of our efforts, we found the following:

- *Higher customer satisfaction, better timeliness, and problem resolution on claims.* The number of telephone inquiries from customers versus the number of claims processed is 6 percent less than at the sister division, which is not as advanced in teams implementation. Claims processing has been 15 percent faster than the government standard because of the reengineering of the claims process cycle allowed by the team structure.
- *Continuous improvement.* This quality initiative idea, generated in the Teams Implementation Steering Committee, was developed by Teryl Scholes, one of its members. The E members (excellence) of the CORE teams get involved to promote and gather information to submit "bright ideas" to the Quality Initiative Task Force. They contribute ideas that have originated with and are refined by the entire team. That process encourages the participation of members that would not get involved otherwise. This team-based component is in addition to the submission of ideas by specific individuals that has proven to be very valuable.

- *Career pathing and higher quality trained employees.* The C members (coaching) of the CORE teams get involved in determining the training needs and coordinating training schedules on the basis of direct feedback from each team. The composition of the PODS teams with members assuming the role of peer coaches also enhances the quality of training.
- *Increased morale.* The employee morale index is consistently 10 percent to 12 percent higher than that of the sister division, which is not as advanced in team implementation.

From the initial implementation as well as from the redefined implementation strategy that continues to take place, we at BCBSSC have learned many lessons. Some of the most important lessons we have learned during this implementation include the following:
- Assess the current situation as accurately as possible.
- Involve key stakeholders when developing the strategy to build commitment.
- Clearly define what the future culture should be.
- Clearly communicate agreed-upon strategy.
- Don't promise paradise. Team implementation is a learning experience that also involves frustration for some employees.
- Implement solutions as quickly as possible.
- Build internal consulting capabilities.
- Be prepared to commit to a lengthy process.
- Prepare management for the changes expected of them as they move from old-style supervision to team-style coaching.
- Design individualized development plans for managers with initial needs assessment.
- Implement accountability systems for managers and team members.
- Change!

Are there challenges ahead? We need to concentrate more on developing CORE teams, because they are vital to the success of the teams. We still need to work on holding managers and team members accountable for team implementation. It is important to minimize any management resistance so that eventually the managers will welcome the team implementation as they notice the benefits enjoyed by those who are fully supportive of the changes. We also need to work on developing partnerships of managers and team during interventions so that lasting improvement will occur. Finally, our biggest challenge lies in systems alignment. Managing team performance, the use of peer assessments, compensation, and selection for teams are areas to be explored.

Questions for Discussion

1. What was the major goal of Blue Cross Blue Shield of South Carolina in designing a team-based organization?
2. What kinds of changes were implemented to redesign the work process? What was the impact of the changes?
3. Why is it important to build internal consulting capabilities?
4. Why was The Dream Team Workshop a valuable team intervention?
5. Why did the organization experience some resistance to change from the old-style supervision to team-style coaching?

The Authors

Myriam G. Alonso oversees the Training and Career Development function at Blue Cross and Blue Shield of South Carolina, TRICARE Services. The health insurance claims-processing business has more than 2,500 employees. TRICARE Services processes millions of claims every year for a total of 36 states. Alonso is responsible for assessing training needs, developing and delivering the technical and customer service curriculum, and developing and administering the Job Progression Program and the Competency and Performance Testing Program for career development. She is also responsible for the organization-wide team strategy implementation and computer-based and multimedia training. Previously Alonso had been a training consultant for General Electric, Caribbean Operations, and held positions as Industrial/Organizational Psychologist at G. Cirino Gerena and Associates and the Medical Services Administration in San Juan, Puerto Rico. In addition, she taught undergraduate and graduate courses at the University of Puerto Rico, San Juan Campus. Alonso holds a bachelor's degree in psychology and a master's degree in industrial and organizational psychology from the University of Puerto Rico. She will complete her Ph.D. degree in the same field in 1999. Alonso can be contacted at Blue Cross and Blue Shield of South Carolina, 8733 Highway 17 Bypass, Surfside Beach, SC 29575; phone: 803.650.6100.

Robin Tebben is a PODS team manager at Blue Cross and Blue Shield of South Carolina, Myrtle Beach Operations. Her responsibilities include all functions necessary to adjudicate claims accurately and timely and provide related customer service in accordance with the regulations of the Department of Defense. Prior to that, she was a priority services representative for the same company. She also held management positions in the retail industry for Jones New York, Ames Department Store, Woodward & Lothrop, and US Shoe Corporation.

She has completed course work in business, accounting, commercial art, and real estate sales.

Frances Cahill is a PODS team manager at Blue Cross and Blue Shield of South Carolina, Myrtle Beach Operations. Her responsibilities include all functions necessary to adjudicate claims accurately and in a timely manner and provide related customer service in accordance with the regulations of the Department of Defense. She has been a priority correspondent for the same company and a claims associate III. Cahill has a bachelor's degree in business administration from the College of Charleston.

High-Performance
Top-Management Teams

United States Navy

Jay J. Janney

This case study examines how a high-performance federal agency achieved greater teaming performance. It examines the creation at the same federal agency of two top-management teams for two organizations with different training assumptions. By implementing one reorganization focused on eliminating all barriers to teaming (including physical, financial, and organizational barriers), the federal agency was able to implement several initiatives that reduced costs and improved its overall performance. A second reorganization that didn't follow the same processes had less success across the board.

Introduction

Perhaps the most difficult time for an organization to change direction is when everyone in it believes it is already headed in the right direction. Previous success strengthens this conviction that it's doing well, making change even more difficult. To change how an organization functions often requires altering the elements that support the structure, rather than altering the organizational structure itself. This case study analyzes a government agency whose executive director understood at an early date the agency's vulnerability to closure under the Base Realignment and Closure (BRAC) commission. The executive director needed to lead managers toward embracing changes to counter a threat they did not believe existed. Rather than attempt to convince managers of the seriousness of the threat, he chose to alter support systems in ways that required managers to change

This case was prepared to serve as a basis for discussion rather than to illustrate either effective or ineffective administrative and management practices.

how business was conducted. He did so through a reorganization that created two new organizations from the old one. The two were created three months apart. Although both organizations emphasized teaming, they operated under different assumptions and experienced different performance levels. This case study examines the two reorganizations' approaches to managerial teaming and the impact the changes had on managers and employees.

NAC's Environment

The Naval Avionics Center (NAC), in Indianapolis, Indiana, opened in World War II as the Lucas-Harold plant, producing the then top-secret weapon guidance system known as the Norden Bombsight. After the war ended, ownership of the center transferred to the Department of the Navy. The center expanded into aircraft avionics, communication systems, and missile guidance systems. NAC was a nonappropriated facility, which means Congress provided no money to run it. Funding came entirely from its successful bids for work from other government agencies. By law, if NAC failed to cover its costs, the center would be closed.

At its 1992 peak, the center employed over 3,400 employees, comprised of roughly 1,500 engineers and scientists, 1,200 technicians and skilled workers, and support personnel. The organization structure featured a dual military and civilian management team. A navy captain primarily focused on maintaining effective liaison with headquarters, and a civilian executive director guided strategy and policy. Beyond the dual executive structure, the facility featured a typical functional structure made up of 10 departments: project office, engineering research and development (R & D), engineering, quality, manufacturing, security, personnel, comptroller, procurement, and public works and information systems, as figure 1 shows. Each department branched into divisions and then into branches, sections, and sometimes work groups.

Early in the 1990s, NAC found itself in a puzzling environment. The 1991 BRAC commission had indicated to the executive director that the facility was vulnerable for closure, although its workload and employment levels hovered near record levels, hourly cost rates remained among the lowest of nonappropriated government agencies, and customer satisfaction ratings appeared respectable. The end of the cold war necessitated significant cuts in budgets and capacity—as much as 40 percent in certain areas. Accordingly, the navy faced significant pressure to close some facilities in order to reduce manufacturing capacity. NAC was indeed vulnerable.

Figure 1. NAC pre-1992 reorganization.

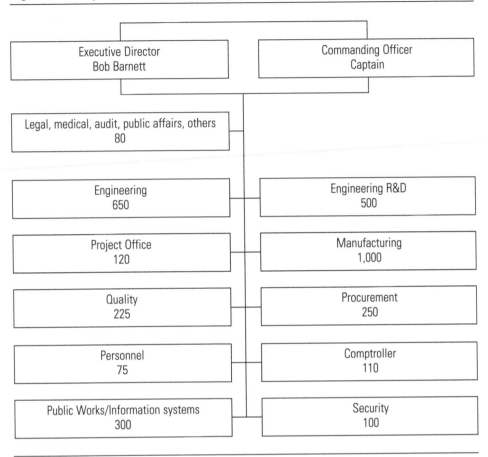

Despite the BRAC announcement in 1991, no managers or employees expected NAC to be closed. Their assumptions were that there were too many wasteful bases to be closed before NAC would be threatened. Generally the bases that were closed suffered from low workload and excess capacity, whereas NAC had solid workloads projected for several years. Managers believed if hiring freezes were lifted, NAC could easily employ another 1,000 employees.

Unlike the managers and employees, however, the executive director, Bob Barnett, was troubled by what he saw. He had spent his entire career at the Naval Avionics Center, beginning as an entry-level electronics engineer in the 1960s. Having served as executive director for 10 years, he wanted to leave the legacy of a viable facility. He considered closure a real threat, but faced the daunting task of convincing managers of it. In fact, it was not until after the BRAC 1993 results were published that any of the department directors became concerned about a possible closure. For the rest of NAC's employees, the threat of closure did not seem real until January 1995, when a local newspaper ran a front-page story indicating the mayor was lobbying the federal government to consider a privatization plan to keep the center open.

Prior to the Reorganization, 1988-1992

Before the reorganization took place, each NAC department had a director, at least one deputy, and a secretary, but beyond that there was no consistency. Some departments had one or two additional staff members, and some had as many as 25 with some redundant duties. For example, manufacturing employed a staff public affairs officer to support a joint venture created with a local university, whereas the center had a public affairs office for similar functions. Sometimes each department performed a similar function, but handled it somewhat differently. In engineering, for example, a department-level staff member might perform budget preparation, whereas a branch-level employee might be responsible for it in manufacturing.

NAC's reputation for customer service was for excellent cost, quality, and design, but also for frequent customer delivery delays. The monthly on-time shipment rate rarely exceeded 30 percent. A contributing factor to low delivery rates was an operating culture that could best be described as having a friendly rivalry among departments. Department directors were not deliberately uncooperative, but they rarely consulted one another when they attempted to improve their own departmental operations. By acting independently, they often created problems in the other departments. The so-called white wire improvement initiative exemplifies this problem.

The federal procurement system prohibits transferring certain types of materials among differently funded programs. For some commodity items, this greatly increases procurement, warehousing, and record-keeping costs. The manufacturing department, acting upon a submission to its suggestion program, purchased a $30,000 machine that could stamp words on the ends of the wire sleeves. The department then began buying only one color of wire (white), and stamping on the ends of wire the "color" the wire represented in the drawings and documentation. This procedure eliminated the need to buy seven other wire colors. Annual estimated cost savings exceeded $300,000. Manufacturing shipped several white wire radio boxes to the fleet without notifying the engineering department that the white wires were installed. The fleet learned about the switch from an extremely angry two-star field admiral! To avert a crisis, engineering rushed new radio boxes through manufacturing (disrupting other programs in the process), and dispatched several engineers to the fleet to remove the radio boxes that contained the white wire and replaced them with boxes that had the appropriately colored wires. The cost to engineering's overhead budget from the scrapped materials, lost time, and the like was more than $100,000. But no manager was fired, demoted, reprimanded, or rotated because of the fiasco.

Previous Efforts With Limited Results

Like most organizations that consider themselves progressive, NAC heartily tackled major management initiatives, such as total quality leadership, total quality management, ISO 9000, synchronized manufacturing, cycle time reduction, and concurrent engineering. From 1988 to 1992, the center spent over $3 million on different training initiatives, with mixed results. The center conducted two major reorganizations and several minor ones. In each reorganization the top-management team structure remained constant. Turnover occurred rarely beyond the occasional retirement. This constancy came at a cost. Before the reorganization, the Personnel Department's employee surveys indicated that employees increasingly believed the top-management team was out of touch with customers and employees. Typical comments were, "We only see Mr. Barnett on the floor when there's a tour." His and the directors' offices were known as Mahogany Row.

David Fogleman, the director of the Human Resources Organization, initially advised Barnett to make incremental changes. From 1988 to 1991, Barnett converted the executive cafeteria to general purpose conference rooms, eliminated reserved management parking spots, and directed each department to conduct weekly roundtables at which employees could discuss issues with their department director. Surveys indicated that employees considered the changes cosmetic or otherwise insignificant and compared reorganizations with games of musical chairs. For real change to occur, nonincremental changes were necessary.

Step One: Planning for the New Organization, Spring 1992

During the spring of 1992, Barnett ordered a new NAC-wide reorganization. Its stated mission was to tear down vertical chimneys—the organizational structure and culture that discourages employees in one department from communicating with employees in other departments—in order to improve customer satisfaction. The white wire episode exemplifies the problem companies with vertical chimneys have. Had employees in the manufacturing area notified anyone in engineering of their intention to send the white-wire radio boxes, they would have learned that the fleet would not accept them.

Unlike previous reorganizations, this one was the responsibility of the director of the Human Resources Organization, who formed a tiger team of all 10 department directors or their deputies. The Naval Avionics Center describes a tiger team as a cross-functional temporary problem-solving team of eight to 15 employees, who work full-time to propose solutions to a specific problem. Before any new organization charts were drawn, the team argued for two months on what systems the new organization would need to satisfy customer needs. Barnett hired a local university professor to facilitate the discussions. He scheduled off-site meetings so the teams could focus on the new organization. After an initial one-week meeting, the team continued meeting off-site one full day each week for further discussions.

The group agreed that cross-departmental teaming was a top goal, and it identified three initiatives to improve managerial teaming:
- Design the organization structure around teams.
- Design all work processes to encourage teaming where possible (including office layouts).
- Design teams to include a customer focus.

The team's immediate recommendation was to reduce the 10 departments to five. Departments would be part of the Avionics Group Operations (AGO) or the Corporate Operations (CO), as figure 2 shows. The AGO would include engineering, the project office, manufacturing and acquisition, and customer and fleet support departments, whereas the CO would include six divisions—comptroller, personnel, public works, legal, information systems, and total quality management (TQM). The AGO had 2,750 employees, and Corporate Operations about 650. The reorganization occurred in two stages. The AGO organizations were created on June 15, 1992, whereas the Corporate Operations organizations did not begin operating until September 15, 1992.

Step Two: The New Department Office Layouts, May 1992

For the AGO, the most radical and visible change was the department directors' move from Mahogany Row into a common cubicle area on the first floor in the center of the building, which they shared with

Figure 2. NAC post-1992 reorganization.

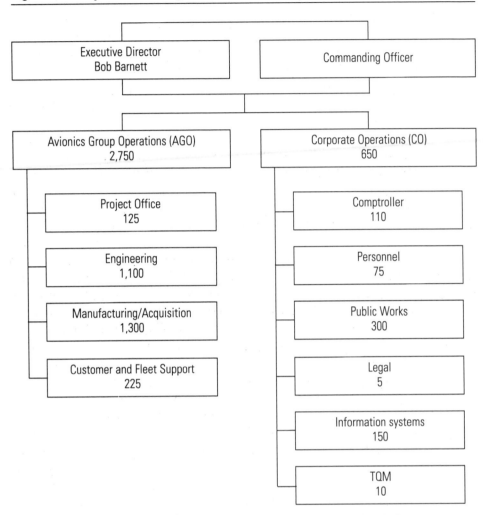

Note: AGO and CO were not layers of management, but represent the two separate reorganizations.

their respective staff. Their previous location in a building wing in which each office had private doors "protected" by a secretarial area had effectively discouraged informal traffic even among department directors.

In contrast, the new AGO area was at the intersection of two high-traffic corridors. The two outer walls along the corridors were 8 feet high, with windows every 12 feet. Managers were prohibited from covering any of the windows along the outside walls. Inside the glass fish-bowl, all walls were 4 feet high and any furniture taller than 4 feet had to be placed against an outer wall. The effect of the design allowed anyone to look into any of the offices from the hallway and observe any manager in a meeting or at work. In addition, offices were sited by function and not by department. This meant all the different department managers assigned to process improvement sat next to each other, rather than next to their department director.

The AGO concept intentionally promoted informality, encouraging fewer formal meetings, and more back-fence discussions at which employees could lean against a wall to chat with another employee. It took six months before employees felt comfortable walking into the area without a formal appointment to see someone, but eventually the concept took hold and employees began conducting business inside the AGO area, informally, without an appointment. Eventually, all new office renovations inside the plant incorporated the AGO open area concept wherever possible.

Step Three: Training Employees in the New Processes, June 1992

A week prior to the reorganization, the center conducted two separate two-hour sessions for each employee, training each employee on the new organizations and the new teaming emphasis. Barnett took care not to emphasize fears of BRAC's closings. Instead he emphasized how the center could grow despite the shrinking budgets if customers were better satisfied. The first session focused on how teams would improve customer service. The second session centered on teaming logistics (who would approve overtime, time cards, and the like). After the training sessions, people development associates (staff assigned to support the department directors) interviewed a sample of employees about the training. Although the new office layouts had caught their attention, the employees' show-me attitude consistently surfaced in the interviews.

Step Four: Fighting the Vertical Chimneys, July 1992

Although the departmental offices promoted communication among the departments, the problems related to vertical chimneys remained. Employees still identified themselves as departmental employees and focused their attention on improving departments. The problem was not that employees resisted teaming because they teamed well within their own smaller organizations. The resistance was to teaming across departments. To counter this, Barnett's tiger team recommended removing the vertical chimneys through intentional vertical-horizontal matrix teaming beginning with the department and division managers. The first step involved creating identical structures within each department where possible. In a break from past reorganizations, each AGO department and division now contained identical staff positions. The extra staff positions were either eliminated or consolidated at a division level.

Each department now featured a director and five managers ("associates") for process improvement, people development, and master scheduling. There were no deputies. In addition, each department received secretarial and business officer support from a team organizationally based in Corporate Operations. Each set of associates had a primary task of horizontally teaming with their fellow associates from the other departments. Their tasks focused on centerwide applications, not departmental.

Step Five: AGO Department Directors Begin to Team, Summer 1992

Initially the four AGO department directors operated independently of each other. They agreed to team and wanted to team, but found their schedules precluded regular meetings. During the first summer, they met with associates who themselves were struggling with making the teaming successful. One of the associates commented on how "the associates were at least trying to team, and this was more than the department directors were doing." In the directors' opinions they had teamed. They had given up their private offices and personal secretaries. They gave up staff members and funded cross-functional teams to improve interdepartmental processes. The departmental directors considered themselves good team players, so the criticism about their lack of teaming stung each one personally. Because their organizations were teaming, they felt they had sufficiently teamed. But employees felt otherwise.

Initially the teaming was limited by the managers' personalities. The friendly rivalry culture promoted individual achievement-oriented behavior, and rising to the top meant one had shown an ability to step in and direct a crisis to a successful outcome. NAC rewarded "firefighters" not "fire preventers." All four department directors were good friends in and out of work, but each had his own way of doing business. Each one's view was that his method had worked well in the past, and the others were welcome to adapt it to their use. The various styles contrasted greatly. Two managers had take-charge, but informal, styles; the third was very deliberate; and the fourth, a micromanager. Two were personal computer (PC) literate, but one refused to touch his PC. One spent considerable time at headquarters, and another rarely traveled at all.

Where the lack of teaming most manifested itself was in how the four department directors responded to common requests for information. The federal government constantly requests information, and many of these requests come from the center's customers who need the information to respond to congressional inquiries. One department manager ignored these requests, one attempted to plan months ahead in anticipation of them, and the other two typically responded as requests occurred. Some handled them personally, whereas others assigned a staff member to coordinate them.

It took the directors approximately three months to recognize that they didn't team well, and nearly two years to define the problem and solve it. The solution focused on incremental changes. They began with administrative procedures and then gradually worked toward full integration. Ultimately, responding to BRAC requests for information spurred them toward full teaming.

After a month, their first agreement involved having one secretary track all of their schedules on the same information system and provide them with daily printouts. From a practical perspective, this move finally allowed them to be electronically scheduled into a meeting together. It took almost two weeks to schedule the second meeting!

During a trip the four directors made to headquarters, they met for dinner and discussed how the new organization increased their workload. In comparing notes, they recognized that they faced several common duties, including performance appraisals and budget preparations. They agreed to delegate budget preparations to their business officers. In a subsequent meeting, the business officers requested that a single unified process be developed. It would save time and allow them to cover for each other. The directors agreed to try it. They each listed their individual requirements and agreed not to dictate how the requirements were to be met. In a meeting with Barnett, they proposed the same unified process for performance appraisals. Barnett readily agreed. He further encouraged them to respond to requests for information with a unified process.

That summer, the business officers implemented both processes, and the results pleased the department directors. There were two important outcomes. Because the business officers went out of their way to involve the divisions in the processes, they attained buy-in from the people who had to supply the input. One trick they used was to give each division manager a list of 10 requests for information pertaining to the previous year. The process they prepared gathered the information needed to address all 10 requests. If the division managers used the process, there was a good probability it would save them time. Given some prodding by the department managers, the division managers agreed to try it that summer.

As expected, requests for information arrived that fall, and the budget submission contained enough information to address most of them. The business officers were able to demonstrate to department and division managers that the summer process had saved them time.

To continue addressing the requests for information, the department managers rotated the assignment among staff members. If a request reached one director, the staff member who was assigned to coordination provided it to the other directors as well. Each saw the others' requests. The coordinator implemented a unified plan to save time. They developed a key rule that three directors could bind the fourth if he were absent from a meeting. This created periodic conflict, but the senior department director took it upon himself to privately "mentor" department directors who acted out of line. The coordinators took care to document the coordination that provided the department managers with an estimate on the time savings. It also provided encouragement to continue using a coordinator and the unified process. As the next round of BRAC requests for information neared, the department managers resolved to appoint an AGO BRAC coordinator.

One Fateful Day for Teaming

Having a coordinator helped the department directors to team, and having their staffs work together helped them team. But the need for teaming hit home in January 1994, when Barnett and the four directors attended an off-site meeting in Washington, D.C. Each site was asked to identify a skilled coordinator of the highest possible caliber. A top-flight person might reduce the damage the sites would face in the next round of closures. The message was clear to all in attendance: NAC could be closed.

The effect was immediate. Rather than employ a coordinator, the managers devoted most of the workday to meeting the BRAC response themselves. They met with each other frequently and soon began to delegate the lead for meeting certain reporting requirements. The Project Office Department manager took the lead on coordinating customer response evaluations and determining the impact on projects should NAC be closed. The manufacturing director took the lead on developing environmental impact statements. The coordinators took the lead on developing response kits to enable the directors to gather input more quickly. Facing a common enemy, they teamed together well.

Step Six: Funding Associate Team Initiatives, Summer-Fall 1992

The four AGO directors asked the various associate teams to improve centerwide processes. The center had previously employed tiger teams, but never funded them to actually implement their solutions. Employees were demoralized because the solutions had not been implemented. To counter this, the department directors shifted more than $15 million from divisional budgets directly to the departmental associate teams so they could allocate the funds back to the divisions. The goal was to encourage centerwide improvement and, in effect, to fund tiger teams and get results. At first the different associate teams encouraged the divisions to submit funding requests, which they would then prioritize. Two things happened. First, they received over $43 million in funding requests, which was nearly triple the amount available. Second, they recognized that the requests focused on improving divisions, not the center.

The department directors acted. They formed a tiger team of associates and assigned them the task of identifying the highest priority for improving the center before any funds could be spent. After 60 daily meetings led by a professional facilitator, the team's reported priority was to improve delivery times by decreasing cycle times. Because this seemed to be a process improvement effort, the department directors asked the process improvement associates to implement it. They asked the divisions to identify barriers to improving the center's process improvements. The results were first parochial, but, after having the division process improvement associates meet and review each other's complaints, several common themes emerged. The most important was a need to align and coordinate technical requirements.

Some engineering design requirements caused significant costs for manufacturing. If these could be changed, costs and time could be saved. After much argument, the engineering divisions found ways to revise their requirements while maintaining product quality and greatly reducing manufacturing process time.

The process improvement associates recognized that the changes were primarily a training issue. They next met with the people development associates and requested they implement the training portion of the solution. At first they resisted, but after a month of twice-weekly meetings, the process improvement associates persuaded them to coordinate and fund the training. It took a year for substantial changes to occur. For example, the scrap rate caused by drilling holes too near metal bends was halved (saving nearly $50,000), and changes in printed wiring boards improved the yield by 50 percent (saving nearly $100,000 annually).

Step Seven: Launch of Corporate Operations, Fall-Winter 1992

The Corporate Operations reorganization occurred differently from the AGO reorganization, and that group faced different problems. The original six CO divisions included legal, comptroller, human resources, information systems, public works, and TQM. Initially there was to have been a director for Corporate Operations position, which the executive officer (a navy commander) was to have filled. The six CO directors felt they would have less authority dealing with the AGO directors if they were only divisions, so they lobbied to be classified as departments. Despite protests from the AGO directors, Barnett agreed, so the number of departments went back up to 10.

The first significant problem that Corporate Operations faced involved developing a reporting structure for several semiautonomous groups that had previously reported directly to the executive director. All the groups dealt with centerwide issues, but did not easily fit any organization chart. Examples include the legal staff, sick bay, small business coordinator, safety office, command evaluation, and public affairs. Arbitrarily it was decided to absorb some of these groups and to create departments out of others. The primary consideration appeared to be whether or not the group's leader could identify any regulation that mandated a separate organizational form. Several of these groups continued to do business as usual and contributed little to teaming. Some departments attempted to integrate them. Others simply left them alone.

In addition, the six division directors and their associates in CO never truly had offices together. The AGO moved into an open area of the plant at a fortuitous time, but the CO initially had no area in which to locate. After 18 months, four of the departments located together inside an old conference room not far from the AGO area. The conference room had walls that prevented visitors from being able to see if managers were in the area. Because this was a temporary move, the offices were created out of makeshift office panels of varying sizes and colors. Labyrinth looking, the layout further discouraged visiting. Within a year, the four directors were moved to new offices in various locations throughout the plant.

The CO directors shared two secretaries. Business officers, failing to come to agreement on common reporting requirements, retained largely the same structures as they had prior to the reorganization, with the exception of having eliminated first-line supervisors. Where the AGO had three levels of management, the CO had five. The CO business officers compiled requests for information by hand, taking longer to complete than did the AGO business officers. This is ironic given that both sets of business officers organizationally reported to the same Corporate Operations branch!

The Human Resources Organization embraced teaming most quickly, establishing support teams for each AGO department. Members of the support teams began attending AGO departmental standing meetings and the people development associate team meetings. Acting as human resource subject matter experts, they joined in managerial discussions offering advice when concerns arose. This enabled managers to reach better staffing decisions faster. Likewise, the comptroller office located business officers with their customers. These analysts were present at standing meetings offering real-time answers to financial questions.

NAC Performance Results With Teams

Did improved teaming help NAC? By focusing on cross-functional teams, the center improved several customer satisfaction measurements. The center decreased costs and increased output while employing fewer employees. At the same time, however, general anxiety about the future clouded internal employee satisfaction measurements. When the BRAC commission announced its results, all performance indicators decreased, some substantially. In 1995, the BRAC Commission recommended closure. All performance indicators then fell, some substantially, and leave soared nearly 40 percent. What we don't know is whether it would have been worse without the teams' support for employees. Table 1 shows the changes in various performance measures from 1991 to 1996.

BRAC and the Future of the Naval Avionics Center

Half the closing criteria was based on performance and cost. On these measures, NAC looked solid. The other criteria for closure included "impact to the community." During this time, the Indianapolis area enjoyed one of the lowest unemployment rates in the country, less than 4 percent. The commission concluded that it was cheaper to close the facility and prop up other facilities that would

Table 1. NAC performance measurements.

Performance Measures	1991	1992	1993	1994	1995	1996
Head count	3,250	3,400	3,100	2,750	2,650	2,250
Workload orders (backlog, in months)	23	25	28	38	31	28
Customer satisfaction	3.2	3.2	3.4	3.6	3.35	NA
On-time delivery	30%	33%	35%	39%	40%	42%
Cycle time (months)	27	29	34	26	22	24
Employee satisfaction	NA	NA	3.3	3.2	2.5	NA
Sick-leave usage	55	58	53	65	105	111

cost even more to close. During final hearings, the commission concluded that the initial findings were flawed. Closing costs were greater than expected, and savings were less than forecast. Nonetheless, they let the closure finding stand, with amendment.

The NAC top-management team accepted the findings, but, in concert with the city of Indianapolis, it proposed a privatization plan featuring an even lower-cost alternative. The final BRAC commission recommendation included language encouraging the navy to accept the privatization plan. In a year of negotiations, over 15 Department of Defense contractors made proposals. The winning bidder, Hughes Technical Services Corporation (Hughes Electronics), won the right to privatize the facility. Two thousand employees were privatized in January 1997, and 80 percent of the remaining 165 government contingent employees were phased out in September 1997. The 25 or so remaining government positions coordinate BRAC issues for the facility and should do so through 1999. Virtually every employee was offered a position, and roughly 300 declined. Nearly all were government employees who were within two years of retirement eligibility and who sought to remain federal employees at other locations.

Lessons Learned

Because the AGO and the CO were formally established only a few months apart, but under different circumstances, several comparisons can be made about the relative successes of each. NAC documented some of these lessons, passing them along to NAC's headquarters as they reorganized. Some of these changes merit additional discussion.

A Unified Reorganization

Corporate Operation employees did not begin employing teams as soon as the AGO employees did. Although timing is primarily a reorganization concern, it did have an impact on teams. Many of the initiatives the AGO associates implemented never occurred in the corporate operation organizations. Funding for improvement initiatives excluded the corporate operations groups, which left them feeling cheated about the budget process.

Eliminating Physical Barriers

The AGO area was designed to facilitate teaming, whereas the CO never received a full common working area. It wasn't only the low walls that supported teaming, but also the emphasis on maintaining a clear visual appearance. The low walls concept has been incorporated into other areas of the plant, but with less success. This difference was partly because the AGO area looks open, whereas other areas allowed employees to barricade themselves with tall file cabinets and bookcases.

Customer Alignment

For Corporate Operations, teams were most successful when they aligned themselves with their customers. The AGO included the Corporate Operations employees as members of their teams, and greater cooperation ensued. Those employees recognized for their support continued to align with the AGO, whereas other corporate operations employees didn't. Providing customer feedback at formal performance appraisal times appears to have helped encourage teaming in both reorganizations.

Vertical and Horizontal Teaming

The AGO was most successful in developing horizontal teams of associates and in maintaining departmental teams. It was least successful in getting the different departmental associate teams together. Corporate Operations had its best success with departmental teams, but less success developing horizontal teams. Asking employees to team tridimensionally may introduce too many loyalty conflicts for most employees. Having budgets for both vertical and horizontal teams helped by fostering enough autonomy to accomplish goals while requiring teaming to accomplish others. The vertical teams had enough money to run a bare bones operation (payroll and some overhead). To acquire anything beyond that, the executive director required them to form horizontal teams, which he delegated to the AGO directors. For example, departments were not allowed to budget for new personal computers. NAC formed a team to develop a new personal computer acquisition program, which was then fully funded.

Focused Organizational Missions

The AGO teams found it easier to work together because they had fewer priorities to satisfy. The AGO directors centered on a customer-performance issue that employees understood. The most successful Corporate Operations teams were customer focused; the least successful were those that inherited most of the smaller semi-autonomous task groups. It is difficult finding common ground in one department for the safety, public works, sick bay, and library groups. It may be better to have these semiautonomous groups report to the executive director or commanding officer.

Conclusion

NAC may have lost the closure battle, but it won the long-term war. Despite massive downsizing occurring in the Department of Defense, NAC remains open with solid workload planned for the next five years. Indianapolis retains an employer that annually pumps over $300 million into the local economy. Hughes Electronics has identified several promising revenue streams that the NAC can pursue, and employment growth appears certain. Although the turmoil has impaired employee satisfaction, it will improve as the transition proceeds onward. Costs to the navy remain reasonable, and employees were not required to take pay cuts. The executive director could not stop the center from getting on the BRAC closure list, but he did keep the center from closing. For the employees who depend upon the center for their livelihood, privatization's impact has been little more than that of some of the reorganizations they endured during their long government careers.

Questions for Discussion

1. Despite the numerous management initiatives, employees initially remained skeptical about the new reorganization and the need for teams. What underlying cause might have caused this skepticism?

2. The center never really addressed the "passive resistors" to the new organization. It offered incentived retirements to some of the dissenters and created new roles for the others. How could this have been handled better?

3. Did you agree with upgrading the Corporate Operations divisions into separate departments? How would you have advised Barnett on the upgrade?

4. Why did the department directors act slowly to acknowledge they were not teaming well? Do you believe the incremental process was appropriate, or would some form of full immersion have been more effective? Would they have teamed as effectively at the end had they not faced the BRAC crisis?

5. Both the Human Resources Department and the various semiautonomous groups (for example, command evaluation, sick bay) served the entire center, but the Human Resources Department was better able to align itself with its customers. How important do you believe the changed organizational structure affected this? How might you have handled the dilemma of organizationally assigning the semiautonomous groups?

6. What changes would you have made to the Corporate Operations reorganization?

The Author

Jay J. Janney is currently working toward completing his dissertation in strategic management at the University of Kentucky. Prior to beginning his doctoral studies, he spent nine years as a management analyst and budget officer at the Naval Avionics Center, in Indianapolis, Indiana. He served on several teams, including one which created the administrative support plan for the Avionics Group Operations. He assisted in designing the Competency Aligned Organizations employed by NAVAIR. Prior to leaving federal service, he coached a 27-employee team which provided financial support to the entire center. Publications include *Business Horizons, Academy of Management, Strategic Management Society,* and *International Conference on Work Teams* proceedings. Janney can be contacted at 7637 Blackthorn Court, Indianapolis, IN 46236; phone: 606.257.2966; e-mail: jjjann0@sac.uky.edu.

Note

The author wishes to thank Keith Lusk for his cooperation in developing this case study. Any errors are the responsibility of the author; the views expressed in this article are solely those of the author and do not represent any official viewpoint of the United States government.

About the Editors

S teven D. Jones is an associate professor at Middle Tennessee State University and a member of a self-directed team with the industrial/organizational psychology program. He received a Ph.D. from the University of Houston in 1986. Jones teaches graduate courses in team performance measurement and training and has published 22 articles and book chapters in his field.

Since 1983, Jones has measured team performance in a wide variety of client organizations, including manufacturing, health care, retail, insurance, and military installations as well as his own university. He conducts several workshops each year on team performance measurement at national and international conferences and is currently writing a book on the topic.

Jones is certified as a Zenger Miller trainer by the international consulting, training, and education company in San Jose, California. He is also certified in return-on-investment training evaluation by Jack Phillips. He conducts most of his training for managers and team leaders.

Jones can be reached at the following address: Industrial Organizational Psychology Program, Middle Tennessee State University, Murfreesboro, TN 37132; phone: 615.898.5937; fax: 615.898.5027; e-mail: sdjones@acad1.mtsu.edu.

Michael M. Beyerlein is director of the Center for the Study of Work Teams and associate professor of industrial/organizational psychology at the University of North Texas. His research interests include all aspects of work teams, organizational transformation, job stress, creativity-innovation, knowledge management, the learning organization, and complex adaptive systems. He has published in a number of research journals, is a member of the editorial boards for *TEAM Magazine* and *Quality Management Journal,* edits *Team Performance Management Journal* and *Infrastructure: Sustaining Systems,* an e-journal, and is senior editor of the JAI Press annual series of books *Interdisciplinary Studies of Work Teams.* In addition, he has been co-editor with Steve Jones of two case books about teams, and he is currently co-editing a book with Sue Beyerlein on sustaining teams.

Beyerlein graduated with a major in philosophy from the University of Oregon in 1969, earned a master's degree in counseling and guidance from Oregon College of Education in 1976, and completed a Ph.D. in industrial/organizational psychology at Colorado State in 1986. He taught industrial/organizational psychology at Fort Hays State University in Kansas for three years.

Michael M. Beyerlein can be reached at the following address: Research Office Center for Study of Work Teams, University of North Texas, Terrill Hall, Room 346, Box 311280, Denton, TX 76203-1280; phone: 940.565.4551; fax: 940.565.4806.

About the Series Editor

J ack J. Phillips has more than 27 years of professional experience in human resource development and management, and he has served as a training and development manager at two *Fortune* 500 firms, senior human resources executive at two firms, president of a regional bank, and management professor at a major state university. In 1992, Phillips founded Performance Resources Organization (PRO), an international consulting firm specializing in human resources accountability programs. Phillips consults with clients in the United States, Canada, England, Belgium, Sweden, Italy, South Africa, Mexico, Venezuela, Malaysia, Indonesia, Australia, and Singapore. PRO provides a full range of services and publications to support assessment, measurement, and evaluation.

A frequent contributor to management literature, Phillips has been author or editor of 15 books including *Return on Investment in Training and Performance Improvement Programs* (1997); *Accountability in Human Resource Management* (1996); *Measuring Return on Investment* (vol. 1, 1994; vol. 2, 1997); *Handbook of Training Evaluation and Measurement* (3d edition, 1997); *Conducting Needs Assessment* (1995); *The Development of a Human Resource Effectiveness Index* (1988); *Recruiting, Training and Retaining New Employees* (1987); and *Improving Supervisors' Effectiveness* (1985), which won an award from the Society for Human Resource Management. Phillips has written more than 100 articles for professional, business, and trade publications.

Phillips has earned undergraduate degrees in electrical engineering, physics, and mathematics from Southern Polytechnic State University and Oglethorpe University; a master's degree in decision sciences from Georgia State University; and a Ph.D. in human resource management from University of Alabama. In 1987, he won the Yoder-Heneman Personnel Creative Application Award from the Society for Human Resource Management for an ROI Study of a return-on-investment (ROI) study of a gainsharing plan. He is an active member of several professional organizations.

Jack Phillips can be reached at Performance Resources Organization, P.O. Box 380637, Birmingham, AL 34238-0637; phone: 205.678.9700; fax: 205.678.8070; e-mail: roipro@wwisp.com.